Piccadilly
in Three Centuries

Piccadilly
in Three Centuries

ARTHUR IRWIN DASENT

NONSUCH

Cover illustration: *The Piccadilly Nuisance, Dedicated to the Worthy Acting Magistrates of the District* (29 December 1818), an etching by George Cruikshank (1792–1878). The scene takes place in front of Hatchett's Hotel, which was a terminus for stage-coaches.

First published 1920
Copyright © in this edition Nonsuch Publishing, 2007

Nonsuch Publishing
Cirencester Road, Chalford, Stroud, Gloucestershire, GL6 8PE
www.nonsuch-publishing.com

Nonsuch Publishing is an imprint of NPI Media Group

British Library Cataloguing in Publication Data.
A catalogue record for this book is available from the British Library.

ISBN 978 1 84588 363 8

Typesetting and origination by NPI Media Group
Printed in Great Britain

Contents

Introduction to the
Modern Edition

Today, Piccadilly is a vibrant area in the heart of London. Looking past the throng of locals and tourists, an observer will see the Ritz and numerous other luxury hotels on Piccadilly itself. On the other side of this wide street one can also find the Royal Academy, for centuries the spiritual home of the greatest artists in the land as well as host to some of London's most exciting exhibitions; numerous shops; and some of the grandest mansions in the whole of London. Adjoined by Old Bond Street, Regent Street and St James's Street, Piccadilly is one of the most significant and best-known areas of London. But what is known about this bustling hub of activity and culture? What is the history behind the buildings photographed countless times every day?

The origins of Piccadilly can be traced from the seventeenth century. In 1612 Robert Baker acquired from John Golightly just over one acre of land in Windmill Field for the costly sum of £50. He was able to afford this because he had been successful as a tailor, making and selling picadils (the scalloped edge at the armhole or neck of a dress, very much in vogue at the time) from a shop he owned on the Strand. On this plot of land, Baker constructed a number of buildings, including a mansion where he lived, which would soon become known to the public as Piccadilly Hall. In 1618 Baker enlarged his estate by purchasing over twenty-two acres of land, and increasingly he was able to add to the number of buildings (as well as to the number of cattle) that he owned. Eventually, when he died in 1623, the valuable property that he owned would provoke his relatives to squabble over their inheritance rights for nearly a century. Baker's wealth inevitably created widespread interest throughout London, resulting in a vast expansion in the mid-seventeenth century. Indeed, Piccadilly '... entered upon a new phase of existence as a residential quarter second to none in the West End.'

The area was particularly appealing for the rich, and a number of the aristocracy had houses built here. Famous mansions include Berkeley House (later Devonshire House, the town residence of the Dukes of Devonshire), Cambridge House, where George III's son Prince Adolphus, the Duke of Cambridge, lived and Apsley House, also known simply as Number One, London, home to the first Duke of Wellington. The appeal of the area as both a temporary and a permanent residence for the rich has continued ever since. In 1906 the Ritz Hotel was built: a magnificent neoclassical building boasting 133 rooms and famous for being the first major steel-frame structure in London, today the Ritz is the epitome of the luxury hotel.

In *Piccadilly in Three Centuries* Arthur Irwin Dasent explains how the area evolved from a patch of open countryside to the west of the City of London into one of the most significant urban districts in Britain and the heart of the capital's West End. Thoroughly researched and meticulously detailed, he provides an intriguing narrative of the rapid transformation it underwent, supplemented by fascinating anecdotes. More than just a description of the development of one particular area of London, this is a valuable account of both the history of London and of British social history from the seventeenth to the nineteenth centuries.

Preface

In the following pages I have based my researches into the history of Piccadilly—the mother superior of the dear disreputable Haymarket—on precisely the same materials which I employed in writing the "History of St James's Square"; namely, the parochial rate-books of St Martin's-in-the-Fields, St James's, Westminster, and St George's, Hanover Square.

I have been enabled, after long and patient examination and comparison of these invaluable records, to trace with substantial accuracy the pedigree and successive ownership of every house in Piccadilly and Berkeley Square mentioned in the text.

I have, however, refrained from printing in an appendix the full results of this—the most laborious part of my self-imposed task, because I found, when I dealt with the much smaller area of St James's Square, that statistics such as these appealed to comparatively few readers, and it was even represented to me that to reproduce them *in extenso* was a waste of space.

In the case, however, of some of the more important houses described in the following pages I have given the name of every individual tenant, distinguished or obscure, at the risk of detracting from the general interest of the narrative.

I may be induced to revert to my original method when I come to deal, as it is my present hope and intention, with the Curzon and Grosvenor estates in a companion volume, already far advanced, on the Heart of Mayfair.

ARTHUR IRWIN DASENT
February, 1920

I

Before the Houses

It is the pardonable ambition of the topographer to trace the origin of place-names in this vast metropolis to an earlier date than has hitherto been assigned to them by workers in the same field. In searching the records of the past not only must every clue be diligently followed up, in the hope of finding the first occurrence of a familiar name, but documentary evidence buried in deeds, wills, and parochial accounts must be studied and digested before a logical decision can be arrived at.

It is advisable to descend even into the sewers, which in many places follow the track of former watercourses, in order to secure first-hand information respecting the main thoroughfares of London, and every printed source of knowledge must be ransacked before the local historian dare take up his pen.

The *terrain* of the district to be described must be compared on the spot with the most trustworthy maps known to exist either in public or private collections.

After all this has been conscientiously performed, it will sometimes happen that a chance allusion to a London place-name in contemporary literature may prove more illuminating than the considered judgment of the historian.

The constant rebuilding of old houses, the merging of two buildings into one in the process of reconstruction, and an increasing tendency to dispense with numbers, especially in the case of business premises, render the task of the conscientious local historian annually more difficult.

In order more readily to identify the former homes of distinguished Londoners not only should all new buildings be compulsorily numbered, but in every case the date of rebuilding should be affixed in a prominent position upon the frontage.

The laudable practice of placing memorial tablets in our streets, initiated by the Society of Arts, is being continued and extended by the London County Council—though, so far, Piccadilly has not received attention at its hands, perhaps from reluctance on the part of private owners to allow these unobtrusive medallions to be placed upon their residences.

In Lincoln's Inn Fields, London's largest and oldest Square, private enterprise is responsible for a new departure in this direction. Not only have the names of the former owners of Newcastle House been inscribed on its outer walls, but their heraldic achievements have been blazoned in their proper colours on the front, with results pleasing to the eye and instructive to the increasing number of Londoners who take an intelligent interest in the history of the metropolis. This practice might, however, if extensively followed, lead to difficulties unforeseen by its promoters.If, for instance, some of the older houses in St James's Square were to be similarly treated, their entire frontage would be studded with medallions, owing to the inevitable changes of ownership which have occurred in the course of two centuries.

Maps of London in Elizabethan times are few in number and meagre in detail, but a glance at the well-known bird's-eye views of Agas or Braun shows that the site of what we now call Piccadilly was, at the close of the sixteenth century, open fields devoted to the pasturing of cattle and the bleaching of linen by herdsmen and washerwomen of the Royal parish of St Martin-in-the-Fields. Roadways are usually of more ancient date than the houses which line them, though for an enduring boundary there is nothing so immutable as water. "Hedge Lane," starting from Charing Cross a little to the westward of the King's Mews, represents the modern Whitcomb Street, and another unnamed field track, a little further to the westward, follows the lines of the present Haymarket. Both these lanes were bounded on the north by the "Way to Reading"—the very earliest name of what is now, and has been for more than two centuries, the most surpassingly interesting thoroughfare in the West End. Till the coming of the Thames Embankment, in the Victorian age, it was, moreover, London's only *boulevard*.[1]

To the enterprise of an inhabitant of St Martin-in-the-Fields, a humble tradesman in the Strand, we owe the first buildings to be erected on any part of the site of what is now called Piccadilly.

So early as 1612, one Robert Baker, a tailor, who lived at the west end of the Strand, opposite Britain's Burse (till recently the premises of Coutts's Bank)[2] paid Lammas money to the parish for ground which he had enclosed and built upon "near the windmill,"[3] and in 1615 he was rated at twenty pence for ten acres of agricultural land behind the King's Mews "at the Town's End."

This land he surrounded with a brick wall, and in addition to his larger holding he paid thirteen shillings for a separate tenement dwelling.

In no book hitherto published on the history of Piccadilly has the nature of Baker's occupation been stated, although it has an important bearing, as will be shown directly, on the origin of a name which has long baffled topographers.

The King's Mews, on part of which the National Gallery now stands, were of great extent, and in later years they were divided into several sections, such as the Blue Mews, the Orange Mews, etc. Hence the derivation of Orange Street, running from Charing Cross Road to the Haymarket.

These Lammas lands were private property until the month of August, after which they were subject to Common rights until the following Candlemas. Under this arrangement, as soon as the crops were off the ground, the arable land resumed the character of common pasturage until the spring.

The parishioners of St Martin's were very jealous of any infringement of this immemorial custom.

In 1549 certain lands described as being respectively in "St Martin's Field," "a close behind St Giles'," another called the Ledstalle, a "great Common ffield" enclosed by one Randall Kerby, "Brookshot Close" (which was watered by the Tyburn stream), St James's Fields, Ebury Farm, the Neate, and Hill Field were presented by the Vestry as being included in those lands which "ought to be Comen[4] when the croppe is awaye."

A similar claim was made in respect of Mr Pulteney's broad acres to the north of the "Way to Reading," where now stands Mayfair, or rather that immensely valuable part of it comprised by the Sutton estate. Singular indeed were some of the reasons adduced by the Vestry for the close cropping of hedges and the periodical scouring of ditches in these outlying pastures. It was solemnly placed on record that "in these same dyches and hedges theves and harlots do lye and resort unto destruction of the Kynge's subjects in wynter season, and in the somer tyme all the harlots contynew and lye there."[5]

The windmill referred to in 1612 is shown in Faithorne and Newcourt's map of London issued during the Commonwealth. It stood on the northern portion of Robert Baker's land, and from it the existing Great Windmill Street derives its sylvan name.

The modern history of this short street is not of much general interest, and the bucolic connections of the immediate neighbourhood in earlier and healthier days are separated *longo intervallo* from the unsavoury mementos of the Argyll Rooms, a dancing saloon which stood here (and next door to a church!)

until finally closed about forty years ago. Mention of the fact that Baker's enclosures are described in some of the parochial records as lying at the Town's End supplies a clue to the origin of the word "Piccadilly," by which name one at least of the houses built by the ex-tailor of the Strand eventually became known.

In the reign of James I residential London stopped short at St. Martin's Lane, beyond which there were no houses to the westward until an aristocracy, wearying of Lincoln's Inn Fields, Drury Lane, and Great Queen Street, overflowed into Leicester Fields, and, ultimately, when the great increase in building took place after the Restoration, into Piccadilly and Pall Mall. Leicester Fields is outside the scope of the present work and those who founded a residential quarter there are all but forgotten. Yet the cognizance of the Dudleys and the Sidneys, who acquired this valuable building site from the Howard family—the bear and ragged staff—is still to be seen on a public-house at the corner of Charing Cross Road. The house was rebuilt in 1878, but the old sign escaped destruction, though its significance is little understood at the present day.

When a paternal legislature, in its haste to bring about compulsory abstinence, sweeps away this ancient tavern (a relic of the days when heraldry had some real meaning to the wayfarer in quest of food and lodging), Bear Street should remain to mark the connection of the Earls of Leicester with the Square in which Hogarth lived and Reynolds died. When few could read but all could see, signs and badges were of positive value to Londoners, a fact which may in part account for the practice of numbering houses having made little progress until the close of the eighteenth century.

After his retirement from the tailor's bench it is doubtful if Robert Baker carried on any public employment. It has been surmised that he became a *traiteur*, and that an ordinary, which attained considerable fame hereabouts, was established by him. A house at the corner of Windmill Street was undoubtedly his place of abode after his removal from the Strand; and it soon became popularly known as "Pickadilly Hall," a free rendering, according to some authorities, of the old Dutch word "Pickedillekens," signifying the extremity or utmost part of anything.[6] But though the building may have been used as an eating-house at some time or other, the balance of probability is on the side of its never having been anything but a private dwelling when Robert Baker lived in it.

Townsend House would have been quite as suitable an appellation in the reign of James I as Piccadilly Hall, but it is conceivable that whether the name was first applied to a place of entertainment or public resort by its customers, or had been invented to distinguish a hitherto-unnamed private house, it was in the nature of a nickname, and that its owner did not approve of the selection. However this may have been, Robert Baker did not allude to his house by name in the recital of his estate contained in his will.[7]

Blount in his "*Glossographia*" hazarded the suggestion that Piccadilly Hall was built by one Higgins, a tailor, and maker of a fashionable ruff or collar, called a "Pickadel" in the seventeenth century. While no trace of the mysterious Higgins is to be found in any of the parochial records[8], it is possible that Baker's neighbours wished to cast ridicule on the retired tradesman's new abode, and that they nicknamed it after an article of apparel formerly sold by him and others, Higgins perhaps among the number, in the Strand.

Lacemen, mercers, and tailors are known to have abounded in that part of London, especially in Bedford Street, whilst the New Exchange was devoted entirely to the sale of millinery. In the Strand, immediately west of the Adelphi Theatre, were standing within the last few years, two houses which must have been at least as old as the reign of James I, and Baker's shop was doubtless similar in appearance to those relics of seventeenth-century street architecture.

That the house near the windmill at the top of the Haymarket represented a "peccadillo" of its owner appears too far-fetched a derivation to deserve serious consideration; nor is the ingenious theory, originated by Mrs Stopes,[9] that the district was called "Pick a dilly," from the wild flowers which Gerard found hereabouts in abundance when he was writing his "Herbal," capable of general acceptance.

The *provenance* of Piccadilly has puzzled many topographers ere now, but the fact that Robert Baker was a tailor being definitely established, it does seem within the bounds of possibility that his new house would be connected in men's minds with his former trade.

The entry of his burial in St Martin-in-the Fields on April 16th, 1623, reads: "Robertus Baker, scissor, sepult erat in ecclesiâ nocte," and all the circumstances point to the name of Piccadilly being a jocular allusion to an article of wearing apparel made by him in trade, much as if a retired pork butcher's house were to be nicknamed "Sausage Hall." It was not unusual to apply canting allusions to places of public resort in the seventeenth century, and Tart Hall in Pimlico, which was probably a house of recreation so early as the reign of Charles I, is a case in point.

This oddly-named house adjoined the Mulberry Garden, and to this day there are mulberry trees growing in the back gardens of the houses in Buckingham Gate. As rebuilt by Nicholas Stone, Tart Hall was the town house of the ill-fated Lord Stafford, beheaded in the Popish plot of 1683, and Walpole averred that after his execution the main gateway was never again opened. The name is preserved in Stafford Row in the immediate vicinity of Buckingham Palace. It may not be generally known that Buckingham Palace is in Pimlico, and was long officially so described, though in modern times the use of the word has come to be restricted to the district of which Eccleston Square is the true centre.

The gaming house at the north-eastern corner of the Haymarket was commonly called Piccadilly, and in consequence it has often been confused with Piccadilly Hall on the northern side of the roadway. The great gambling establishment, which sprang up after Robert Baker's death and entirely eclipsed the memory of the Strand tailor's house, has a totally distinct history.

Baker's name appears regularly in the rate-books until 1622, in which year the additional information is vouchsafed that he had bequeathed the sum of £3 to the parish. Probably these accounts were not made up until the new year, for it was not until April 4th, 1623, that his will was made.

Mr. Wheatley stated in "London, Past and Present," that "Piccadilly" does not occur as a street-name until 1673, but after a minute search amongst the manuscript records preserved by St Martin's parish, I find the following entries nearly fifty years earlier, which that eminent writer on old London overlooked.

In 1627, only four years after Robert Baker's death, the rate-book includes under the heading "Pecadilly" the names of:

Mary Baker, widdowe	...	...	...	xi[8.]
John Woode	...	...	...	...	ii[8.]
Isabel Ridley	...	...	...	...	iiii[8.] iiii[d.]
George Gunner	...	...	...	...	xviii[d.]
Paul Tracy	...	...	...	...	x[8.]

Thus, simultaneously with the building of Piccadilly Hall—the skirthouse of the Metropolis, if the alternative, and, to our mind, the more likely, theory of the tailor's ruff is discarded—occupiers of dwelling-houses or agricultural holdings adjacent to it were rated under the same place-name, and Piccadilly became a district as well as a local habitation. All these buildings lay to the eastward of the present Piccadilly Circus, and were understood by the rate-collector to refer to a district at the top of the Haymarket. The first houses built in the new region clustered around the windmill near the "Cawsey Head" and the springs of sweet water which supplied the King's Palace of Whitehall.

In after days these springs were declared to have been polluted by the buildings round about the windmill, and Mrs. Baker, as will be shown hereafter, got into serious trouble with the Court in consequence. Soon after her husband's death, she must have leased her house to Mary Cavendish, dowager Countess of Shrewsbury, for among the State Papers there is a note of priests and Jesuits in London in 1630, amongst the number being one John Blundstone who "is now much at Piccadilly Hall, at the Countess of Shrewsbury's."[10]

Mass was reported to have been said there by another priest, and a regular system of espionage was instituted by the authorities to cope with the imaginary danger to the community. Lady Shrewsbury, daughter of the famous Bess of Hardwick, had suffered imprisonment on suspicion of having connived at the flight of her niece, Arabella Stuart. Less fortunate than her aunt, Arabella was kept a close prisoner in the Tower of London until her death. Lady Shrewsbury's daughter Alethea became Countess of Arundel, and lived at Tart Hall, where a portion of the Arundel marbles was stored. She was therefore, in a sense, the connecting link between Pimlico and Piccadilly Hall.[11]

It has not, I think, been hitherto stated in print that another "Piccadilly Hall," also in a lonely situation, existed in the marshlands of Norfolk, at a place called Walton, in 1636. It probably received its name from an occupier, who had been a visitor to Robert Baker's house on the outskirts of fashionable London, and who retained an agreeable recollection of the locality.[12] A Piccadilly is to be found in Manchester and a Pimlico in Dublin; but Tart Hall, so far as our knowledge goes, remains unique.

It will now be convenient to pass from "Number One Piccadilly," as it may justly be called, across the highway to a spot where, early in the reign of Charles I, there sprang up the most notorious gaming house which ever existed in the West End. Though often confused with Robert Baker's "Hall," the gambling establishment was quite distinct from the house occupied by the retired tailor of St Martin's and afterwards by Lady Shrewsbury. The situation of both is clearly laid down in Porter's scarce map of London.[13]

The good old English game of bowls, severely repressed by the legislature in the reign of Philip and Mary as tending to encourage gambling, experienced a great revival under James I. No longer banned by the Parliament, gaming, dicing, and betting were freely indulged in at the various establishments ostensibly intended for bowls alone.

St Martin's had its own particular green "behind the Mews,"[14] but the famous gaming-house at the top of the Haymarket owed its erection to a scandal which led to the closing of an earlier bowling green patronised by the Court of Charles I at the Spring Garden, near Charing Cross.

The Rev. George Garrard, Master of the Charterhouse—and a first-rate gossip, as his letters abundantly show—wrote as follows to Strafford, then Lord Deputy in Ireland, on June 3rd, 1634:—

"The bowling green in the Spring Garden was by the King's Command put down for one day, but by the intercession of the Queen it was reprieved for this year, but hereafter it shall be no common bowling place. There was kept in it an ordinary of six shillings a meal (when the King's Proclamation allows but two elsewhere), continual bibbing and drinking wine all day long under the trees, two or three quarrels every week. It was growing scandalous and insufferable; besides my Lord Digby being reprimanded for striking in the King's garden, he answered that he took it for a common bowling place, where all paid money for their coming in."[15]

This Spring Garden at Charing Cross, the last vestige of which was lately swept away on the formation of the Processional Road through the Mall, on approved Teutonic lines,[16] was presided over by Simon Osbaldeston, who held office by patent dated July 8th, 1631. He was also a Knight Harbinger and the holder of several profitable concessions. In earlier days he had been gentleman barber to the Earl of Pembroke, one of that incomparable pair of brothers to whom Shakespeare dedicated his plays. Lord Pembroke's grandson Philip, seventh Earl, was implicated in a drunken brawl at another well-known place of entertainment in the Haymarket.

On a Sunday evening (February 3rd, 1678, to be exact) Lord Pembroke, who was married to a sister of the Duchess of Portsmouth, one of the least attractive of Charles the Second's many mistresses and the pet aversion of Nell Gwynne, was drinking with some boon companions at Long's, a famous ordinary in this street of taverns.

Every member of the party had reached an advanced state of intoxication, when a tentative proposal by Mr Goring (one of the principal witnesses at the subsequent trial of Lord Pembroke for murder) for a throw at hazard against Lord Pembroke for a stake of £500, was withdrawn.

This so infuriated the Earl that, in the course of a general scuffle, he felled Mr Nathaniel Coney (a total stranger to him up till that moment) to the ground with his fists, trod upon his prostrate body, and kicked him so severely that he died in agony a week later. At his trial before his peers in Westminster Hall, the Lords, after hearing the evidence tendered on both sides, withdrew to their own Chamber and deliberated in secret session for two hours.

Returning to the Great Hall they pronounced Lord Pembroke guilty, not indeed of murder, but of manslaughter.

Six peers found him guilty on the graver charge and eighteen not guilty. No less than forty adjudged him guilty of manslaughter.

But when the verdict of the majority was communicated to the prisoner at the bar, Lord Pembroke claimed the privilege of his order, under a statute passed in the reign of Edward VI,[17] and was immediately discharged from custody.

He was warned that no man could obtain such exemption more than once and cautioned as to his future conduct, but there seems to be little doubt that the trial was a grave miscarriage of justice. Such scandals were only too frequent in the seventeenth century, though a man of lesser degree would hardly have escaped the gallows or a long term of penal servitude.[18]

The Lords as a body were evidently ill-satisfied with the recurrence of such incidents, for later in the century they amended their Standing Orders so that such privilege should not thereafter be understood or construed to extend to charges of murder or felony.[19]

Lord Pembroke's criminal record is an extraordinary one even for the boisterous times in which he lived.

Before Mr Coney's murder he had nearly killed a man in a duel,[20] and in January, 1678, he was sent to the Tower by the King for "uttering such horrid and blasphemous words as are not fit to be repeated in any Christian assembly."[21]

On another occasion one Philip Rycaut petitioned the Upper House for protection against his violence, declaring that the Earl had made an unprovoked attack upon him in the Strand, nearly knocking out one of his eyes, and threatening to take his life.[22]

For this outrage he was compelled to enter into a recognisance for £2,000 to keep the peace.[23]

Only a few months later he quarrelled with the Earl of Dorset (another notorious libertine, a brilliant wit, and a spirited writer of verse) at Locket's Ordinary at Charing Cross, on the site of Drummond's Bank. Both Lords were confined to their respective houses by order of their Peers, Pembroke being subsequently permitted to retire to Wilton.[24]

In 1680 he killed an officer of the watch whilst returning from a drinking bout at Turnham Green, but, pleading the King's pardon, was once more discharged from custody.

In 1683 he died, prematurely worn out by dissipation and drink, at the early age of thirty.

Wine and wenches, cards and dice, bowls and wagers, week-days and Sundays year in and year out, whilst they helped to make the fortunes of the gaming houses, ruined many another man of fashion in the riotous days of the seventeenth century.

Sir John Coventry, who lived in Suffolk Street, had his nose slit to the bone by a gang of hired bullies who professed to resent a casual remark of Coventry's on the King's fondness for the stage. It should be added that Moll Davis, one of Charles the Second's especial favourites at the time, lodged in the same street.

A few years later, another cold-blooded murder was committed within a stone's throw of the scene of both these outrages.

Mr Thynne of Longleat was assassinated in St. Alban's Street, at the lower or Pall Mall end of the Haymarket, at the instigation of Count Köningsmark. This Swedish nobleman had been a disappointed suitor for the hand of Lady Elizabeth Percy, heiress of the last Earl of Northumberland, and then quite recently married to "Tom of Ten Thousand."[25]

The Haymarket, truth to tell, has never at any time been too respectable. Other and less innocent wares than hay were openly bought and sold in it until it became, in process of time, a recognised mart for human frailty. Yet for many years the sweet scent of real meadow hay, brought here for sale by the farmers of the Home Counties, was the only perfume wafted into the Haymarket.

With the lure of the footlights firmly established in the West End a new atmosphere was introduced.

The exotic odours, the paint and artificiality of the stage, effectually destroyed its former rustic charm.

The farmers' waggons were eventually driven to other quarters, and such legitimate trading as survived was thrust into the narrow courts and alleys of St James's Market, where milk and vegetables were still sold within my recollection.[26]

As private dwelling-houses replaced the haunts of licence, the Haymarket took upon itself something of a new shape, although it remained, until recently, a street of sharp contrasts. One of its earliest aristocratic residents was the Lord Scarborough who so largely contributed to Monmouth's defeat at Sedgemoor.

A Duke soon after came to live in it, probably on the eastern side, though I have not identified the actual site of his house.

This was Lionel, first Duke of Dorset, father of Lord George Sackville Germain. He did not, however, stay here very long, as he removed, on taking office under the Crown, to the Cockpit in Whitehall.

Most of the inns, according to Strype, were on the west side of the street. The Black Horse, which still exists, at the corner of Jermyn Street, as a public-house sign, the Nag's Head, the Cock, the White Horse, the Phœnix, and the Unicorn were all on this side. From the latter, so early as 1681, a coach went to and from Windsor every day in the week.[27] Opposite were the King's Head, a noted hostelry, and Paulet's ordinary at the corner of James Street, the especial resort of the tennis players.

Addison, one of the pioneers of modern journalism, rented a garret in the Haymarket at one time of his brilliant career. Anne Oldfield shed something of the reflected lustre of the stage upon it, and, like Addison, achieved the distinction of burial in Westminster Abbey.[28]

George Morland, an inimitable painter of animal life and rusticity, was born in it—only to die in a sponging house—and Dr Garth, a famous physician and a bit of a poet in his day, is said to have practised the healing art in it.

It became the earliest home of opera in England. Vanbrugh's great playhouse, "The Queen's," covered the site of the late Sir Herbert Beerbohm Tree's His Majesty's Theatre and the Carlton Hotel, and on the opposite side of the road still stands the oldest theatre in central London, with the exception of Drury Lane. Its well-proportioned portico, just a century old, redeems the street, to some extent, from the stigma of the commonplace and the vulgar.

Old vices have a tendency to reappear under new labels, and in the early Victorian age the night houses of the Haymarket and Panton Street gained for the neighbourhood an unsavoury reputation which long retarded its commercial development.

The sordid scenes nightly witnessed at Kate Hamilton's and similar dens of infamy—the squalid successors of the bagnios and brothels of earlier days—are not of general interest. Their red lamps, beckoning the unwary to certain physical and moral degradation, twinkled no more after the Early Closing Act of 1872 put an end to their mischievous activities. The alterations then made in the hours of sale for intoxicating liquors have undoubtedly made London a soberer and healthier place to live in, and, at the present day, the character of the Haymarket as a business centre stands higher than ever it did before.

Returning, after this digression, to the seventeenth century, I find that the Spring Garden's misfortune was Sim Osbaldeston's opportunity. He conceived the idea of establishing a new bowling green and gaming house in the growing district at the top of the Haymarket, which should eclipse anything hitherto enjoyed by the Cavaliers for whom he especially catered.

Garrard, in another gossiping letter to Strafford, shows how the project was put into execution. Writing on June 24th, 1635, he said:

"Since the Spring Garden was put down, we have by a servant of the Lord Chamberlain's a new Spring Garden erected in the fields behind the Mewes, where is built a fair house, and two bowling greens made, to entertain gamesters and bowlers, at an excessive rate; for I believe it hath cost him above four thousand pounds, a dear undertaking for a gentleman barber. My Lord Chamberlain much frequents that place, where they bowl great matches."[29]

There was a gaming house in Bell Yard, Lincoln's Inn Fields, visited by Pepys, and another and earlier bowling green was, as we have seen, in Leicester Fields, but when Lord Pembroke's barber conceived the idea of a place of entertainment where the flower of London society could meet and dine and drink, a new chapter was added to the history of London's amusements. Yet another letter from George Garrard (written, on this occasion, to Edward, Viscount Conway), is valuable for our purpose, as it shows how the new gaming house obtained its slang name.

"Simme Austbiston's house is newly christened. It is called Shaver's Hall, as other neighbouring places thereabout are nicknamed Tart Hall, Pickadel Hall. At first no conceit there was of the builder's being a barber, but it came upon my Lord of Dunbar's losing of £3,000 at one sitting, whereon they said a Northern Lord was shaved there; but now, putting both together, I fear it will be a nickname of the place, as Nick and Froth is at Petworth, as long as the house stands. My Lord Chamberlain[30] knows not of it yet, but he'll chafe abominably when he comes to know it."[31]

Garrard's spelling of surnames was occasionally faulty, but it occurred to the present writer on reading the above letter that "Simme Austbiston" must be one and the same with Osbaldeston, late of the Charing Cross Spring Garden, and on searching the rate-books of St. Martin's for the year 1636, he was rewarded by finding, in respect of the gaming house at the north-east of the Haymarket, the latter's name entered as paying thirty-four shillings and eightpence, a larger sum than was levied upon anyone else in the vicinity, towards the relief of the poor of the parish.

It will be noted that though Garrard speaks of the new establishment being nicknamed Shaver's Hall, he does not definitely state that Tart Hall and Pickadell Hall were places of public entertainment, a fact which strengthens our contention that "Number One Piccadilly," as we have ventured to call it, was a private residence, just as Tart Hall is known to have been at the same period.

The bowling greens, the gardens and the tennis court occupied practically the whole of the eastern side of the Haymarket, and were bounded on the south by Lord Suffolk's garden wall. Apparently he did not like the new departure, for in another letter written by Garrard to Strafford in 1635, it is said that: "The Earl of Suffolk intends to change his dwelling, he will leave London altogether."

It seems probable from an entry in the State Papers that Mrs Mary Baker retained something of a proprietary interest in the site of Osbaldeston's Gaming House or premises immediately adjacent thereto, for in a list of cases to be heard in the Star Chamber in January 1637–1638 was that of the Attorney-General *versus* Mary Baker and others for erecting buildings contrary to proclamation, whereby the springs of water running to Whitehall and to Somerset House were putrefied. A marginal note by Secretary Windebank reveals the fact that Mrs Baker was fined £1,000 and that her house was ordered to be demolished.[32]

It may be that Mrs Baker only came into collision with the Court in respect of buildings erected on her lands north of the Haymarket, but from the fine being such a heavy one it seems probable that the gaming house or some of its appurtenances was included in the list of her delinquencies.

Yet it was not demolished, and for years it flourished exceedingly.

What was this famous place of resort like, and who were its principal patrons? A survey of lands and buildings in and about Piccadilly in 1650[33] gives a good idea of Shaver's Hall, as it existed in the hey-day of its fame.

It was a three-storeyed house (including the ground floor), substantially built of brick and roofed with lead, and it had three entrance doors.

On the ground floor, which was ten steps above the level of the roadway, were four fair rooms with Purbeck stone floors "well-fitted and joynted." These were presumably the dining-rooms. On the first floor were four good rooms devoted to cards and dice, one of which opened on to a pleasant balcony overlooking the gardens and bowling alleys to the south.

In the top storey were six smaller rooms, and the flat leads of the roof formed an agreeable promenade "enclosed with rails," presumably lest the diners should overbalance themselves and fall into the garden. Nor must the staircase be forgotten—it was curiously carved and wrought, and a pleasing feature of the architecture.

In the basement were cellars, but the kitchens, of which there were no less than three, with living-rooms over, were in a separate range of buildings.

The Survey states that they stood to the north of the principal edifice, which looks almost as if they formed part of Mrs Baker's dwelling house over the way.

The tennis-court at the southern extremity was strongly built of brick and covered with tiles, and "well accommodated with all things fitting for the same." There were, as has been said, two separate bowling alleys, an upper and a lower, approached by entrance gates from the Haymarket. They were divided from one another by a roadway or footpath occupying the site of what is now Panton Street: another proof of the contention that roads in London are in the majority of cases older than the houses to be found in them. Access to the lower alley was obtained by a subterranean passage. In the grounds, which covered no less than three and a half acres, were a banqueting house and another apartment called the "green-room" in which refreshments were served in summer time. There was also an orchard "planted with several choyce of fruit trees," there were "gravily walks," and a conduit house, from which an abundant supply of water was obtained. This conduit may have been the head and front of Mrs. Baker's offending against the powers of Whitehall. Two small turrets, or summer-houses, adjoined the garden walls which effectually hid the property from the vulgar gaze.

From an examination of the structure the mind is led by a natural transition to a consideration of the games which were played there. Although the great increase of gambling in London did not occur until the eighteenth century—when numerous clubs at which high stakes were the rule, and mushroom gambling hells, all more or less disreputable, sprang up in Piccadilly and St James's Street—card-playing and dicing had been fashionable in England at least as early as the time of the Tudors.

There is record of a sermon preached by Bishop Latimer at Cambridge in 1527 in which that eminent divine illustrated the meaning of his discourse according to the terms then current amongst card players. "I propose to deal unto you," he said, "another card almost of the same suit, for they be of so high affinity that one cannot well be played without the other."

Roger Ascham also drew a vivid picture of the tricks played by dicers on the unwary in the reign of Queen Elizabeth.

Primero was the favourite game in the sixteenth century. Sir Walter Raleigh played it at Court in company with Shakespeare's patron, Lord Southampton, and the poet makes Falstaff say: "I never prospered since I forswore myself at Primero." Maw or Macaw, which closely resembled Five Cards, a game still popular in Ireland, came into fashion early in the seventeenth century.

Ombre is said to have been introduced into England by Charles the Second's Queen, who, according to Pepys, also instituted the practice of playing cards on Sunday. Whist is unknown before the eighteenth century, but picquet and écarté were played in France far earlier.

Apart from cards, the favourite occupation of the Cavalier gambler was the playing of hazard. For this only two dice were required, but as many as twenty people could play at the same time. The chief objects of the game were the *chance* and the *main*; the former representing the caster's chance and the latter the setter's. In old country houses there may still be seen round tables with deeply bevelled edges. These were to prevent the dice from falling onto the floor, which, at hazard, would be accounted "no throw."

So much for the place and the games, now for the players who made Piccadilly famous.

Here would be met with on a summer afternoon that gifted amateur poet, gambler, and man of fashion Sir John Suckling, of whom Aubrey has preserved a tradition that his sisters came crying to the bowling green for fear he should lose all their portions at play. Like many another poet, Suckling lived hard and died young and miserably. Holding love to be a delusion, pursuit to be everything and enjoyment nothing, his outlook on life was summed up in the cynical lines:

Women enjoy'd (whate'er before they've been)
Are like romances read, or sights once seen;
Fruition's dull, and spoils the play much more
Than if one read or knew the plot before.
'Tis expectation makes a blessing dear;
Heaven were not heaven, if we knew what 'twere.

Here, too, as a young man just entering the House of Commons, came plain Ned Hyde (afterwards to be known throughout the civilised world as the Earl of Clarendon), more for recreation and the society of his friends than from a love of play.[34]

Clarendon mentions his meeting the Earl of Bedford here in 1641, and the fact of the "best quality" resorting to the place for exercise and conversation, it was perhaps owing to his early visits to the neighbourhood that he conceived the idea, when at the zenith of his power, of building a great house for himself looking down upon St James's. Osbaldeston was succeeded in the management of the gaming house by a Captain Geare, who carried on the business from 1641 until about 1653, though little is heard of the place whilst the gaiety of London suffered a temporary eclipse under the Commonwealth.

After Geare's name disappears from the rate-books, the owners of Piccadilly House and the bowling greens paid £4 annually to the parish of St. Martin in respect of the property, and in 1664 the name of a very notorious gambler, Thomas Panton, replaces those of the original owners. This remarkable man, who made a fortune of £1,500 a year in a single night (after which we are told that he could never be persuaded to handle cards or dice again), seems gradually to have acquired the freehold of all Mrs Baker's lands hereabouts, and about 1670 he began to develop his property as a building estate. The Pantons are inextricably bound up with the history of Piccadilly and the sporting world, especially in connection with Newmarket, at the close of the seventeenth and throughout the eighteenth century.

The gambler who laid the foundations of his family's fortunes had a daughter, Elizabeth. She married the head of one of the oldest families in England, the fifth Lord Arundell of Wardour, hence the name Arundell Passage at the top of the Haymarket which isolates to this day the site of the Gaming House. Mrs Panton's name is found in the Haymarket for some years after her husband's death, and at least one other bearer of the name will be mentioned on a later page.

In 1671 Sir Christopher Wren, who, as Crown Surveyor, had been directed to report on Panton's building schemes, wrote to the King that the new landlord, "having purchased the two bowling greens fronting the Haymarket and on the north of the Tennis Court upon which several old houses were standing" with a design to build, had demolished them to improve his property and to render it more uniform. One of the new houses subsequently erected was the shop owned by the tobacconists Fribourg and Treyer (No 34) since the first quarter of the eighteenth century. From Wren we also learn that the opening of a projected street from the Haymarket into Leicester Fields[35] would, in his opinion, be for the public advantage as it would ease in some measure "the great passage of the Strand" and cure the "noisomeness" of that portion of the West End.

Panton was bound down to build with brick, with party walls and sufficient scantlings, to pave the newly formed streets, and to construct sewers.

These improvements entailed the destruction of the great gaming establishment and after an existence of less than half a century it finally closed its doors about 1670.

A few years later it had become a mere memory when Phil Porter wrote in his "Wit and Drollery":

Farewell my dearest Piccadilly,
Notorious for great dinners
Oh, what a Tennis Court was there,
Alas! too good for sinners.

There is a public-house called the "Hand and Racquet" to this day in Panton Street, and the tennis court on the south side of Orange Street, formerly James Street, existed in a mutilated condition until 1866.

When the court was dismantled the Earl of Warwick bought the stone floor, polished after two centuries of use to an exquisite smoothness, and had it carefully removed to his ancestral castle. It came originally from a famous French quarry, and Lord Warwick intended to relay it in a new court which he desired to construct. The project was, for some reason, abandoned, and these time-honoured stones are, I believe, lying idle at Warwick Castle to this day.

Henry Coventry, Secretary of State to Charles II, an elderly bachelor with a good diplomatic record behind him, came to live on the site of the gaming-house, perhaps in the original building after some necessary alteration, about the year 1673, and here he stayed till his death,[36] coming to and fro in his coach from a country house which he owned at Enfileld Chace.

Henry Savile, writing in June 1686 to Lord Halifax, speaks of the secretary's town residence as Piccadilly House, but as the distinguishing mark of a private house the name did not long survive, any more than when revived nearly 200 years later at the other extremity of the street, by Baron Lionel de Rothschild in respect of his new house (now No 148), next door to Apsley House. Henry Coventry's connection with Piccadilly is preserved in Coventry Street, whilst a block of shops recently erected at the top of the Haymarket has appropriately been called Coventry House.

Having now dealt at some length with the pioneers of London life in Piccadilly and the Haymarket—the tailor and the barber who first brought the locality into prominence—this chronicle has next to relate the coming of the great houses of the Restoration period.

II

The Coming of the Aristocracy to Piccadilly

Even before the shuffling of the last pack of cards, the muttering of the last gambler's oath, the expiring rattle of the dice-box and the final game of bowls at Shaver's Hall, Piccadilly entered upon a new phase of existence as a residential quarter second to none in the West End.

A portion of the new thoroughfare replacing the country road "from Knightsbridge unto Piccadilly Hall," as it is called in Faithorne and Newcourt's map,[37] was named after Catherine of Braganza so early as 1663, only a year after that unhappy lady's arrival in England.

Portugal Street, to give it its new designation, is officially recognised in the rate-books for 1664, and its boundaries were gradually extended westward to Ayr Street, to Sackville Street[38] and a little beyond, though the name does not seem to have been very generally applied to the houses built in after years to the west of St James's Street.

Its true centre was always where the Albany now stands, and though the use of the name of Portugal Street lingered in the parochial records until nearly the close of the eighteenth century, it gradually became merged in the more popular and wider appellation of Piccadilly.

The north side was the first to be rated to the relief of the poor, but a year later the south side "towards the Haymarket from the Poet's Head"[39] also contributed its modest quota towards the parochial funds. The first houses erected were mostly business premises let at very low rentals. Richard Groome, who issued a token in Piccadilly in 1665, was one of these humble occupiers, but it was not long before the new street began to attract a wealthier class, and to exercise an increasing fascination for such of the Cavalier nobility as were in search of the *rus in urbe* which never fails to appeal to the connoisseur in his choice of a London abode.

The present writer has been able to show in a former work[40] how the Earl of St Albans drew the flower of the aristocracy from Drury Lane, Lincoln's Inn Fields, and the Strand to the grassy meads of St James's, and how the apple orchards to the north of Pall Mall came to be replaced by mansions of brick and stone under the fostering care of the Jermyn family.

The second great expansion of habitable London in the seventeenth century was also primarily due to one man's ambition.

About the time that Harry Jermyn was projecting the great piazza in St James's Fields another and infinitely greater personage at the Court of Whitehall conceived the idea of obtaining from the Crown a grant of land, which, though it lay further to the westward, was still in proximity to the occasional residence of the Sovereign.

In 1663, Edward Hyde, Earl of Clarendon (Keeper of the Great Seal of England and, technically, of the King's conscience, if Charles II can be said to have had such a thing), whom we have already met with at the bowling-green in the Haymarket, thought himself ill-housed in the Strand, although Worcester House was probably little inferior to an earlier residence of his in Fleet Street called Dorset House.

Worcester House stood on the site of Beaufort Buildings, swept away in the Strand improvements of the last few years. It had a large garden sloping to the riverside and must have been at least as desirable a place of abode as Arundel House and other peers' residences in the immediate vicinity.

Clarendon, as his fame and power increased, turned his eyes steadily westward, and in 1663, when his share in the discreditable sale of Dunkirk had not received its full meed of public condemnation, there was no effective bar to the realisation of his craving for territorial expansion.

He took Worcester House, offered to him rent free by the gentle author of the "Century of Inventions,"[41] on lease at £500 a year, but it was not grand enough for the vaulting ambition of a man who aimed at dividing the sceptre of England between the Stuarts and the Hydes. Clarendon then moved for a time to Berkshire (now Bridgewater) House, but apparently he had set his heart upon acquiring a freehold estate of his own, looking right down upon the Royal Palace of St James's.

In August, 1664, he succeeded in obtaining a grant by Letters Patent from Charles II, "in consideration of his eminent and faithful services," of no fewer than thirty acres lying to the northward of the high road leading to Hyde Park and Knightsbridge. This extremely valuable site, a little Hyde Park of his very own, included (1) the Stonebridge Close of eleven acres, of which the western boundary was the then open and unconfined Tybourne stream, (2) Pennyless Bank Close of nine-and-a-half acres, lying to the eastward of the former, and (3) Stone Conduit Close, which comprised another nine acres to the eastward again. This last was bounded on the east by Swallow Close, which in after years gave its name to a street almost wholly obliterated in the formation of Regent Street.

In addition to this grant Clarendon secured another twenty-four acres formerly in the occupation, no doubt for purely pastoral purposes, of one Widow Austin, of the "Eagle and Child" in the Strand, and on this unique site he began to build from the designs of Sir Roger Pratt.

To understand the history of this part of Piccadilly aright, it is necessary to point out, what has hitherto been but imperfectly understood, that, before the first brick of Clarendon House was laid, its owner, having obtained the freehold of a great deal more land than he actually wanted, proceeded to part with two several plots to the westward of his intended mansion, one of them to Lord Berkeley of Stratton and the other to Sir William Pulteney, who thus acquired between them the sites of what are now Devonshire House and Bath House respectively. A third and equally valuable plot to the eastward of Clarendon House, comprising the site of Burlington House and the Albany, was granted to Sir John Denham, the poet architect, with whom Pulteney was closely associated.

The date of Clarendon's grant from the Crown on the Patent Rolls is August 23, 1664, and the conveyances to Berkeley, Pulteney and Denham, which are to be found on the Close Rolls, were made on the day after.

The great house built by Sir Roger Pratt for the Chancellor, at a cost of between £40,000 and £50,000, was begun immediately after the grant was obtained, and the progress of the works in Piccadilly is duly recorded by both Pepys and Evelyn, who vied with one another in praising the design as one of the noblest they had seen.

The lower orders viewed its erection from the first with less satisfaction. Their suspicions were aroused when it was rumoured that the Chancellor (much after the manner of Protector Somerset, who was popularly supposed to have utilised portions of old St Paul's and other religious edifices for the mansion in the Strand which still bears his name), was obtaining building materials from similar sources.[42] So much grandeur, they said, was incompatible with honesty, and it was asserted that the Chancellor was converting to profane uses stone designed for the repair of the Cathedral before the Civil War, but subsequently acquired by

Clarendon with gains derived from the sale of Dunkirk. Andrew Marvell, in "Clarendon's House Warming," summed up the popular attitude towards the new palace in Piccadilly:

Behold, in the depth of our Plague and our Wars,
He built him a Palace outbraves the stars
Which house (*we* Dunkirk and *he* Clarendon names),
It looks down with shame upon St. James;
But 'tis not his golden globe [43] will save him,
Being less than the Custom-house farmers gave him;
His chapel for consecration calls,
Whose sacrilege plundered the stones from St Paul's.

Another, and graver, charge brought against Clarendon was that the house was furnished, for the most part, with Cavaliers' goods sent in as peace offerings to the all-powerful Chancellor. The Lord Paulett of that day humbly craved permission to take copies of two of his ancestors' full-length portraits by Vandyck, purloined from Hinton St George to swell the collection of representative Englishmen in the new Piccadilly galleries, and, if Burnet is to be trusted, poor Lord Paulett had great difficulty in obtaining even this modest request, as their new owner thought that to take copies of these paintings might lessen the value of the originals. Thanks to Evelyn, who compiled a rough list of the principal pictures at Clarendon House, unfortunately without mentioning the names of the artists, we are enabled to form some idea of the amazing variety and interest of what was, in the fullest and truest sense, a National Portrait Gallery. It included the great Chancellors, Ministers of the Crown, judges, divines, commanders naval and military, and Parliamentary leaders of the later Tudors and the three first Stuarts, with some examples of even greater antiquity. Burleigh, Walsingham, Cecil, Bacon, and Coke were to be found there in the company of Sir Thomas More, Sir Walter Raleigh, and Sir Philip

Sidney. Amongst the poets were Chaucer, Shakespeare, Beaumont and Fletcher, Spenser, Waller, Cowley, and Samuel Butler, the portrait of the author of "Hudibras" being hung in the principal dining-hall. Divinity was represented by Laud, Juxon, Sheldon, Fisher, and Fox. There were in all more than one hundred of the choicest works of art collected with infinite pains and judgment, but their stay in Piccadilly was all too brief. Some of the Vandycks are now, or were lately, at The Grove in Hertfordshire, and some are mentioned at a later page, in the chapter devoted to "Old Q." who inherited a portion of the Clarendon estates and treasures.

As the Chancellor's popularity waned, the common people, growing more daring and resentful, cut down the trees which grew before the house, smashed the windows, and even set up a representation of a gallows before the principal entrance gate, inscribed:

"Three sights to be seen: Dunkirk, Tangier, and a barren Queen!"

This was in June, 1667, not many months after its owner had first gone into residence in Piccadilly. Before the close of the year Clarendon fled the country, never to return to it alive, though his bones were suffered to be laid to rest in the North Ambulatory of Westminster Abbey. For nigh two hundred years they lay beneath a nameless stone, until, in 1867, Dean Stanley caused an inscription to be cut recording the Chancellor's interment and some twenty of his relatives and descendants. Both Clarendon's mother and his mother-in-law are buried in the same vault. After the Chancellor's disgrace the great house in Piccadilly was occupied for a year or two by his son, Lord Cornbury, but he was soon replaced by the Duke of Ormond, who was living here when the infamous Colonel Blood, who stole the Crown Jewels from the Tower, made an unsuccessful attempt upon the Duke's life. In 1675 the second Duke of Albemarle, son of General Monk, bought the house for about £25,000, but he too only stayed in it for two years. Having got into pecuniary difficulties, he sold the freehold to Sir Thomas Bond and other speculators in landed property, who promptly pulled down the house and built Bond Street and Albemarle Buildings in its stead. The second Duke of Albemarle died in Jamaica, of which island he was Governor, in 1688, "burnt to a coal with hot liquor."

Two Corinthian pilasters which formerly stood one on each side of the "Three Kings" Inn gateway were supposed by Isaac Disraeli, writing in the "Curiosities of Literature," to have been the last remaining relics of the ill-fated Clarendon House, but they, too, have shared the fate of the original mansion.

Another pioneer of fashion in this new quarter of the town was Lord Berkeley of Stratton, a Royalist Commander of distinction in the Civil Wars. He was a kinsman of Henry Jermyn and, like him, an especial favourite with Queen Henrietta Maria. Charles the Second raised him to the Peerage during his exile, and after the Restoration he was constantly employed in the service of the Crown.

On his coming to Piccadilly he did not, like Clarendon, employ Sir Roger Pratt, for he built the mansion which preceded the present Devonshire House from the designs of Hugh May, a minor architect in great favour at Whitehall.

The original house had a fine cedar-wood staircase and the façade towards the street was surmounted by a white marble figure of Britannia, said to have cost £3,500. Evelyn, whilst not wholly approving the design, thought the fore-court noble and the gardens, which were of vast extent, incomparable. On his advice Lord Berkeley planted holly hedges on the terrace walk, but I do not think that any of these have survived to the present day, for the holly does not thrive in London smoke.

The mansion cost in all about £30,000, and its owner appears to have entered into residence on his return from Ireland, where he had been sent as Lord Lieutenant, in 1672.

He died in 1678 and was buried at Twickenham, where his monument is still to be seen in good preservation under the tower, though the remainder of the old riverside church has been practically re-built since the seventeenth century.

His widow, Christian,[44] lived in Piccadilly for a time, but in 1692 the house was taken for Prince George of Denmark and the Princess Anne, and it is their arms which are blazoned on Kip's admirable view.

Lady Berkeley was back again in 1695, but shortly before her death[45] the freehold was acquired by the first Duke of Devonshire, and the long connection of the Cavendishes with Piccadilly began with the builder of Chatsworth.

Lady Berkeley built Stratton Street and Berkeley Street on a portion of her grounds, and whilst Evelyn deplored the curtailment of the gardens he had assisted in laying out, he added that there was some excuse for their owner's action, since a similar fate had overtaken the pleasaunces of Clarendon House. Moreover, the formation of these two streets increased Lady Berkeley's ground rents to the extent of a thousand a year.

An even more valuable portion of surplus land remained to swell the fortunes of the family in after years. On this was subsequently built Bruton Street and the greater portion of Berkeley Square, a notable instance of unpenalised "increment value" which would make the land-taxers of the present day mad with envy. The Duke of Devonshire was burnt out of Montagu House (on the site of the British Museum) in 1686, and five years later his apartments at Whitehall were greatly damaged by fire. He removed to St James's Square for a time, but for years he and Lord Normanby[46] had been trying to acquire Berkeley House. As both claimed to have bought it, a lawsuit followed which terminated in the Duke of Devonshire's favour. The unsuccessful litigant thereupon bought Arlington House, where Buckingham Palace now stands, from the Duchess of Grafton and soon afterwards rebuilt it.

The first Duke of Devonshire died in Piccadilly in 1707, as did his successor in the title in 1729. The Cavendishes were destined once more to be sufferers from the fire fiend, for in October, 1733, Berkeley House was totally destroyed, the famous cedar staircase perishing in the flames and the statue of Britannia crashing to the ground in the general wreck and ruin. A violin painted by a Dutch artist on one of the doors, and so cleverly as to deceive the eye, escaped the conflagration, and is now, I believe, at Chatsworth.[47] The high brick wall which divides the fore-court from the roadway is part of Hugh May's original design, and is, moreover, the only bit of seventeenth-century Piccadilly remaining in an unaltered state. The ornamental iron gates in the centre were brought here from Chiswick by the late Duke a few years ago, and after two centuries and a half Devonshire House, as rebuilt by William Kent, remains one of the more desirable of the private palaces of London, although its exterior is plain and homely to a degree.

The cedar-wood staircase, the especial pride of the old home of the Berkeleys, reminiscent in its sweet odours of Trinity College Chapel, Oxford, on a summer afternoon, has given way to one of gleaming white marble with a balustrade of glass. This and other internal decorations were added by the sixth Duke, an untiring collector of rare books and coins, in the middle of the last century, when artistic perception was not invariably of remarkable clarity. The marble staircase serves its primary purpose admirably when the house is thronged, as it frequently has been in recent years, on the occasion of political receptions.

Prominent amongst the series of family portraits on the walls is that of Duchess Georgiana, the "Piccadilly beauty" *par excellence* of the eighteenth century.

Born in 1757 her father[48] was then plain Mr John Spencer of Althorp. He had just entered the House of Commons as member for Warwick and was married to Miss Poyntz, a member of an ancient Berkshire family seated at Midgham in that county. At the time of his daughter's birth he was living in Grosvenor Street, but soon removed to Arlington Street, and early in the reign of George III he built Spencer House in St James's Place, which is still in the possession of his family. His services to the State are somewhat difficult to estimate, for, although he received no fewer than four Peerage creations in as many years, he never filled any public employment except that of President of the Lying-In Society.

Duchess Georgiana, the prototype of lady canvassers—she is said to have kissed a butcher in Long Acre to secure a party vote—married when only sixteen, though within a few days of her seventeenth birthday, the fifth Duke of Devonshire. In the prime of Georgiana's womanly beauty and charm (bred as she was of the finest flower of English aristocracy), Devonshire House was destined to become the leading social factory of Whig politics.

And in Piccadilly she died in the course of the year in which the grave also closed over Charles James Fox, for whom she worked indefatigably in the memorable Westminster election of 1784. It was happily said at the time that she and her sister, Lady Duncannon, were the two loveliest portraits that ever appeared on a *canvas*.

This election, the longest and most hotly contested ever known in the City of Westminster, a constituency notorious, before and after, for strenuous party fights, was mainly conducted by Fox from Devonshire House. Even before the dissolution of Parliament was announced, the struggle began. A general meeting of the electors was held on March 14th in Westminster Hall, of all places, but in consequence of the prevailing uproar Fox found it impossible to obtain a hearing, and his supporters bore him shoulder-high to the King's Head Tavern in Palace Yard. The Friends of Liberty, as they styled themselves, took the horses from his carriage and dragged him, amidst deafening cheers, all the way back to Piccadilly.

The poll opened in Covent Garden on April 1st, but not until May 17th, after six weeks of speech-making, feasting and rioting, accompanied by the most unblushing bribery and unscrupulous vilification of opponents by both sides, were the numbers declared.

In spite of all the forces of the Crown having been arrayed against him, for George III had very imperfectly grasped the lessons of the seventeenth-century struggle between King and Commons, Fox was returned second on the poll, less than 500 votes separating him from Lord Hood, a popular admiral, whose election to one or other of the two seats was a foregone conclusion from the first. The third candidate, Sir Cecil Wray, demanded a scrutiny, and not until March in the following year were Lord Hood and Fox declared to have been duly elected.

Debrett, a Piccadilly bookseller, published a complete record of this memorable contest, the anonymous authors describing themselves as "Lovers of Truth and Justice."

The lives of the Dukes of Devonshire, and there have been nine of them in 200 years, no fewer than eight of whom became Knights of the Garter, are written large in the history of their country, therefore their solid services to the State need not be touched upon here. But one cadet of the family, Henry Cavendish, the scientist, though not, I think, actually resident in Piccadilly at any time of his life, comes into the picture of either Devonshire House or of Burlington House. At one or other of them he was an occasional and reluctant visitor when a family christening, a marriage, or it might be a funeral, compelled his attendance.

Henry Cavendish lived the life of a hermit, and, though he died worth a million of money, he was only allowed £500 a year by his father in his younger days, even less, some say, including five shillings a day for his dinner, which he was accustomed to eat at the Crown and Anchor Tavern in the Strand, where the Royal Society then held its meetings. He has been called "le plus riche de tous les savants, et probablement aussi, le plus savant de tous les riches." He lodged, remote from the haunts of fashion, in Bloomsbury, and, like Richard Heber, he had a separate house for his books in Soho. For change of air he would retire to Clapham, in his day a pleasant suburban village. He saw but little of his family, though his cousin, Lord George Cavendish, who ultimately inherited his fortune, is said to have visited him twice a year for half an hour at a time.

Morbidly shy, he had the reputation of being a misogynist, but the beautiful Duchess Georgiana, to her credit be it recorded, used to visit him on the sly. When her husband discovered this, he forbade her to continue the intercourse, saying, "He is not a gentleman, he *works*!" Such, unfortunately, was, with rare exceptions, the prevailing attitude of the leisured aristocracy of the eighteenth century towards men of science and literary taste. Henry Cavendish died in 1810, supposed by the family to have been a woman-hater; yet there were found amongst his belongings, after his death, a quantity of extremely valuable jewels, including a diamond stomacher.

The history of Burlington House, so long as it remained a place of private residence, is closely bound up with the inter-allied families of Boyle and Cavendish, who succeeded one another in Piccadilly, with scarcely an exception, at what is now the Royal Academy, until the house was sold to the Government in 1854.

The first house built on the site was a plain red-brick building, begun soon after the Restoration for Richard Boyle, 2nd Earl of Cork, and 1st Earl of Burlington, Lord Treasurer of Ireland.

It is said to have been constructed from the designs of Sir John Denham, a minor poet with architectural leanings, to whom the land on which it stood, seven acres in extent, had been assigned by Lord Clarendon. His merits as a writer of verse were inconsiderable, and perhaps his best-remembered composition is

"Cooper's Hill"—almost the first example in the English language of a poem devoted entirely to local description.

The original Burlington House was first rated to the relief of the poor in 1670,[49] by which date Denham was dead and had found honourable burial in the Abbey in the company of Chaucer, Cowley, and Dryden.

After Denham's death the house was in all probability completed by his deputy, John Webb, represented in London street architecture until recently by two interesting old houses, numbered 54 and 55 in Great Queen Street. On these Webb is believed to have worked under the far greater Inigo Jones, whom he eventually succeeded as Crown Surveyor.

These houses have only been swept away in the last year or two in order to enlarge the Freemasons' Hall, and London is distinctly the poorer for the change.

The 3rd Earl of Burlington, an amateur architect of more eminence than Denham, made it the ambition of his life to foster the talents of his contemporaries in the respective domains of literature, music, painting, and artistic design. He greatly altered the house, in or about 1718, encasing it with stone in the Palladian style, and adding the famous colonnade, so much admired by Horace Walpole.

Seeing it for the first time, after his return from Italy, on the occasion of a ball, he wrote: "At daybreak, looking out of the windows to see the sun rise, I was surprised with the vision of the colonnade that fronted me. It seemed one of those edifices in fairy tales that are raised by genii in a night time."

The mistake has often been made in the past of calling a patron of architecture the actual architect, in the modern sense of the word, of a particular building. For example, the biographical dictionaries, almost without exception, attribute the design of Henry VII's Chapel to Sir Reginald Bray. This he certainly was not directly responsible for, any more than he was for putting the finishing touches to St George's Chapel, Windsor, in which he lies buried without a monument. The design of the famous Piccadilly colonnade is usually attributed to Lord Burlington, but this is by no means a matter of certainty, though he was unquestionably a man of keen artistic perception and rare taste. Colin Campbell, in his "Vitruvius Britannicus," claimed it as his own work, and the claim was undoubtedly made, and not specifically denied, in Lord Burlington's lifetime.

This fine architectural conception, which could not be seen from the street—standing, as it did, behind what has been called "the most expensive wall in England"—was removed to Battersea Park in 1866, where the stones are still lying neglected on the ground.

The vestibule and lower storey of the Royal Academy buildings are portions of the second, or Palladian, mansion and retain, in part, some of its mural decorations.

In Burlington House, William Kent, a much over-rated Georgian architect, who began life as a coach painter, died in 1748, and was buried in Lord Burlington's private vault at Chiswick.

Handel lived in the house for three whole years and Gay was a constant visitor.

Hogarth's caustically cynical "Man of Taste," first published in 1731, but promptly "suppressed," shows us Kent's ponderous entrance gateway with the architect perched on its summit, flanked by the reclining figures of Michael Angelo and Raphael!

On a lower platform Pope is depicted as a plasterer whitewashing the front (incidentally bespattering the Duke of Chandos of "Canons" fame), whilst Lord Burlington, ascending a ladder, bricklayer's hod in hand, appears in the capacity of a humble labourer.

The Earl of Burlington died at Chiswick in 1753, and the great house in Piccadilly passed into the possession of the 4th Duke of Devonshire. He had married the Boyle heiress, Lady Charlotte

Elizabeth, when she was only sixteen. She brought the valuable Burlington estates, including Bolton Abbey and Lismore Castle, into the Cavendish family and died at the early age of twenty-three.

The 3rd Duke of Portland[50] lived here for a time, after his marriage with the Duke of Devonshire's only daughter. In 1815 the 6th Duke of the house of Cavendish sold Burlington House for £75,000 to his uncle, Lord George Cavendish, the projector of the Burlington Arcade. He sat in the House of Commons for over fifty years, almost a record to that date, and the title of Earl of Burlington was revived in his favour at the coronation of William the Fourth.

In 1854 the Cavendishes sold Burlington House to the Government for £140,000, nearly double the sum realised only 40 years earlier, with a view to the erection of a new National Gallery on the site. This project was not finally abandoned until 1866, when the house was leased to the Royal Academy of Arts, in whose occupation it remains. When the beautiful colonnade was removed, the old wall facing Piccadilly, well shown in Boys' view of the street, was pulled down, and a rather ineffective new front added in order to accommodate various learned societies who desired to make their permanent home in Piccadilly. The garden at the back was also built over to house the newly created University of London.

No sooner had Burlington House risen from its foundations than several other well-inhabited houses were built between it on the west and what is now Sackville Street on the east.

They embraced the site of what is now the Albany, or Albany without the prefix, as the residents within its gates prefer to call it. Proceeding eastwards from Burlington House, these houses were severally in the occupation, when first they attracted the notice of the rate-collector, of Jeremiah Clarke, Sir Thomas Clarges, Sir Thomas Ingram, Lord Townshend, and Sir William Petty.[51] The two most important, Sir Thomas Clarges's and Lord Townshend's, stood well back from the road, after the usual manner of capital mansions of the better class, and had ample fore-courts of their own. Even before the close of the seventeenth century the process of absorption had begun, as after 1699 I find only four houses enumerated in this section of the street, and in parochial maps of the first quarter of the eighteenth century there appear to be only two of any considerable size. Sir Thomas Clarges, one of the members for Westminster, was a great speculator in house property in Piccadilly and St James's.

In common with that of Sir William Pulteney, who represented Westminster from 1678–79 till 1691, when he died, I find his name again and again in deeds relating to new buildings which sprang up with lightning rapidity in this quarter of the town. It was Clarges who advised Lord St Albans in the planning of St James's Square, and in that favoured spot he secured for himself a plot of ground on the north side.[52]

He did not, however, inhabit it himself, and its first occupier was Lawrence Hyde, afterwards Earl of Rochester, a son of the fallen Chancellor.

A brother-in-law of General Monk, Clarges contrived to enrich himself out of the public purse whilst posing in Parliament as a rigid economist. He died in 1695, and was succeeded in the representation of Westminster by Sir Walter Clarges.[53]

Lord Townshend's house was successively inhabited by Dorothy, Lady Stanhope (from 1676 to 1686), and her son, Charles Livingston, Earl of Newburgh.

He was followed by Mary, Countess of Denbigh, and after her began the long connection of the Spencers with Piccadilly.

Charles, Lord Spencer, the first of his family to settle here, came in 1696, on attaining his majority. Four years later he married Anne Churchill, daughter of the great Duke of Marlborough, and with her marriage portion he greatly improved the property.

At his father's death in 1702 the Earl of Sunderland, as he had now become, resigned the Piccadilly house to his mother (who, according to Queen Anne, was "the greatest jade that ever was"), and went to live in St James's Square, where he remained for five years at a house on the site of the present Norfolk House.[54]

In 1709 Sunderland was back in Piccadilly, and having bought the freehold of Clarges's house for £4,600 he proceeded to throw it into his own, and to build a library at the back, 150 feet long, to contain the books it had been his life's passion to collect. These formed the nucleus of the famous Sunderland library at Blenheim, brought to the hammer in 1881.

Scattered to the four corners of the globe, they experienced a worse fate than the literary treasures of Althorp, which, when parted with by the late Lord Spencer, "the red Earl," were, fortunately for the nation, preserved *en bloc* in the Rylands Memorial library at Manchester.

Sunderland began life as an active Whig, but became unpopular with his party. Setting himself up in opposition to Walpole, he succeeded in ousting him from office and became Prime Minister in 1718.

Rumours connecting his name with the South Sea speculation eventually drove him from office. Though he was technically acquitted of actual corruption by a strictly party vote, his Chancellor of the Exchequer (John Aislabie) did not fare so well, for he was expelled from the House of Commons for gambling in the same stock. Aislabie attempted to justify his conduct before a Committee of the House of Lords, declaring that he regarded his dealings as an investment, and not as a speculation. But he signally failed to convince his accusers of his *bona fides*, and he retired from public life to Studley Royal, where he passed the remainder of his days in seclusion.

Robert, 4th Earl of Sunderland, also lived in Piccadilly, but his son, the 5th Earl, who became 3rd Duke of Marlborough, sold the house in June, 1745, to the Duke of Bedford. After the death of Duchess Sarah, Marlborough House in Pall Mall became available, and the Duke soon removed to it, altering and improving the house by the addition of an upper storey.

The Duke of Bedford's tenure of Sunderland House was a very brief one, for in the summer of 1746 he entered into negotiations for its sale to Lord Monson, who ultimately acquired it for the small sum of £6,000.

His Grace of Bedford was anxious that the new owner should take over the Sunderland bookcases and he did so, but the 2nd Lord Monson pulled the library down in 1758 and, five years later, sold the house for £16,000 to Henry Fox, 1st Lord Holland, leader of the House of Commons in the Newcastle and Bute Ministries.

He, in his turn, parted with it to Peniston Lamb, 1st Viscount Melbourne, who rebuilt it from the designs of Sir William Chambers, and eventually exchanged it with the Duke of York for Melbourne House in Whitehall, now the Scottish Office.

In 1775, the leasehold interest of Melbourne House, or York House as it was by then called, was sold for only £8,000. Sir William Chambers acquired something of a proprietary interest in it, probably on account of professional fees owing to him. Thomas Coutts, the banker, lent a large sum of money on the freehold to the Duke of York, as did several others.

Its last owner before its conversion into Chambers seems to have been Alexander Copland, a builder in St. Martin's Lane, who paid Coutts £95,000, and the Duke of York £9,300 for the freehold.

The high wall screening the house from Piccadilly was demolished about the same time, and four shops were built on the vacant space. The well-modelled figures of eagles supporting their balconies have been supposed to be an allusion to the Duke's heraldic bearings, but this is at least doubtful. The Duke of York is commemorated in the West End by the column in House Terrace. His effigy on the summit was humorously said to have been placed so high up in order to keep him out of the reach of his creditors!

In 1803, York House became the Albany Chambers. Amongst the first tenants were Lord Althorp and George Canning, both of whom occupied rooms in the mansion house towards Piccadilly.

The garden at the back was subsequently built over to provide additional suites. Macaulay's rooms were in Block E, and No. 1 on the west side, and Bulwer Lytton's in Block H, and No. 6 on the east.

Space does not admit of a catalogue of the many distinguished men who have chosen to make their home in the Albany, to enjoy within its gates a semi-collegiate life in the heart of London. Numbers and labels are of little account nor, at this distance of time, does it much matter, except perhaps to their humbler successors, which were the actual rooms occupied by Byron, Bulwer Lytton or "Monk" Lewis. I believe, however, that a late resident left, at the time of his recent death, an exhaustive list of former Albanians which may some day be given to the world. I lived in Piccadilly for some years and learned to love it, but, in spite of the fascination which the Albany seems to possess for men prominent in all walks of life, I have never been quite able to understand their predilection for this rather gloomy place of abode. It may be that the quiet and isolation of this residential backwater appeals strongly to them but, personally, I prefer the full tide of human existence which sweeps along the main thoroughfare, ever changing but never ceasing.

It is interesting to remember that Mr Gladstone was always partial to this neighbourhood. On first entering Parliament he lodged in Jermyn Street with a relation of some of his constituents at Newark, migrating thence to the Albany, where he remained till his marriage. In the evening of his laborious days, after occupying numbers of other houses besides the official residence in Downing Street, he took No 10 St James's Square, which had been Chatham's London abode at the zenith of his power.

I used frequently to see Mr Gladstone in the Square during the Parliamentary session of 1890, and it was from him, personally, that I learnt of his early association with St James's. He told me that though he was aware of Lady Blessington having lived at No 10, when he was a young man, and of Lord Derby's subsequent tenure of the house, he had not the slightest idea, until I informed him, of the much greater historical interest attaching to it in the eighteenth century.

Mr. Gladstone's knowledge of London was extraordinary. His remarkably accurate memory enabled him to recall not only the habitations of nearly all his friends and acquaintances for a period of more than sixty years, but also the successive ownership of shops and business premises in every quarter of the town. Always, until old age overtook him, an untiring walker, no other Prime Minister of modern times was to be seen so often on foot in the West End.

Where Palmerston habitually rode, Gladstone, if he could possibly spare the time, preferred to walk.

After a late sitting of the House of Commons, (and perhaps a heated debate in which he had borne the principal burden), I have met him, on a fine summer's night, proceeding briskly along Piccadilly, evidently enjoying the fresh air at a time when less active men would have gone straight to bed.

His ghost may walk in Albany, in company with that of Canning and other giants of his youth, but rather than meet with it in that sombre and rather airless environment, I would prefer to think of him revisiting his former haunts—the humble lodgings over the corn-chandler's shop in Jermyn Street or the more dignified and spacious surroundings of his later days in St James's Square.[55]

So far I have dealt only with the coming of the aristocracy to Piccadilly as regards that portion of the thoroughfare lying to the eastward of Devonshire House.

With the accession of the House of Hanover the street, as a place of residence, increased rapidly in favour.

The masons' and statuaries' yards, and the small inn-holders' premises towards Hyde Park were gradually replaced by private houses.

On the abolition of the fair, held in Brook Fields in the month of May from time immemorial, the building of substantial mansions, commanding a view of the Green Park, received a great impetus.[56]

Yet something of the old leaven lingered until well into the reign of George the First. I gather from a periodical publication of the time that one Jane Symonds, of evil memory, was sentenced to be whipped from the lower end of the Haymarket to the upper end of Piccadilly where she kept a seraglio of female traders.[57]

By leaving Devonshire House behind and crossing one of my Lady Berkeley's new streets a landmark is reached in the extension of the historic thoroughfare dating only from the accession of George the Third.

If there is one house in Piccadilly more generally known to the man in the street than any other, with the possible exception of Apsley House, it is the plain, bow-fronted brick building at the corner of Stratton Street. Not a beautiful house, judged by any standard of taste, its honest exterior bespeaks respectability, and its design proclaims that firm dependence on utility characteristic of the period of its erection. Thousands who never entered its doors have paused to stare at the white cockatoo which has hung for more years than I care to remember in the dining-room window overlooking the Green Park. Working men as they passed to their morning's toil have felt themselves cheered by its familiar presence and have recognised No 1 Stratton Street as the home of one of their best friends—the philanthropic Baroness Burdett-Coutts—a lady whose good deeds and heartfelt interest in the poor require no extraneous advertisement.

There is a pretty story connected with the cockatoo which deserves to be rescued from oblivion. An ugly-looking mob composed of the riff-raff of the East End, on its way to a strike meeting in Hyde Park, once halted opposite the house whilst its leaders argued amongst themselves with much heat whether the bird was a live one or only a counterfeit. So engrossed were they in the controversy that they forgot the immediate cause of their assembling, and the procession, which had at first threatened to give serious trouble to the police, allowed itself to be summarily dispersed. Three cheers were raised for the Baroness and an impending riot was averted solely through the peaceful agency of the china cockatoo. Long may it continue to exercise a beneficent influence on the changing passions of the crowds which pass through Piccadilly from time to time *en route* to the Reformers' tree.

The history of Lady Burdett-Coutts's house, inextricably bound up as it is with the adjoining No 80 Piccadilly (in the same ownership), is a long one and takes the reader back to the middle of the eighteenth century.

This corner house (at one time officially designated No. 77 Piccadilly during one of the street's periodical renumberings) was built, probably from the designs of Matthew Brettingham, at a cost of £8,500, immediately after the accession of George the Third, for the tenth Earl of Eglinton. It took three years to build under the direction of a Mr. Cameron, who stipulated that he should be the only person employed in all branches of the work. The Earl was a friend and contemporary of "Old Q" and had been his schoolfellow at Winchester. He was also associated with him in the celebrated carriage match on Newmarket Heath (see Chapter IV). A representative peer for Scotland and a Lord of the Bedchamber in his later years, Lord Eglinton took a more serious view of life than "Old Q," devoting himself untiringly to the improvement of his Ayrshire estates. He introduced new and improved methods of agriculture to the notice of his Scotch farmers, who clung with the tenacity of their race to what they had always been accustomed to and viewed with suspicion any alteration emanating from south of the Tweed. Lord Eglinton also displayed considerable aptitude for Parliamentary business and was largely responsible for the passing of an Act which abolished the optional clause enabling the Scottish banks to refuse payment of their notes until six months after demand.

His death, at the early age of forty-seven, was regarded as a national loss and took place under tragic circumstances. He was engaged to be married at the time, which increased the general sympathy at his untimely fate. Whilst driving near Eglinton Castle he noticed an excise officer named Mungo Campbell, whom he had formerly caught poaching on his estate, with a gun in his hand. When told to give up the weapon, Campbell refused, and, after a long altercation, fired at and mortally wounded Lord Eglinton. The murderer was tried and convicted at Edinburgh and only escaped the gallows by hanging himself in gaol. (For a circumstantial account of this tragedy see Wood's edition of Douglas's "Peerage of Scotland," 1813, Vol. I, p. 506.)

Lord Eglinton's house did not stand empty long, for in 1771 the second Earl Fitzwilliam (distinguished in after years when Lord Lieutenant of Ireland for his broad-minded views on Catholic Emancipation) came to live here on his marriage. He altered the house by the addition of the attic storey and made other minor improvements at a cost of £1,600. On the death of his uncle the Marquis of Rockingham in 1782, he succeeded to the Wentworth estates, including the house in Grosvenor Square where his descendants have lived ever since.

Earl Fitzwilliam's aunt, Lady Rockingham, changed houses with him and lived in Piccadilly until 1791, being succeeded by Lord Beauchamp (Francis Seymour Conway, Viscount Beauchamp, afterwards second Marquis of Hertford, K.G., born 1743, died 1822), who stayed here for only one year.[58] In 1794 the house was empty, but in the course of the following year Thomas Coutts, founder of the Bank in the Strand, acquired it, adding the library and some extra bedrooms. He bought for this purpose two adjoining houses, Nos 5 and 6 Stratton Street, and made at the back a small garden which still exists.

With characteristic caution, Coutts instructed Robert Mylne, surveyor of St Paul's Cathedral, to make a detailed report of the value of the house, from which I gather the following facts.

As originally designed the house had a frontage only thirty-one feet six inches towards Piccadilly, but stress is laid in the report upon its great depth of substantial building on the Stratton Street front, extending, as it does in part, behind No. 80 in the main thoroughfare.

In 1795 the ground rent was only £28 and the site was not, in Mylne's opinion, likely to be "diminished by any probable event."

At Lord Eglinton's death it had been sold at auction by Christie for £7,500, and, in concluding his valuation, Mylne advised Mr. Coutts that, "in these times of advanced price of workmanship and diminished value of money," he ought not to offer more than £11,000 to £12,000 for the property.

Three months after the death of his first wife[59] Coutts married Harriet Mellon, an actress of Irish birth and considerable beauty. He was then in his 80th year and she only thirty-seven. Making her first appearance on the London stage at Drury Lane in 1795 as Lydia Languish, she became friendly with Coutts before her retirement from the boards in Waterloo year.

Coutts died immensely rich in 1822, leaving everything he possessed to his widow.

Her second husband was the ninth Duke of St Albans, and the marriage took place, by special licence, at No 1 Stratton Street. On this occasion the ages of the contracting parties were reversed, for the Duke was only twenty-six and Harriet close upon fifty. It seems to have been a marriage of affection, and though, at her death, she bequeathed the bulk of her fortune to Mr. Coutts's daughters by his first wife, she was able out of her savings to leave the Duke £10,000 a year.

Coutts's youngest daughter, Sophia, married Sir Francis Burdett, the champion of free speech, popularly known as "Old Glory," and their youngest daughter, Angela, created Baroness Burdett-Coutts in 1871, was born at No 80 in 1814.

Only a few years before, her father had been committed to the Tower by the House of Commons. The sensational incidents of his forcible arrest in Piccadilly by the Serjeant-at-Arms are well known: a warrant for his arrest being issued by the Speaker, Burdett barricaded himself inside his house, but the Serjeant, escorted by soldiers, forced an entry and he was conveyed under guard to the Tower. Sir Francis was again imprisoned in 1820, on this occasion for three months, for a libel on the Government. He became more moderate in his political views as he grew older, and after representing the City of Westminster for thirty years as a democrat he ended his Parliamentary career as a Tory county member.

It is not often that one hears of a man dying of a broken heart, but Burdett is said to have grieved so much at the death of his wife that he died in less than a fortnight after her, and they were both buried in one grave on the same day.

No 80 is interesting if only from the fact that it is believed to be the first stuccoed house ever built in London. The site was granted in 1737 by Lord Berkeley of Stratton to Mr Boswell at a rental of £15 per annum. Sir Richard Lyttelton pulled the original house down and built the existing one in 1764–65. Other occupiers were his widow Rachel, Duchess of Bridgwater; Richard Willoughby, fourth Lord Middleton, and his widow, who re-married Sir Edward Miller Mundy. In 1802 Mr. Coutts bought the house at auction and allowed his son-in-law the use of it. Another of Coutts's daughters, the Countess of Guildford, lived in it until her death in 1837. The Duke of St Albans was here from 1838 to 1849, Thomas Assheton-Smith from 1854 to 1857, and Dr James Blundell from 1858 to 1878. It is now part of the premises of the Royal Thames Yacht Club and the freehold property of Mr Burdett Coutts, MP

The Baroness remained constant to Piccadilly during the whole of her long life, removing from No 80 (after the death of Duchess Harriet) to Stratton Street, where she died in 1906. At the time of the Chartist rising the Duke of Wellington, with a keen perception of the military advantages of the position, stationed a company of riflemen in the bow windows of the first floor in order to command a direct line of fire, east and west, in case their services should be required.

Bath House, at the western corner of Bolton Street, and formerly reckoned therein, though rated as in Piccadilly since 1773, deserves more than a passing glance.

Built by the Pulteneys, lords of the soil in the immediate neighbourhood from the reign of Charles I, if not earlier, it forms the connecting link with Lord Clarendon's grant from the Crown and what is known as the Sutton estate.

The Pulteneys, now extinct in the male line, could trace an unbroken descent from Sir John de Pulteney, who was Mayor of London on four separate occasions in the fourteenth century.

Prospering exceedingly as he did in the wool trade, Sir John's position was so well established in the reign of Edward III that he was able, on several occasions, to lend the king money.

His house at Cold Harbour, not far from the modern Cannon Street, was of such magnificence that, after his death in 1349, it was used as a Royal residence by Edward, the Black Prince.

For close upon 500 years the Pulteneys made the accumulation of wealth their principal business in life, and in process of time they acquired vast estates in town and country.

Their name endures to this day, in the City of London, in Lawrence Pountney (or Pulteney) Lane, and, in the West End, in Pulteney Street. The best-known street in all the City of Bath is also called after the same family. The original Bath House in Piccadilly was pulled down and rebuilt in its present shape in 1821 by the first Lord Ashburton, but a view of the old mansion of the Pulteneys, shortly before its demolition, is given in plate 3.

Plain and unpretentious, with a large garden at the back extending almost to Curzon Street, it is clearly marked in Rocque's great map of London published in 1746.

It might appropriately be re-christened "The Millionaire's Home," for since its erection in the eighteenth century it has been continuously inhabited by a succession of extremely rich men, not all of them of English origin and none, perhaps, of outstanding eminence in political or social life apart from their great wealth and such influence as springs from the power which wealth confers when wisely used.

Imagination fairly reels at the thought of the aggregate fortunes of some half a dozen families who have made Bath House their London home since William Pulteney removed to it from Arlington Street in 1740.

His father, another William Pulteney, died in 1715, and it is a singular coincidence that after his death no one member of this ancient family left a male heir.

William Pulteney, Earl of Bath, was Walpole's most persistent opponent throughout his political career. Possessed as he was of oratorical powers far above the average, Sir Robert said that he feared his tongue more than another man's sword. Arthur Onslow, the *doyen* of Speakers, had also the highest opinion of his Parliamentary capacity.

"Bill, of all Bob's foes, the wittiest in verse and prose," was Prime Minister in 1746 for exactly two days, but "sinking into obscurity and a peerage" he died in 1764, leaving behind him a fortune of £1,200,000, almost unremembered by posterity. His portrait, by Sir Joshua Reynolds, in the National Portrait Gallery, is one of the finest and most vigorously painted of that master's works.

He was succeeded in Piccadilly by his only surviving, and unmarried, brother General Harry Pulteney, Lord Bath's only son, Viscount Pulteney, having predeceased his father.[60]

Lord Bath left his brother—though, according to Lord Chesterfield, he never loved him—not only his fortune but a large landed estate formerly belonging to Lord Bradford. This, Chesterfield more than hinted, had been acquired from a lunatic owner by undue influence. General Harry only enjoyed his inheritance for three years, for he died in Piccadilly in 1767 in his 82nd year, leaving directions in his will that his house should be called Bath House for evermore.

He left the Earl of Darlington, whose grandmother had been a Pulteney, £200,000 in the funds.

The next owner of the house was Sir William (Johnstone) Pulteney, who assumed the family name on his marriage to Frances, fourth daughter and eventually sole heiress of Daniel Pulteney of Harefield. General Harry left her £28,000 a year including the Bradford estate. She died at Bath House in 1782.

Sir William Johnstone Pulteney, who in his old age made the daughter and co-heir of Sir William Stirling his second wife, is said to have been the richest commoner in England. When he died intestate, in 1805, his funded estate alone amounted to two millions sterling.

The largest holder of American stock known to that date, his daughter, Henrietta Laura, created Countess of Bath in her own right, is said to have paid in stamp duties alone £6,000, the largest sum then on record, on succeeding to his estate.

In her youth Lady Bath is supposed to have been betrothed to Charles James Fox. Rumours to that effect were current in London society in 1788, in which year they were both in Italy. Fox was travelling abroad at the time with his mistress, Mrs Armistead, whom he eventually married in 1795, though his belated union was not publicly avowed until 1802.

Had the engagement to the great Pulteney heiress not been broken off, who can tell how Fox's after career might have been affected?

The fact remains that they drifted apart and, in 1794, Lady Bath married, by special licence at the family house, her cousin the Right Honourable Sir James Murray, who promptly assumed his wife's maiden name. Lady Bath died without issue in 1808 at the comparatively early age of 41, and was buried from Piccadilly in the south cloister of Westminster.

There, and in the Abbey itself, are to be seen the graves and monuments of so many generations of Pulteneys as almost to lead one to believe that the family enjoyed a prescriptive right of burial at Westminster. Lord Bath lies in the Islip chapel, securely sealed down under a flat blue stone with his wife, brother, and only son near him. There is a ponderous monument to him by Wilton in the North Ambulatory, but the medallion portrait which surmounts the marble pile is placed so high up as to be almost invisible in the dim light of that portion of the Abbey. When the family vault became too full to allow of any more interments in the Abbey the Pulteneys overflowed into the south cloister where, formerly, the only graves allowed to be dug were those of the Norman Abbots.

With the death of Henrietta, Countess of Bath, the race of Pulteney became extinct in the direct line. I have been unable to trace a portrait of this lady, but some particulars of her character have been recorded by an anonymous writer in the "Annual Register."

In her earliest youth she is said to have been of such a benevolent nature that she would give the shoes and stockings from her own feet to beggars at her mother's carriage door.

Cultivating habits of application and business in the exclusive management of her vast estates, she would never sign a paper without carefully perusing it, "frequently," we are told, "correcting the mistakes of her lawyers." Her "almost-uninterrupted continuance of ill-health rendered her retirement at last equal to a perfect seclusion from the world."

Of unassuming simplicity of manner and unaffected good nature, she found, we are also told, her greatest solace in religion.

Lady Bath's husband enjoyed the income from the Pulteney estates, estimated at £50,000 a year, until his death in 1811 from an accident caused by the bursting of a powder flask in his hand.

He left £600,000 to his half-brother John, eighth Baronet of Clermont, and £200,000 to another half-brother.

Nearly a million of Lady Bath's great fortune passed to her cousin, Mrs Elizabeth Evelyn Markham,[61] who had lived under Lady Bath's roof for years, having been divorced by her husband the Dean of York—an unusual happening in the life of a dignitary of the Church of England.

Mrs Markham's second husband was John Fawcett (afterwards of Northwood Park, Lyndhurst), who also, "from grateful and affectionate regard" to the memory of Countess Henrietta, assumed the name of Pulteney.

The freehold London estates devolved upon Sir Richard Sutton, Lady Bath's kinsman. To understand aright the succession of the Suttons to the Pulteney millions it should be mentioned that Lady Bath's maternal grandmother was Margaret Tichborne (daughter and co-heiress of Benjamin Tichborne), wife of Daniel Pulteney of Harefield; and that her sister Judith [Tichborne], third wife of the third Earl of Sunderland, took for her second husband Sir Robert Sutton, K.B., father of the Sir Richard who was created a baronet in 1773.

The second baronet of this name, whom we shall meet with again in the next chapter, succeeded his father at the early age of two, and during his long minority the Piccadilly property so increased in value that he became eventually one of the richest men in England.

The family mansion in Piccadilly was let for a few years to the fourth Duke of Portland at what was then considered the enormous rent of £2,500.

General Sir John Murray, eighth Baronet of Clermont aforesaid, was the next occupier and after him came the first Lord Ashburton, head of the great financial house of Baring Brothers, or Behring, as the name was habitually spelt until the family removed from Bremen to London.[62]

Lord Ashburton was a connoisseur of the Arts and a first-rate judge of pictures. His collection, especially rich in examples of the Dutch and Flemish schools, long adorned the walls of the rebuilt Bath House, but has now been dispersed.

His three successors in the title carried on the Baring family connection with the old home of the Pulteneys, but on the death of the fourth Lord Ashburton, in Piccadilly, in 1889, the house passed into the occupation of the late Baron de Hirsch, an international financier of a distinctly different type from the Barings.

He died in 1896 and was succeeded at Bath House by yet another multi-millionaire. This was Sir Julius Wernher, who died in it in 1912.

Its Georgian exterior is in no way remarkable except for the solidity and excellence of the brick work, but the interior was lavishly redecorated by Sir Julius in the modern French style, extremely ornate but of an almost overpowering richness.

In the Sutton family the freehold remains to this day, though repeated offers to acquire it have been made unsuccessfully from time to time by various millionaires who have rented it from the ground landlord.

The late Sir Richard Sutton, who lost his young life on active service in the great war, is said to have contemplated taking up his abode either here or at Cambridge House when the lease of the latter to the Naval and Military Club should expire.

One word more about this interesting abode of mammon before passing westward and its record is finished.

Though it does not look at all like a public bagnio or wash-house it is said that ingenuous passers-by, seeing the name of the house inscribed on its outer walls, have been known to ring the bell and ask if a hot bath could be obtained there and at what charge!

There are not nowadays many private houses remaining in this part of Piccadilly which require to be noticed separately, most of those which are now occupied by clubs being treated of in the next chapter.

No 129, formerly 19, Piccadilly West, was built in 1787 and first occupied by Sir John Lade, a sporting baronet, and one of the ultra-fast set surrounding the Prince Regent.

Being reduced to something like beggary in his old age, Lord Anglesey induced George IV to give him £500 a year out of the Privy Purse. William IV reduced the allowance to £300, but in the very last letter which Creevey ever wrote, dated January 27th, 1838, it is stated that the young Queen, having enquired whether Sir John was not over eighty years of age, declared that, rather than allow the pension to be reduced, she would continue to pay it out of her own private means. Lade's name disappears from the rate-books after 1796, and the next occupier of the house was the Margrave of Anspach.

No 137, at the west corner of Old Park Lane, was until recently Gloucester House. It was built for the Cholmondeleys early in the reign of George III, before the family removed to Egremont, or, as it afterwards came to be called, Cambridge House.

It was a homely-looking building with a green balcony towards the park, and it became a Royal residence when the Duke of Gloucester on his marriage acquired it from Lord Elgin.

In it the famous Elgin marbles were stored before their removal to the British Museum.

George, Duke of Cambridge, Commander-in-Chief of the Army, lived in it for many years, and I have before me, as I write, a letter from him to Delane, written in 1868, asking him to lend his powerful aid to prevent him from being turned out of house and home by the Government of the day.

The appeal to Jupiter was not made in vain, and the old Duke remained undisturbed in Piccadilly till his death. When a statue, on a prancing steed, was set up to his memory in Whitehall, the inscription on the base wrongly assigned the date of his death to the year 1903, instead of 1904. The mistake was soon discovered, and the blunder corrected, but the earlier date is still visible beneath the altered figure.

The house was pulled down after the Duke's death and replaced by a hideous block of flats with a top-heavy façade towards the street. Out of all proportion to its surroundings it constitutes a perpetual eye-sore, viewed from any standpoint in Piccadilly or the Green Park.

When it was first erected, as much as £1,000 a year was asked for a suite of rooms here, but I believe that not many were let at anything approaching such a figure; at all events not until recently, when the most extravagant sums are asked and obtained for houses and flats in the immediate neighbourhood.

III

The Club-houses of Piccadilly, their Former Owners, and the Coming of the Rothschilds to the West End

Sixty years ago, strange though it may appear, there was not a single Club in Piccadilly, from end to end, though, as has been pointed out in an earlier chapter, there had been gambling hells, in the thin disguise of social circles, scattered here and there along the street for years before. At the present day, west of Devonshire House and right up to Park Lane this historic thoroughfare threatens to become a serried mass of Club houses. Nor is the reason for this rapid change in the face of the West End far to seek.

The ever-growing volume of traffic, carried on without intermission by night and by day, has rendered Piccadilly less desirable for purposes of private residence on account of the noise, which the introduction of wood-paving has been powerless to mitigate, until, at the time of writing, few family houses remain within its boundaries. Some half-dozen mansions near Hyde Park Corner, fortunately for their owners, stand back from the overcrowded roadway and so escape the disadvantages which confront their less favourably situated neighbours in the hollow of the street.

Existing Clubs have enlarged their premises, sweeping away the former homes of private individuals in the process.

Vast caravanserais, like the white marble palace of the Junior Constitutional, pretentious without and luxurious within, have absorbed whole blocks of smaller houses. Many of these had interesting histories of their own as will appear hereafter, dating, for the most part, from the latter end of the eighteenth century. Even the sacrosanct precincts of Hamilton Place have been invaded, owing to the increased demand for Club accommodation by all sorts and conditions of men who, fifty years ago, would not have required a Club at all.

The gradual relinquishment on the part of private owners of once-coveted sites overlooking the Green Park has left less than a dozen private houses between Devonshire House and Hyde Park Corner. These are now far outnumbered by Clubs, social, political, diplomatic, literary, naval and military, by Clubs admitting ladies (and even dogs) as guests. Some of them have proved to be of the purely agaric order, but some there are whose histories deserve fuller consideration, dating as they do from mid-Victorian times when the Club-habit received its greatest impetus.

Horace Walpole, writing to Montagu in 1759, was amazed at the rapid development of a neighbourhood which he only remembered as the recognised haunt of livery-stable keepers and purveyors of leaden figures.

"I stared to-day at Piccadilly, like a country squire. There are twenty new stone houses. At first I concluded that all the grooms that used to live there had got estates and built palaces."

Evidently he had Lord Egremont, Lord Coventry and the Duke of Grafton in his mind, for their mansions were rising from their foundations when George the Third came to the throne, and others, at least as important, followed in the wake of these pioneers of fashion. Nearly all of these great private houses are now occupied by Clubs, as are several other large houses erected in Piccadilly within the next decade.

Far and away the most celebrated of these mansions are Cambridge House and Coventry House, two well-designed eighteenth-century houses whose exteriors present to-day much the same appearance as they did when first built.

No 81, an unpretentious-looking house at the east corner of Bolton Street,[63] had in earlier days an evil reputation as a gambling house.

Originally built in the middle of the eighteenth century, its first occupier was Sir Sidney Meadows, who was succeeded by Sir John Fleming Leicester, afterwards Lord de Tabley.

In 1805, or at the beginning of 1806, the house was taken by Watier, the Prince Regent's cook, and in partnership with Maddison, the Prince's page, and Augustus Labourie, another of the Royal cooks, it became, under the thin disguise of a harmonic assembly,[64] a gaming club which acquired a sinister reputation for high play and extravagant living.

Catches and glees were soon superseded by cards and dice. Macao was the principal game, just as it had been at the seventeenth-century Piccadilly gaming-house.[65] Byron and Brummell were constant visitors and, in the long run, heavy losers. The former cared only for the rattle of the dice and disliked cards, but the Beau was once so fortunate as to win £1,500 here in ten minutes. Half of this he insisted on giving to Sheridan, saying: "There, Tom, go home and give your wife and brats a supper, and never play again."

"The play at Watier's is *tremendous*," wrote Sir Harry Featherstone to Arthur Paget in May, 1811. "Charles Manners has won £3,000 or £4,000, which he was much in need of. There has been a grand commotion among the cooks, the Prince having debauched three from their places, Lord Granville Leveson's, Lord Bathurst's and another; mine was attempted, but he resisted."

Watier's name is not found in connection with the house after 1811, but the rates were paid by Labourie as late as 1823, though by that date most of the original members were either dead or ruined.

John Maddocks cut his throat, Brummell levanted to Calais, where Charles Greville saw him in 1830, "full of gaiety, impudence and misery." Byron shook the dust of London off his feet and retired to the Continent, never to return to England.

In 1824 a man named Joshua Taylor took the house and entered into partnership with Crockford, who had started life as a fishmonger near Temple Bar. They set up a hazard bank at No 81 and won a great deal of money, but, having quarrelled, they separated at the end of the first year. Taylor remained where he was in Piccadilly, had a bad year, and failed. Crockford moved to St James's Street, and being remarkably successful in attracting the *jeunesse dorée*, he built the large house which is now the Devonshire Club.

He furnished it regardless of expense, and the curious in petty details can still see in the modern club some of the crimson and gilt chairs on which the gamblers sat. Crockford engaged Ude as cook and provided free suppers for his patrons. One of them, a Member of Parliament, developed such an enormous appetite, that after he had breakfasted off a whole covey of partridges, Crockford had serious thoughts of offering him a guinea to take his supper elsewhere. Theodore Hook, who was a pretty constant visitor, when he had anything to lose, used to excuse himself for not going to bed by saying that he always made it a rule not to expose himself to the night air. The "fishmonger," as he was familiarly called by the members, retired in 1840, much as an Indian Chief deserts a hunting country when there is not game enough left for his tribe. He is supposed to have made a million by the profits of the bank, even after making allowance for half that sum in bad debts.

After Crockford's departure from Piccadilly, No 81 returned to respectability, and continued to be used as a private house until the premises were acquired by the Royal Thames Yacht Club a few years ago.

There are no very interesting associations connected with the houses numbered from 83 to 93 inclusive, with the possible exception of the Turf Club, in former years the town house of the Dukes of Grafton, which belongs not so much to Piccadilly as to Clarges Street, in which it is No 47.

Proceeding west, when No 94 in the main thoroughfare is reached, we are once more on classic ground.

The large stone-fronted house, with its " In" and "Out" entrance gates, standing well back from the road,[66] was built in 1760 for the second Earl of Egremont, by whose name it was known for many years subsequently.

When Dodsley wrote his interesting book on old London it was the last house of any account built in Piccadilly proper, though long before 1760 there had been a number of small dwelling-houses round about Hyde Park Corner, most of them taverns frequented by drovers attending the periodical cattle markets held in Brook Fields. These flowery meads, in which Gerard loved to botanise, have long been obliterated by the fashionable district vaguely called Mayfair.

Lord Egremont began life as a Tory, but gradually weakened into Whiggism, so much so that, when the elder Pitt was driven from office, he accepted the post of Secretary of State for the Southern Department under the Duke of Newcastle.

His connection with political life was not of long duration, for two years later he died in the house which he had so recently built. He seems to have been of a gluttonous disposition, for the cause of his death was apoplexy, and only a few days before it occurred he is related to have said: "I have three more turtle dinners to come. If I survive the last of them I shall be immortal."

His son and successor in the title reversed his father's political opinions, for from having been brought up as an orthodox Whig he developed in later years into an irreproachable Tory. Perhaps his conversion was due to his heart having inclined more to art and sport than to politics. He encouraged mediocrity in Haydon and Lucas, recognised talent in Constable, and was one of the first amateurs of art, in common with Walter Fawkes of Farnley, to appreciate the consummate genius of Turner. Sculpture interested him quite as much as painting, and Nollekens and Flaxman owed a great deal in their early days to his generous assistance. From some unexplained cause sculptors always leave larger fortunes than painters. Nollekens, now scarcely remembered, left £200,000 at his death, and Chantrey, whose equestrian statue of George IV in Trafalgar Square cost the country from first to last nine thousand guineas, died worth £150,000.

Turner certainly did make money, though not a tenth part of what he ought to have made had his talents been properly appreciated in his lifetime.

It paid old Nollekens and his contemporaries better to line the walls of Westminster Abbey with memorial busts, wholly out of keeping with Gothic architecture, than it did Reynolds and Gainsborough to paint the same subjects on canvas. Neither of those great masters ever received for a single portrait anything like the prices now readily given for mezzotints after their works. Romney never received more than one hundred and twenty guineas for a picture, Raeburn and Constable died poor, and Haydon, an indifferent artist no doubt, was so mortified at the scant recognition of his talent that he committed suicide. Turner was always a welcome visitor at Petworth, where he had a studio fitted up for his private use, to which access could only be obtained by the noble owner on giving a pre-arranged tap at the door. In that agreeable seclusion he painted more than one view of the glorious deer park and the smiling landscape scenery of Sussex between Cowdray and Arundel.

An unfinished picture in the national collection was a study for "Petworth park with bucks fighting," in the possession of Lord Leconfield.

Turner made several water-colour drawings of the interior of the house which well illustrate his mastery of light and shade. Some of these, dating from about 1830, are now in the Tate Gallery at Millbank. It is probable that many an obscure artist, whose memory has not survived, had reason to bless Lord Egremont's name, for it is said on excellent authority that he gave away £20,000 a year (about a fourth of his total income) in works of charity.

He apppeared on the turf in 1787, when "old Q's" was still a name to conjure with at Newmarket. As the fortunes of the "Star of Piccadilly" declined, the Egremont colours rose to achieve a remarkable series of successes in the classic races, carrying off, as they did, both the Derby and the Oaks no fewer than five times. The local races at one time held at Petworth were transferred to Goodwood at the beginning of the nineteenth century, and after the course there had been relaid and greatly improved under the fostering care of Lord George Bentinck, the Duke of Richmond's home meeting became a formidable rival to many older racecourses.

Again and again Lord Egremont swept the board between 1802 and his death in 1837. He secured the Gold Cup, then, as now, the principal trophy to be won at Goodwood, the first year it was offered for competition, and later on, in two consecutive years.

A curious ménage in some respects was the Lord of Petworth's, and one that would be quite impossible at the present day.

Though never married, he was extremely fond of children, and his guests were aware of a numerous young family living happily under his roof and acknowledging him as their father, though all the time his friends knew that no woman had the legal right to call him husband.

The mother of some half-dozen of his natural children was commonly believed to be the wife of one of the assistant masters of Westminster School, where Lord Egremont had been educated. Possessing none of the usual attributes of the rake or the sensualist, of an affectionately domestic nature and imbued with the true spirit of hospitality, his unconquerable dislike to a formal matrimonial alliance never seems to have prevented his entertainments from being shared by many worthy people of a more conventional turn of mind.

At Petworth, where he lived on the best of terms with his tenants, host and visitors were accustomed to go their own way. The artists could sketch at their leisure and roam about the great stag park, the man or woman of literary tastes could spend the day undisturbed in the library, whilst others hunted and shot. Another attraction was the stud farm, where were to be seen between 60 and 70 brood mares, and about 300 horses all told.

All met at dinner-time, when, in good old English fashion, Lord Egremont sat at the head of the table and carved for each guest.[67]

After living for thirty years in Piccadilly he removed to Grosvenor Place, a few doors from Hyde Park Corner, to be succeeded at Egremont House by James Milnes, of whom I have discovered nothing, except that his country house was at Thornes House, near Wakefield. Possibly he was related to Lord Houghton's family. The first Marquis of Cholmondeley came to No 94 from Gloucester House, to call it by the name which it afterwards acquired, early in the nineteenth century, and died in Piccadilly in 1827.

The house then became a Royal residence, as it was taken for HRH the Duke of Cambridge.[68]

The unexpected death of the Princess Charlotte in 1817 having made it necessary to provide for the succession to the throne of England, the Duke of Cambridge and his two bachelor brothers, the Dukes of Kent and Clarence, displayed a dutiful diligence in dismissing their respective mistresses as a preliminary to entering into the holy state of matrimony. They were all married within three months, in the course of the year after Princess Charlotte's death.

The old Duke of Cambridge, with whom alone we are concerned, was a bluff, hearty man with an incurable propensity for thinking aloud. Once on coming down to breakfast at Chatsworth he found family prayers in progress and exclaimed, as he dropped on his knees with the rest of the house party: "And a damned good custom too!"

On another occasion, after listening with attention to the reading of the Commandments in church, he added in an audible whisper, to the bewilderment of his fellow-worshippers, when the seventh was reached: "No, no; it was my brother Ernest who broke that one."

Shortly before his death at Cambridge House Queen Victoria went to see him, and as she was driving out of the courtyard, one Robert Pate, a retired lieutenant, and a lunatic, assaulted her with a stick. Still suffering from the blow, the Queen appeared at the Opera the same evening, where she was received with tremendous enthusiasm by the loyal audience.

In 1851 Sir Richard Sutton, the ground landlord of all this part of Piccadilly, came to live here. He was, in addition to being one of the richest men in the country, a great sportsman and master of the Quorn for many years. From first to last he is said to have spent £300,000 on fox-hunting. He died of *angina pectoris* at Cambridge House in November, 1855. His son Richard, the fourth Baronet, was also fond of sport.

In 1866 his *Lord Lyon*, ridden by Custance, won the Derby by a short head and the St. Leger by a nose. He does not appear to have taken up his abode in Piccadilly, and shortly after he succeeded his father there came to Cambridge House its most distinguished tenant. This was Lord Palmerston, the greatest of Victorian Prime Ministers with the exception of Sir Robert Peel. He had lived previously, for one year, at No 144, but in 1857 he came here to stay until his death.

Madame Flahault, who will be met with at Coventry House,[69] told Henry Greville as an instance of Talleyrand's remarkable insight into character that, when Ambassador at St James's in the reign of William the Fourth, he summed up his impressions of English statesmen by saying: "Mais parmi tous, c'est Palmerston qui est le véritable homme d'état." He then had been Foreign Secretary for only about two years, so the prophecy was an exceedingly shrewd one. Even at that time his gallantry towards the weaker sex had gained him the title of "the venerable Cupid." He realised to the full that wise saying of the Duchesse de Dino that it is by what they demand that men preserve their influence over women, while it is by what they concede that women preserve their influence over men. In later years people were uncharitable enough to say that a facial resemblance to the Prime Minister on the part of Lady Palmerston's children by her first marriage was more than an accidental coincidence.

This is not the place to write even a summary of Palmerston's public life, but it is to be hoped that some biographer may yet give to the world a full appreciation of his career based upon the mass of unpublished documents preserved at Broadlands.

Under Palmerston, the House of Commons was at its zenith. It possessed greater freedom of action than it does now, for its members, once elected, were free agents—at liberty to express their individual opinions—instead of (as now) finding their chief occupation in registering the cut-and-dried decrees of the Cabinet. Within the last twenty-five years the control and initiative in legislation have gradually passed by sure, if imperceptible, stages from the House to the Executive. Altered rules of procedure have tended to enhance the power of the Government at the expense of the independent member, and even the debates (once the admiration and the wonder of the civilised world), as conducted under the oppressive shadow of the guillotine, have lost half their reality. The late Professor Lecky maintained that the world has never seen a better political system than England enjoyed between 1832 and 1867, and Mr Gladstone, writing in 1877, made the significant admission that, in his judgment, "our level of public principle and public action was at its zenith in the twenty years or so which succeeded the Reform Act of 1832, and that it has since perceptibly gone down."

Opposed though he was to democratic change, Palmerston was superior to his immediate successors in his jealous regard for British interests. His common sense, his imperturbable good humour, and that inborn talent for leadership which ranks far above mere oratorical display, entitle him to a niche among the greatest figures of the Victorian age.

The outstanding feature of the General Election which immediately preceded his death was that it was practically a vote of continued confidence in himself, and the expression of a desire on the part of the country at large for political repose. Lord John Russell, who lacked the bodily vigour and elasticity of mind of his late leader, started at a great disadvantage. Skilled though he was in the dead lore of the English constitution, he signally failed to grasp the living spirit of a free and self-governing nation when, in 1865, he replaced, not only one of the truest of Englishmen, but one in whose nature there was not to be found a particle of bitterness. It would be difficult to name a first Minister of the Crown more unlike the great "Pam" than his successor. Lord John's icy manners, the outcome of an innate and unconquerable shyness, effectually prevented him from endearing himself to his followers.

A loquacious hairdresser, who was in the habit of waiting upon Palmerston, summed up his character rather neatly with a simile drawn from his own calling. "You ask me, sir, what I remember of Lord Palmerston! Well, he was what I should call a very *emollient* man." This far-seeing tradesman, had he also, in his professional capacity, attended Bishop Wilberforce of Oxford and Winchester, would have appreciated the aptness of the nickname by which he is best remembered.

A solitary specimen of Palmerston's ready wit may be given here. When a deputation of busybodies from Rugeley waited upon him urging him to use his influence to change the name of their town, in consequence of a slur alleged to have been cast upon it by William Palmer, the poisoner,[70] the Prime Minister briefly replied: "Well, gentlemen, if you must change the name, I can only suggest that you call it Palmerstown!"

Whereupon the deputation hastily withdrew, and Rugeley is Rugeley still. This love of a joke often stood him in good stead at Westminster, where humour is one of the most valuable assets which a leader of the House of Commons can command. Those who only knew him superficially, felt a certain sense of disappointment that a man who played so conspicuous a part in European affairs should habitually adopt a jocose style in private life, but his more intimate friends knew that this light-heartedness had an inner meaning not apparent to all and sundry.

He had a positive horror of bores and the loss of time which any protracted toleration of them entailed. Hence the cheery enquiry: "How's the old complaint?"—a formula which he invented with the deliberate intention of escaping, at the earliest possible moment, from pertinacious members of his party who attempted to buttonhole him in the lobby or at his wife's receptions in Piccadilly.

It was his invariable habit, even in old age, to write his letters standing at a high desk. This interesting piece of furniture is still preserved in the library at Broadlands. Asked why he adopted this singular mode of conducting his correspondence, he replied "I have so many letters to write in the course of my day's work that if I was once to sit down I should fall asleep." I have a letter before me, written to Delane in December, 1859, on the subject of the Suez Canal scheme, of nearly seven quarto pages, but without an erasure, a verbal alteration or even a blot.

Palmerston was, I think, the last Prime Minister who habitually rode to the House of Commons. His love of horses was proverbial, and Tenniel, who always drew him in *Punch* with a straw in his mouth, was careful to emphasize his fondness for the stables. In the 'sixties morning calls were constantly paid on horseback, grooms holding their masters' mounts the while, and quite a considerable number of Members of the House of Commons rode to Westminster.

Though there is still a covered shed for saddle-horses in Palace Yard, it has of late years lost its original function, though I have known it to be used as an ambush for the police on the eve of a suffragist raid.

I cannot myself recollect having seen any Prime Minister on horseback in the streets of London. Delane, one of the great forces of the Victorian era, was almost the last of his generation to ride through Fleet Street from Serjeants' Inn to the West End, though I believe the late Mr Justice Grantham habitually rode to the Law Courts, generally on one of his wife's carriage horses, up to a very recent period.

Invitations to Lady Palmerston's receptions at Cambridge House were much sought after in days when a political *salon* was still a reality. The Dowager Lady Granville, some thirty years ago, revived the practice in Carlton House Terrace, but, at the present day, this particular form of political and social entertainment has practically ceased to exist. Lady Palmerston always wrote her own invitations and caused them to be delivered by hand, for in the 'sixties it was not customary to send out cards for private parties by the penny post. Her correspondence was mainly conducted in the small *boudoir* overlooking the Green Park—a link with mid-Victorian days—wisely preserved in its original state, even to the carpet and curtains, by the Naval and Military Club.

Her portrait by Sir Thomas Lawrence, one of the most fascinating realisations of feminine loveliness ever painted, shows her at the height of her irresistible beauty and charm.

Palmerston once told Delane that it was not until he had set the library chimney at Broadlands on fire in the lengthy process of burning Gladstone's letters of resignation, that he felt it his duty (his Chancellor of the Exchequer having objected to an increase in the estimates for the necessary defence of the country, agreed upon by a majority of the Cabinet) to tell the Queen that: "It would be better to lose even Mr. Gladstone than Portsmouth or Plymouth." With his death in 1865 came the virtual termination of a period during which the distribution and exercise of political power in England had reposed mainly in the middle class. "Our quiet days are over, no more peace for us," said Sir Charles Wood, truly enough, as he came away from the great Pam's funeral in Westminster Abbey.

Thenceforward, though Lord John Russell or Lord Derby might reign, it became obvious that either Gladstone or Disraeli, by means of an appeal to a lower and hitherto unenfranchised stratum of the population, would be the actual ruler of the State.

Though there was as yet no overwhelming demand for reform, the inevitable extension of the franchise in the near future was recognised by both parties, each of them anxious to steal a march upon the other.

As Palmerston's remains were lowered into the vault (after a public funeral punctuated in its progress from Piccadilly to Westminister by genuine manifestations of public sympathy and regard) a sudden darkness overspread the scene, to be succeeded, a moment later, by a solitary ray of sunshine falling on the coffin as it disappeared from mortal view.

With the events of that chill October afternoon the story of Cambridge House as a place of private residence comes to an end.

In 1862 some officers of the Buffs quartered at the Tower, finding themselves without a club to go to in consequence of the long waiting-lists of candidates for the older Service clubs, originated the Naval and Military. With a modest membership of one hundred and fifty they opened a small house in Clifford Street. Mainly composed of junior officers ("spring captains" and junior naval lieutenants), the club long maintained a reputation for youthfulness which has become a tradition of the past.

The new club increased so rapidly that a year after its foundation it was able to take larger premises at 22 Hanover Square, and when Cambridge House became vacant it took a lease of the old mansion and moved into it in the course of 1866. There had been some idea of the site being utilised for the building of a Roman Catholic Cathedral, but objections which proved to be insuperable prevented that great scheme from being brought to fruition until the episcopate of the late Cardinal Vaughan. The tower of the great Cathedral in Westminster, the nave of which actually exceeds in length and breadth that of the neighbouring Abbey, is distinctly visible from this part of Piccadilly.

A unique feature of the Naval and Military, which has earned the reputation of being the best-managed club in London, is the coffee-room standing apart from the main building. It covers a portion of the garden formerly existing at the back (for all the big houses hereabouts had gardens at one time), thus escaping the smell of the kitchen which occasionally pervades the dining-rooms of clubs constructed on the older plan.

The small house No 95, immediately adjoining Cambridge House, deserves a word of mention. It first occurs in the parochial records in 1765 and has had a great variety of owners.[71] John Jones, an ex-army tailor, some time in the 'sixties and 'seventies, filled it from basement to attic with the exquisite collection of old French furniture which he ultimately bequeathed to the South Kensington Museum. The house was rebuilt in 1886 by Cubitt from the designs of Mr Alfred Lovejoy, of Bucklersbury, who cleverly utilised the small space at his disposal.[72]

By crossing White Horse Street, a narrow lane leading into Shepherd's Market, immortalised by Disraeli in "Tancred," a house with very interesting associations is reached.

The Junior Naval and Military Club, formerly the Junior Travellers, an appellation which gave rise to a ribald epigram which I do not propose to print, covers the sites of two older houses, Nos 96 and 97.[73] Both of these were pulled down about twenty-five years ago and the present club-house, built of the peculiar cheese-coloured stone which comes from the Ham Hill quarries, was erected on the vacant site.[74]

No 96 Piccadilly really belonged to White Horse Street, and it will be found entered thereunder in the rate-books, though it was also formerly known by a number in Piccadilly.

Charles Dumergue, Surgeon Dentist to the Royal family, who practised in Bond Street, came to live in it about 1800, and Sir Walter Scott stayed with him here in 1809 (when he was already favourably known as the author of "Marmion"), and again in 1815 and 1820.

If any house in Piccadilly deserves to be marked with a memorial tablet it is this one, but the practice has not, as yet, been adopted by the London County Council in any part of this historic thoroughfare.[75]

No. 97 now incorporated with No 96, was built on, or adjoining, the site of Carter's Statuary Yard which existed here so early as 1734,[76] for Sir John Irwin, a collateral ancestor of my own. He was a prominent figure in London Society and in Parliament for many years, and a friend of Lord Chesterfield, many of whose letters are addressed to him. He was also Governor of Gibraltar

and Commander-in-Chief in Ireland. Extravagance caused him
to leave England and he died at Parma in 1788.

Its next owner was Tom Panton, of Newmarket fame. He lived
here from 1784 to 1805, and won the Derby in 1786 with *Noble*.
A member of the Jockey Club, he formed one of the fast set
surrounding the Prince Regent including "Old Q," Sir John Lade,
and the third Marquis of Hertford. He left money in his will
to his two nieces, Lady Cholmondeley and Lady Gwydyr, both
of whom are mentioned elsewhere in these pages. After Panton's
departure the house was occupied for a long series of years by
Lady Pulteney, widow of Sir William (Johnstone) Pulteney. She
died at this house November 1, 1849, and was the last member of
the Pulteney family, so long connected with this neighbourhood,
whose name occurs in the annals of Piccadilly. From the reign
of Charles the Second to mid-Victorian days is a long family
connection with a single street, and, in a sense, the connection
may still be said to endure, for the Sutton estate is part and parcel
of the original Royal grant to William Pulteney.

No 106[77] is Coventry House, one of the best designed and least
spoiled of all the eighteenth-century Piccadilly mansions.

It appears to have been built, in the first instance, for Sir Henry
Hunloke, about 1760, and it is said, again on the authority of old
Carter the antiquary, to occupy the site of a rambling old inn,
called "The Greyhound," no trace of which has survived.

Sir Henry sold the house in 1764 to the 6th Earl of Coventry
for 10,000 guineas, and dirt cheap it must have been at the money,
though it was then not quite finished.[78] Its design has been attributed
to Kent, but as he died in 1748, the ascription is obviously an
erroneous one. Lord Coventry had succeeded, on the death of his
father, to a house in Grosvenor Square (No 3 on the east side), but
on his second marriage he preferred a view of the Green Park.

I have not been able to discover the name of the actual architect
of No 106, but the interior decorations were by the brothers

Adam, and one, at least, of the ceilings, recently well restored, is undoubtedly the work of Angelica Kauffmann.

It was originally assessed at only £160 a year, as against £200 in the case of Egremont House. The ground rent was £75, and the sum total of the yearly parochial rates £8!

This Lord Coventry, whose first wife was one of the beautiful Miss Gunnings, had been instrumental in procuring the abolition of May Fair, held for many previous years in the fields behind Piccadilly. It had become a public nuisance by the middle of the eighteenth century, and with its discontinuance Piccadilly, as a desirable place of residence, rapidly increased in public favour.

Lord Coventry's two immediate successors in the title[79] both died here, which brings the history of No 106 down to the year 1843. After remaining empty for a few years it was re-opened about 1847 as the Coventry House Club, a short-lived institution which closed its doors in March, 1854.

The house then became the London home of a most distinguished member of the *Ancienne Noblesse* of France.[80] Comte Flahault was a brave, discreet, amiable and trustworthy gentleman. Outliving the 'sixties as the only survivor of that wonderful period, embracing the Consulate and the First Empire, when Europe was shaken to its foundations, he was not by any means the least in days when there were giants in the land.

His military career was as eventful as his diplomatic record. Present at the battles of Marengo and Austerlitz, he distinguished himself throughout the Russian campaign, wherein he lost seventeen horses but escaped without a scratch.

At Dresden, and especially at Leipsic, he showed himself the bravest of the brave, and Napoleon conferred on him the title of Count on the field of battle.

At Waterloo he was in the thickest of the fight, and, when the day was lost, he was one of those who escorted the Emperor off the field. After a long and agonising silence Napoleon exclaimed: "Depuis Crécy c'est impossible de vaincre les Anglais."

On Talleyrand's advice Flahault retired to England when the Bourbons were restored and became a great favourite in society, for his presence was noble and his manners perfect.

He wooed and won the fair heiress of Admiral Keith, that same Meg Mercer who might have married Byron had she chosen. Their eldest daughter married the fourth Lord Lansdowne, father of the present Marquis. It was reserved for the soldier of Moscow, Dresden and Waterloo to take up his abode in a Scotch castle and so contribute to keep up that singular connection which long subsisted between Northern Britain and France.

He consented to serve under Louis Philippe, and in 1841 he was sent Ambassador to Vienna.

After the *coup d'état* of 1851 his old love for the Imperial dynasty returned, and Flahault was one of the first to place his services at the disposal of the President.

In 1860 he was appointed Ambassador to this country, after the recall of Persigny, and at Coventry House he and his charming wife dispensed a splendid hospitality until, in 1864, he returned to Paris as Chancellor of the Legion of Honour. Walewski seems to have been the first of the French Ambassadors to the Court of St. James's to use the house at Albert Gate, just before the Crimean War. Though recently enlarged and greatly improved, it is much inferior to Coventry House in point of interest.

In his boyhood Flahault might just have heard that the Prussians had penetrated into France as far as Valmy, thence to be driven back in disastrous defeat. Twice in later years it was his hard fate to see those same Prussians lording it in Paris, but he was spared the misery of seeing them a third time before its walls.

His wife was scarcely less accomplished than the great soldier who had taken part in every campaign from Marengo onwards.

Shortly before the death of Charles X a current joke in Paris was to the effect that as the King had been unable to form a male administration, he had confided the affairs of the country to a Cabinet of ladies, in which Madame de Boigne was to be his Minister of the Interior, and Madame Flahault his Minister of War.[81]

There can be no indiscretion in so far revealing the carefully guarded secrets of Printing House Square as to state that the obituary notice of Flahault in *The Times*[82] was written by my father. I find amongst Delane's papers a note from him saying: "My dear George, I wish you would write an article upon the death of my dear old friend Flahault, who has died just in time to escape seeing the Prussians in Paris for the third time." From this article some of the above facts have been reproduced. Flahault died at the Palace of the Legion of Honour, aged 85, within a week of the crowning disaster of Sedan.

The St James's Club, first established in a wing of Crockford's former premises at 54, St James's Street, came to Piccadilly in 1869, but adhered to its old name.

Internally, as well as externally, it is one of the handsomest clubs in London. Most of the rooms have been redecorated strictly in accord with the prevailing mode of the Adams' period. In 1912 a fine marble mantelpiece was found boarded up in one of the upstairs rooms and placed in a more prominent position on the ground floor. It represents the Triumph of Love, and was no doubt designed, in the first instance, for Lady Coventry's boudoir.

The staircase, with its double flight of steps and well-executed iron balustrade, is lit by a large window in the Venetian style, and has remained unaltered since the house was built.

The St James's has always included a numerous diplomatic element amongst its members. It possesses among other attractions a music-room, a feature not often met with in West End clubs, unless it may be in some of those confined to ladies.

I well remember a proposition to add a piano, for the use of musically inclined members, shaking another old-fashioned club to its foundations, the scheme being ultimately defeated by an overwhelming majority.

Some mention has been made at an earlier page of the rapid process of obliteration of private houses in Piccadilly owing to the erection of one or more of those huge caravanserais which are such a conspicuous feature of modern Club life in London. Many may think that Clubs cease to be gatherings of congenial spirits, united to one another by a common bond of social and personal acquaintance, so soon as they overstep a reasonable limitation of membership. But when their numbers swell to two and three thousand and upwards what do they become but a congeries of fortuitous atoms, as unknown to one another as the week-end visitors to a seaside hotel?

Yet these mammoth establishments have definite political uses in a democratic age, for the rank and file of their members can generally be recalled to a proper sense of their corporate existence, when patiently listening to the post-prandial utterances of Cabinet Ministers in search of a sympathetic audience during the dull season. There is a non-political Club in Pall Mall, said to be the largest of its kind in the world, whose members number over five thousand. The few who remain in ignorance of its varied attractions can only wonder what sort of man the hall porter must be, and if he can possibly know one-tenth of its members by sight!

One of these club palaces—the Junior Constitutional—has absorbed at least four houses in Piccadilly, and if a paternal County Council ever takes up the task of commemorating the distinguished men and women who formerly dwelt here, its shining marble face will be agreeably relieved by a tesselated pattern of memorial tablets.

Towards the close of the eighteenth century four new houses, rated at from £120 to £150 a year, were built in this part of the

street, representing, according to the modern numbering, Nos
101, 102, 103, and 104. The first occupant of 102 was Sir Thomas
Lawrence, a great artist who is only now coming to be appreciated
at his true value. He was in Piccadilly from 1796 to 1798, but most
of his studio work was done in Soho. Lord and Lady Yarmouth,
who were always changing their place of abode, were the next,
but they soon removed to No 105, where they will be mentioned
hereafter.

In the middle of the nineteenth century the Marquis of Granby,[83]
a strong Protectionist and an ally of Lord George Bentinck, lived
here for a few years. Born in Waterloo year he entered the House of
Commons as member for the family borough of Stamford in the
year of Queen Victoria's succession, and remained a member of
the Lower House until he succeeded to the Dukedom. In 1848 the
Protectionists wanted to depose Lord George Bentinck and make
him their leader, but he felt himself obliged to decline the honour.
When Palmerston, in 1852, succeeded in turning out Lord Derby
on Disraeli's first budget, Lord Granby, alone of the Protectionists,
declared himself unchanged in his opinions and unable to vote
with him, adding that some apology was due to the memory of
Sir Robert Peel from those who had heaped calumny and abuse
upon him. All the other Peelites voted with Palmerston and his
hour was thought to have arrived, but his predominance was not
yet. "I never thought of Aberdeen," he exclaimed, much as Lord
Randolph Churchill "forgot Goschen" when he resigned in 1886.

The next house to Lord Granby's, No 103 (formerly No 23,
Piccadilly East, according to the numbering of the street in use
down to about the year 1820), deserves to be marked with a blue
stone, for here it was that Nelson stayed with Sir William and
Lady Hamilton during his infrequent visits to London.

The house was built for the Hon. John Stratford in 1797, but in
1801 Sir William Hamilton's name is found here, and he died in it
in 1803, holding Nelson's hand.

It must have been from Piccadilly that the Admiral went down to the House of Lords fresh from the triumph of Copenhagen, perhaps the most remarkable of his many victories to that date, to second the Address to the Throne in 1802.

Speaking as a plain seaman, he uttered these remarkable words, as applicable to-day as they were a hundred years ago.

"My Lords, I have seen in different countries much of the miseries of war. I am, therefore, in my inmost soul a man of peace. Yet would I not, for the sake of any peace, however fortunate, consent to sacrifice one jot of England's honour. Our honour is inseparably combined with our genuine interest. Hitherto there has been nothing greater known on the continent, than the faith, the untarnished honour, the generous public sympathies, the high diplomatic influence, the commerce, the grandeur, the resistless power, the unconquerable valour of the British nation. Wherever I have served in foreign countries I have witnessed these to be the sentiments with which Britons were regarded. *The advantages of such a reputation are not to be lightly brought into hazard.*" The prophetic words of our greatest Admiral, breathing as they do the true spirit of patriotism, should be emblazoned in letters of gold on the walls of the Admiralty to remind Ministers of their paramount duty to the State.[84]

Stories directly connecting Nelson with Piccadilly are few and far between, but the following, though little known, is well authenticated.

In the early autumn of 1805, probably some time in September, the Admiral looked in at Fores', the printseller's,[85] to pay his bill and was received by the wife of the then proprietor. Perceiving in a moment with his one remaining eye that an interesting event was imminent in the family, he exclaimed: "If it's a boy, Mrs. Fores, remember that I should like to be his godfather."

Nelson never came back, but the son to which Mrs. Fores subsequently gave birth was duly christened "Horatio Nelson."

This story was told to Mr G P Fores by a daughter of the original owner of the shop, who remembered having clung to her mother's side whilst the Admiral counted his money out of a large silken purse, and her having asked her mother where the gentleman's other arm was.

No 103 was occupied from 1827 to 1832 by old Lady Keith. She was a Thrale by birth and the "Queenie" of Dr. Johnson. She was also one of the original lady patronesses of Almack's, that curious society long the despair of the middle classes, and ruled with a rod of iron by half-a-dozen of the most exclusive ladies in London Society. From 1832 till her death in 1857, at the great age of 95, she lived at No 110, a small house now (1912), in process of being demolished to make way for a big hotel.[86]

The large house, No 105, which is now the Isthmian Club, has had as varied a history as any in Piccadilly. The view of it on the opposite page shows it as it was originally designed for Lord Barrymore, nicknamed "Hell Gate" by the Prince Regent.[87] In the rate-books from 1791 to 1794 an empty house, one to the eastward of Lord Coventry's, was rated at £200, but from 1795 two separate assessments are made, although it was still apparently empty, of £150 and £70 respectively.

Early in the nineteenth century the site was secured for an hotel, of which there were then scarcely any in the West End of London, and in 1811 the proprietors of the Pulteney Hotel, as it was called, were rated, in respect of the whole premises, at the then high figure of £416. Opened in 1812, it was kept going by a restaurateur called John Escudier, but about 1823 he moved from Piccadilly to Albemarle Street, where the business flourished under its original name for many years.

In 1814 the Czar Alexander of Russia was lodged at 105, and his sister, HRH the Duchess of Oldenburg, seems to have rented the whole building for a season.

In 1824 the house became the property of the Marquis of

Hertford, the original of Thackeray's Marquis of Steyne, and the husband of George Selwyn's "Mie-Mie," but it is doubtful if he ever lived here, although his name appears in the rate-books until 1830. Thackeray's caricature of him is well known, but even before the appearance of *Vanity Fair* his portrait had been drawn by another master hand. As Lord Monmouth in *Coningsby*, Disraeli wrote of him as: "In height about the middle size but somewhat portly and corpulent. His countenance was strongly marked, sagacity on the brow, sensuality in the mouth and jaw. His head was bald, but there were remains of the rich brown locks on which he once prided himself. His large, deep blue eyes, madid,[88] and yet piercing, showed that the secretions of his brain were apportioned, half to voluptuousness, half to common sense. His general mien was truly grand, full of a natural nobility, of which no one was more sensible than himself."

Mie-Mie's husband began the great collection of works of art now at Hertford House,[89] though his successor in the title[90] and, after him, his eventual heir, the late Sir Richard Wallace, were responsible for the bulk of it.

The 3rd Marquis, known as Lord Yarmouth from 1794 until his father's death,[91] was the only son of the Lady Hertford who exercised such a powerful influence over the Prince Regent, and as she and "Old Q" were always on good terms, it is not improbable that the match with Mdlle. Fagniani was jointly arranged by them. The marriage took place at Southampton on May 15th, 1798, but did not prove a happy one. Only twenty-one at the time, Lord Yarmouth was nearly six years younger than his bride, a fact which, in itself, constituted an element of danger in the years which were to come.

"Red Herrings," as he was called by the Prince Regent and his friends, revelled in all the voluptuous orgies of that dissipated age, and did not make at all a good husband, judged by any standard of taste. Having landed in France just after the rupture of the treaty of Amiens, he was forcibly detained by Napoleon and consigned to the fortress of Verdun. He was released in 1806 through Fox pleading his cause with Talleyrand. In 1809 he acted as second to Castlereagh in his duel with Canning. His wife remained in France, and after the birth of the youngest of her three children the great heiress, whose interests "Old Q" had so much at heart as to lead the ignorant to suppose that she was his own daughter, separated from her husband and lived a life of pleasure on the Continent, residing mostly in Paris, where she is said, on somewhat doubtful evidence, to have been for a time the *amie intime* of General Junot. Napoleon, who had known Junot since his Toulon days, made him his *aide-de-camp* for his coolness and courage at the siege of that town, and later on created him Duc d'Abrantes. No divorce proceedings, so far as I have been able to discover, were ever instituted, and rumour asserts that Lord and Lady Hertford became reconciled after Junot's death.[92] He left his widow a large sum of money in his will, to which, like "Old Q," he added a number of codicils which caused infinite trouble to his executors. Lady Hertford lived to a great age and, surviving her husband by many years, died at her house at the Rue Taitbout, in 1856, and was buried in Père La Chaise.

After the passing of the Reform Bill her husband conceived a violent dislike to his native country, and he, too, passed nearly the whole remainder of his wasted life on the Continent. A martyr to gout in his later years, he divided his time between Aix and Naples, but returned to England to die. In the unreformed Parliament he practically nominated eight members of the House of Commons, and for Lisburn, one of the family pocket boroughs, he consented to sit for a few years. With the advent of Reform he became disgusted with politics, and devoted his principal attention to buying works of art. But he did not only collect pictures, furniture, snuff-boxes, and armour.

When a small and impressionable boy, he had been taken to see the celebrated striking clock, with its club-bearing giants representing Gog and Magog, at St Dunstan's, Fleet Street.

"When I am a man I will buy that clock and put it up in my house!" he declared in childish delight as he saw the moving figures striking the hour.

It so happened that in 1830, when he was building a villa in Regent's Park, a scheme was on foot for widening Fleet Street and setting St Dunstan's Church further back from the roadway. Lord Hertford seized the opportunity to realise the wish of his boyhood, and offered the Vestry 200 guineas for the clock and bells with three ancient statues removed from Ludgate thrown in. The offer was accepted, and the trophies were removed to the Regent's Park, where the new villa was named in their honour after the old City church. Charles Lamb is said to have shed tears when the clock was taken down from St Dunstan's, for it had long been one of the recognised sights of London, and, as such, duly pointed out to country visitors as one of the wonders of the world.[93] A somewhat similar clock of modern construction is to be seen in Cheapside,[94] and the old church at Rye, in Sussex, with its two "Jacks," is not unlike the one at St Dunstan's. Lord Hertford's villa belonged to Lord Londesborough, before it earned undying fame in the Great War as St Dunstan's Hostel for blinded heroes. It says much for the excellence of its workmanship that the famous clock, which was made by Thomas Harrys of Water Lane, Blackfriars, in 1671, is still in good going order.[95]

"Red Herrings," or the "Yarmouth bloater," as he was also called, was always changing his place of abode in London. He lived at three different houses in Piccadilly, at No. 7 Seamore Place, in the Regent's Park, and he died, in 1842, at Dorchester House, Park Lane, worth, it is supposed, about two millions.

His body lay in state in the library adjoining the great hall, and was visited by a morbid crowd of sight-seers, to whom a

velvet-covered coffin and gilt trappings of death are an irresistible
attraction. The funeral *cortège* proceeded by road to Ragley by
easy stages, halting several times on the way. When at last it
reached Warwickshire the interment was performed at Arrow, by
torchlight, as was then customary in the case of the obsequies
of Knights of the Garter, for they, more than persons of lesser
rank, were the especial prey of the mid-Victorian undertaker. I
notice that Lord Hertford's dressing-case is now displayed, with
other objects of very unequal artistic merit, in the new London
Museum.

No. 105 was reopened shortly after 1830 as the British and
Foreign Union Club, a short-lived society which has left no
history behind it. Yet it appears to have been the first genuine
club in Piccadilly, for Watier's was only a gambling hell disguised
as a social rendezvous for musical amateurs. Various tenants came
to live here after the club ceased to exist, but in 1843 the name of
a Marquis of Hertford is again found in this position.[96]

Mie-Mie's son relinquished the family residence in Manchester
Square to the French Embassy, and lived for a time, during his
infrequent visits to England, at No 13, Berkeley Square, Admiral
Rous's house in later years. He rebuilt the Piccadilly house as it now
stands in 1850–51, employing Cubitt to construct a great saloon
on the first floor in which he intended to house the choicest of
the art treasures he had been sedulously collecting for years. In the
early part of the nineteenth century, and even later, as Sir Robert
Peel knew, really fine pictures could be acquired for what would
now be thought ridiculously low prices, and the competition
which Lord Hertford had to meet was very limited. He bought
largely in Paris and at The Hague, where he probably obtained
the magnificent Cuyps, the great Frans Hals, and other pictures
of the Dutch school now at Hertford House, and so late as 1865 he
bought the pick of the Morny Collection. For some reason or other
he changed his mind as to the destination of his picture gallery

and the other *objets d'art* now in Manchester Square. It is said that he took an unalterable dislike to the house in Piccadilly from an unpleasant smell which occasionally pervaded it owing to the proximity of the Tyburn stream, or sewer, which crosses Piccadilly at its lowest point, flows underground through the Green Park, and after passing by, or as some say under, Buckingham Palace, discharges its foul waters into the Thames near Millbank.

All but the least observant must have noticed how in foggy weather the atmosphere is denser in the hollow of Piccadilly than in other parts of the street, and cabmen say that the neighbourhood of Buckingham Palace presents greater difficulties to drivers than any other part of the West End when London is wrapped in the grimy embrace of a thick black fog. This condition is due partly to the exhalations from the Tyburn and partly to the water-logged state of the soil in Pimlico, which in early times was little better than a tidal swamp known to the Anglo-Saxons and Normans as Bulinga-Fen.

Curiously enough the formation of the Underground Railway has been the means of effecting an improvement in this respect, as the tunnels have helped to drain off the surface water.

Lord Hertford, who spent most of his life in Paris, scarcely visiting England since the days of his youth, eventually sent his pictures to Manchester Square.

Though the collection was not generally accessible to visitors, he condescended to issue orders to view to people either personally known to him or properly recommended.

Henry Greville, who went in 1865 to see the pictures in this way, was told by the housekeeper that the deserted mansion was kept in readiness for its eccentric owner should he wish to occupy it at any moment, but that, as a matter of fact, he had not seen the collection since it was arranged, neither had he set foot in the house for nine years.

Delane, who was similarly privileged to visit the collection, wrote in his diary for March 3rd, 1868: "Went with Sir Hamilton

Seymour" (the diplomatist and a cousin of Lord Hertford) "and Countess Teleki to see Hertford House and the pictures which are above praise."

But with few exceptions the collection was a closed book to connoisseurs of art, and entirely unknown to the general public.

Its owner, if he did not inherit his father's vices, shared many of his eccentricities, for he, too, after passing some years in the diplomatic service, spent an epicurean existence abroad.

His younger brother, Lord Henry Seymour, who also lived almost entirely in Paris, was one of the founders and the first President of the French Jockey Club. He did a great deal to foster sport in Paris and won the Grand Prix in 1835 and 1837. Dying unmarried in 1859, he was buried beside his mother in Père La Chaise. The bulk of his fortune, derived in the first instance from "Old Q's" legacies to his mother, he bequeathed to various Paris hospitals, which are said to have benefited thereby to the extent of nearly £40,000 a year. In the long run, therefore, the greater part of the "Star of Piccadilly's" wealth was devoted to charitable purposes.

On the death of the fourth Marquis the houses in Piccadilly and Manchester Square devolved absolutely on the late Sir Richard Wallace.

The "Dictionary of National Biography" assumed, quite erroneously, that Sir Richard, whose precise origin was long surrounded by an impenetrable mystery, was a natural son of Maria Fagniani, the Mie-Mie of George Selwyn's letters, whose name occurs frequently in these pages.

The assumption was not only a hasty one, but, in view of facts which have recently been brought to light, a cruel and undeserved aspersion on that lady's memory. Another theory, equally untenable, was that the child was a late-born son of the third Marquis by an unidentified mother. Mystery and suspicion of a sort had also surrounded Mie-Mie's own paternity and it may be desirable at this point to recall "Old Q's" words, when writing to Selwyn on August 25th, 1771:—

"Last night Madame Fagniani was brought to bed of a girl. They wished it had been a boy; however, cette petite princesse héritéra les biens de la famille, so that they are all very happy. She is vastly so to have it all over, and to find herself quite well after having suffered a great deal, which I believe women always do on these occasions, but particularly with their first child." Not a word, it will be observed, did "Old Q" write which could give the slightest countenance to the rumours, sedulously circulated in London society in after years, that he was the father.

At the time of Sir Richard Wallace's birth Lady Hertford was within a month of completing her forty-eighth year.

Her eldest son Richard, the fourth Marquis, had a brief intrigue, when a mere boy of eighteen, with a Scotch girl of humble parentage and indifferent reputation, subsequently known as Agnes Jackson, though her maiden name was Wallace.

She became the mother of the child who was ultimately to inherit not only the bulk of the family property, but also the priceless treasures of Hertford House.

Lady Hertford became aware of her son's entanglement and, out of pure kindness of heart, she brought the unwanted child up in Paris under her personal supervision. He appears to have been known in the household as "*Monsieur Richard*," though not regarded, at all events in his youth, as an equal in blood relationship. He dined in the steward's room and was not, until he reached man's estate, accorded even the dignity of a surname. His father was at first inclined to disown him but, as time wore on, he grew to be so fond of him that he eventually left him everything that he possibly could, to the exclusion of his successor in the family honours.

The late Lord Redesdale, who devoted much time and attention to the inception and development of the Wallace Collection, of which he was one of the trustees, tells the full, and, as I believe, the only authentic story of Sir Richard's origin in the supplementary volume of his memoirs published after his death by Mr Edmund Gosse.[97]

Sir Richard Wallace never, I think, occupied the house in Piccadilly any more than Lord Hertford had done. When in town he preferred Manchester Square. A tall, handsome man of commanding appearance, he inherited much of the reserve of the family from which he sprang.

A large landowner in Ireland, as well as in England, he owned an estate of 50,000 acres in County Antrim, which had descended to the Seymours from the Conway family. When he so far overcame the traditional aversion of his forbears to English public life as to enter the House of Commons, it was as Conservative Member for Lisburn. In that long-disfranchised pocket borough of the Seymour-Conways the electors numbered less than eight hundred all told, and, probably, all subsidised. Before the agitation for Home Rule, Lisburn was the safest of safe seats for the ground landlord, whether he were a resident or an absentee. Antrim, it may be added, is an impregnable Unionist stronghold to this day.

Until the Union, Lisburn, one among the many glaring anomalies of the representative system of the sister island, returned two members to the Irish Parliament.

The third Marquis, as Lord Yarmouth, sat for the same constituency in 1802, and his son for the undivided County of Antrim in 1821.

Sir Richard Wallace remained in undisputed possession of Lisburn until 1885, when the little linen town in the north of Ireland ceased to return a member to the Imperial Parliament.

He did not marry until he was fifty-two years of age, and he died without surviving issue. He had, however, an adopted son, the late Sir John Murray Scott, who acted as his private secretary, and his will, by a strange coincidence, recently engaged the attention of the Law Courts.

Sir Richard made good use of his wealth during the Franco-Prussian War, equipping, at his private expense, an extensive ambulance service for the French Army, besides contributing largely to the relief of the poor of Paris during the siege. His donations at that critical period are said to have amounted to two and a half million of francs.

At Bagatelle, his delightful country house beyond the Bois de Boulogne, he occasionally received English visitors, being especially hospitable to members of the English Jockey Club who were interested in the French turf. To some of these he issued a perpetual invitation to stay at his house, whether he was in residence or not. Bagatelle was acquired from his heirs by the Municipality of Paris for a quarter of a million. Sir Richard, in addition to many other charitable donations, founded the Hertford hospital in Paris, where a street has been named after him, and he died in the city of his adoption in 1890. The priceless art collection in Manchester Square, in which he seems to have taken a more practical and personal interest than his predecessors, was eventually bequeathed to the English nation by his widow. With his death the fitful connection of the holders of the title with Piccadilly came to an end, though Yarmouth Mews, behind No 105, commemorates to this day the former association of the Seymours with the spot.

It should be added that the lease of No 105 was put up for sale by Phillips of New Bond Street after the death of the fourth Marquis. It was then described as being held under a lease from Sir Richard Sutton, the ground landlord, for a term of years from December 25th, 1822, at a yearly rent of £212 12s. 0d.

It was sold to Sir Julian Goldsmid, who, presumably, did not find the Tyburn so unpleasant a neighbour as Lord Hertford had done, for he remained in Piccadilly until his death in 1896. The lease was then acquired by the Isthmian Club, which removed here from Walsingham House, where the Ritz Hotel now stands.

Many interesting associations cluster round the unpretentious stuccoed house,[98] which stands one door to the westward of Coventry House, the stately home of the St James's Club. Its earlier history is uneventful, but in 1814 it appears to have been temporarily occupied by General Blücher. He was accustomed to sit in an armchair placed on the top of the flight of steps at the hall door, smoking a pipe in the true German fashion and acknowledging the salutations of the passers-by. Gratified at the notice which Londoners took of him, he is said to have shown himself frequently at the windows of another of his temporary residences in the Ambassadors' Court of St James's Palace. People in England had an idea that Blücher was a coarse, rough old fellow like most Prussians of his generation, but when receiving visitors his manners were good and with a pleasing admixture of heartiness.[99]

The old general is only one amongst the ghosts of Piccadilly, and the more real and permanent interest of No 107 dates from some ten years later than his visit, when Nathan Mayer Rothschild, a comparative stranger to our shores, and the founder of the English line of the great Jewish family which has dominated European finance for a hundred years, came to live at Blücher's old house.

In 1825 Rothschild transferred his place of residence from Stamford Hill to the West End, and in Piccadilly, where perhaps he may have visited Blücher, his descendants have remained ever since. Their earliest home in this historic thoroughfare was then assessed at the moderate figure of £300, not a tenth part of the estimated rental of their present holdings in the same locality.

The third son of his father,[100] and third sons are proverbially lucky, Nathan Mayer was probably the greatest financial genius of a family of great financiers.

He first came to England in 1798 and, before settling in London, he passed a few years in Manchester, where he dealt chiefly in cotton goods and familiarised himself with the conditions of English trade.

Realising from the first that unity is strength, he acted jointly with his brothers in Frankfort, Vienna, Naples, and Paris, who had been planted out in the European capitals by their father much after the manner of Napoleon's brothers. It fell to the lot of the third son to capture London, and in the ten years which intervened between Waterloo and his migration to Piccadilly he achieved such an impregnable position that at a time of great financial depression in the City in 1825, when many business houses were shaken to their foundations, he was able out of his own resources to help the Bank of England to meet its obligations.

After a brief connection with St Helens he established the offices of the firm where they now are in St Swithin's Lane.[101] Being always as good as their word in all business relations, the "five Frankforters," as they have been called, made themselves indispensable to the Great Powers of Europe, who, in their turn, were not slow to realise that what the Rothschilds promised they invariably performed. Co-operation and intermarriage were their watchwords, and by strict adherence to these guiding principles, all of Nathan's sons became millionaires and his grandsons millionaires many times over.

In St Swithin's Lane the whole of the second generation of the English Rothschilds were born. A hundred years ago City men without pronounced social ambitions were content to live where they carried on their business, and in those now remote days the natural aptitude of the family for finance confined its immediate interest to the neighbourhood of the Exchange, although its influence was felt on every Bourse in Europe.

There would seem to be something in the atmosphere of the particular corner of the City of London which Nathan Mayer selected for his office peculiarly favourable to the acquisition of colossal wealth. Within a stone's throw of Salters' Hall in

Wallbrook there dwelt in the fifteenth century those twin extortioners Dudley and Empson.

But here the parallel ceases. While they never devoted any of their gains to relieving the necessities of the poor, New Court has been for more than a century not only the chosen home of the aristocracy of finance, but a business centre rightly associated in the public mind with unbounded charity, freely and unceasingly dispensed without regard to class or creed.

In 1806 Nathan Mayer married Hannah, one of the two daughters of Levy Cohen, a merchant of unblemished reputation who came to London from Amsterdam early in the reign of George the Third, and settled in St Mary Axe and later in Angel Court, Throgmorton Street.

Another daughter, Judith, married Sir Moses Montefiore, the centenarian, who also carried on business in St Swithin's Lane.

Rothschild's real prosperity dated from the period of his marriage. About the same time he became the trusted London agent of the Court of Hesse, gradually superseding in this connection the Van Nottens, who had been settled as merchants in Devonshire Square, an ancient home of Old Jewry, since the reign of George the Second.

At the beginning of the nineteenth century the Jewish merchants had their own especial corner on 'Change. Plans are in existence showing how the space was allotted to the representatives of various nationalities and specific trades. I have one of them before me, at the time of writing, showing the Jewish quarter as distinct from the Portuguese and the Dutch. Rothschild's next great achievement was the purchase of £800,000 worth of gold from the East India Company, by transmitting which, on behalf of the Government, to the Duke of Wellington in the Peninsula he earned a substantial commission. The Government was at its wits' end to supply the Duke with ready money, and where everything had to be paid for in cash, the Treasury bills could only be converted at considerable loss. Rothschild, undismayed by the difficulties and dangers of the enterprise, undertook to send the money in coin through France at his own risk, and the successful accomplishment of his task proved the most lucrative business which he ever undertook. From that day forward he made himself indispensable to the British Government, and as an accurate collector of news from the Continent he out-distanced the very inadequate newspaper services of that now remote period.

The story that he was actually present at the battle of Waterloo, and that, having hurried back to London, he made a fortune in a single day by keeping to himself the knowledge so acquired, is a baseless fabrication.

It is true that he received prior information of the great victory, probably by carrier pigeon, and that he bought stock largely, by perfectly legitimate methods, when no one else had the pluck to enter into heavy commitments on 'Change. It has been alleged that he depressed the funds by hinting at a British disaster, but the facts are that he not only bought largely and openly in face of an incredulous market, but that he communicated his intelligence to the Government as soon as he received it. In 1836 he died at Frankfort, whither he had gone to be present at the marriage of his eldest son, who subsequently largely extended the business reputation and influence of the firm.

This son, Lionel by name, was the first of his race, adhering to the tenets of the Jewish faith, ever elected to the House of Commons, and in the long struggle for the emancipation of the Jews from political disability which ensued between 1847, when he was first returned for the City of London, and 1858, when he at last took his seat, he had the advantage of the powerful advocacy of *The Times*.

Delane's intimacy with Baron Lionel dated from an early period of his career as editor of the paper, and had its origin in a curious incident. Lionel Rothschild and he were in the habit of going to the same hairdresser's in the City in the early 'forties. One day

Rothschild asked the proprietor of the shop who his handsome young customer was, and when he heard that he was the editor of *The Times* an acquaintance sprang up between them which soon ripened into intimacy.

With his three younger brothers, Anthony, Nathaniel and Mayer, and especially the last-named, Delane became intimate in after years, but Lionel was his earliest friend and many were the mutual advantages which followed on the acquaintanceship so opportunely begun in the City hairdresser's shop. When Lionel decided to stand for Parliament, it was Delane who helped him to write his first election address. The young editor, for he was only twenty-nine at the time, advised him to take Lord John Russell's opinion upon it before issuing it to his constituents, and the Prime Minister having signified his entire approval, Rothschild's candidature was launched under most favourable auspices.

The City of London was a tolerably safe Whig seat in those days, and with *The Times* on its side it remained so for many a long day, until the latter-day Whig became practically indistinguishable from the modern Tory.[102]

Soon after his father's death Baron Lionel removed to 148, Piccadilly, next door to Apsley House,[103] but for a country, or rather a suburban, retreat, he was content to live at Gunnersbury, just as his father before him had been content with Stamford Hill (a district now merged in a dreary expanse of bricks and mortar), both places being within an easy drive of the City. It was not until the peaceful invasion of the Vale of Aylesbury in the middle of the nineteenth century, when the introduction of railways made a more distant residence possible for the family, that a number of enchanted palaces rose from their foundations in rapid succession in the home counties served by the London and North Western Railway.

No 107, the earliest home of the aristocracy of finance in the West End, passed into the possession[104] of Lionel's youngest brother Mayer, who, more than any of his predecessors in England, promoted the social reputation of the family, though it must not be supposed that, for all his love of sport and the fine arts, he was devoid of business instincts.

Preferring in early life the countryside to the counting-house, he entered into agricultural pursuits, and having taken up English sports with the enthusiasm of a novice he acquired a large tract of land near Leighton Buzzard, which had formed part of the Duke of Buckingham's estate. Thereon he built Mentmore,[105] a spacious renaissance mansion, modelled to some extent on the lines of Wollaton, from the designs of Sir Joseph Paxton. This, perhaps the most beautiful of many country houses belonging to the family in the Vale of Aylesbury, he proceeded to make a perfect storehouse of the arts. It may be said that with his great wealth it was easy for him to make Mentmore a palace—any millionaire could have done as much—but Mayer Rothschild did far more than the term implies. Under his fostering hand the mansion was gradually transformed into a museum, replete with all that is most beautiful in art. And yet, in all the vast expenditure of wealth which it represented, there was felt to be nothing inappropriate, nothing out of place, because the sense of waste and over-profusion was wholly absent. Great resources had been employed to produce a great result, and the result was something which had, and has, a permanent æsthetic value of its own.

The secret of its owner's success was that he applied to his passion for the arts the same qualities which in business made the fortunes of his house. Sparing no money for his purpose, there was always a purpose in his expenditure. The great copper-gilt lanterns hanging in the central hall, which is the principal feature of the house, were made for the Doge of Venice, in the arsenal of the Adriatic, towards the close of the fifteenth century.[106] For twenty years before the Baron's death they shone down upon a scene of many splendid hospitalities. Their owner was never so happy as when entertaining his friends, whose comfort was enhanced (for the first time, perhaps, in the history of social entertaining in this country) by the running of special trains from Euston on the occasion of the sumptuous balls given at Mentmore from time to time. This practice has been extended by other members of the family, until the Rothschild specials to Waddesdon, Halton and Aston Clinton have become a recognised feature of luxurious railway travelling.

The gardens at Mentmore, also planned by Paxton, are little, if at all, inferior to those at Chatsworth, and the farm buildings on the estate were, and probably still are, the most complete of their kind in every detail to be found in England.

The Baron founded the pack of staghounds called after his name, and hunted regularly with them for many years. He greatly improved the shooting on the estate, although he was never in favour of those *battues* which are, nowadays, sometimes organised more with a view to advertisement than to the legitimate interests of sport. He diligently attended agricultural shows and won his way, as he richly deserved, to the hearts of Buckinghamshire farmers throughout the Vale. Liberal though he was in his political opinions, the family interest was never exerted against the long-continued return of Disraeli for the undivided county. Always rather a silent member at Westminster, he represented one of the Cinque Ports, and not until 1865 did the late head of the family, who by that date was settled at Tring Park, enter the House of Commons as Member for Aylesbury.

The owner of Mentmore and his eldest brother were the first of the Rothschilds to keep race-horses, a departure deliberately entered upon with a view to rendering the family more thoroughly in accord with English tastes. It is perhaps not generally known that the whole of the accounts of the racing stable at Newmarket were kept in New Court as part and parcel of the business of the firm, thus adhering, even in sporting matters, to the principle of collective responsibility which has made the Rothschilds what they are to-day.

The Baron never squandered money in speculative purchases of high-priced yearlings at the Newmarket sales, but he kept a stud which he so improved that when, in 1871, the many successes of the now familiar blue and yellow gave rise to the catchphrase, "Follow the Baron," it was felt that a piece of good and useful work had been justly rewarded. Many costly yearlings and two-year-olds have proved worthless to their purchasers for racing purposes. On the other hand Lord George Bentinck only gave Lord Chesterfield £60 for *Crucifix*, and won the Two Thousand, the One Thousand and the Oaks with her, the latter after sixteen false starts, in 1840.

The blue and yellow were not the first racing colours connected with the great financial house. I find that so long ago as May, 1841, Baron Rothschild's *Consul* won a little race at Gorhambury, a semi-private meeting promoted by the Lord Verulam of that day and long since defunct as a racing fixture.

The next year he registered his colours as "amber body, lilac sleeves and red cap," but in 1843 this gaudy combination was changed to the well-known dark blue and yellow cap so respected on the turf.

The new jacket was carried unsuccessfully on *Emerald*, a two-year-old filly, on three occasions, and in 1844 she ran unplaced in the Oaks. *Mahonia* in the late 'sixties won some important races, but her running in the Woodcote Stakes of 1869 so disappointed her owner that he wrote to Delane to say that he felt he could not go down to see the Derby the next day, so much did he take the defeat of his colours to heart. But the victories of *Favonius* and *Hannah* in the Derby and Oaks of 1871 caused him intense delight, and the tide had now definitely turned in the Baron's favour. The family scored another classic success in 1879, when Fordham had his only winning mount in the Derby. *Sir Bevys*, the winner of the blue riband, ran in the assumed name of "Mr Acton," and was really the property of Baron Lionel.

Of the stud farm in the Crafton paddocks long presided over by *King Tom* I have a distinct personal recollection, for I was lifted on to the horse's broad back by the Baron when I was on a visit to Mentmore as a small boy. *King Tom* did not win the Derby, or indeed any of the classic races, but he was a great success at the stud, and I have somewhere in my possession an album containing the photographs of all his progeny.

To the great regret of a host of friends, the Baron died aged only fifty-five, in February 1874, not at his beloved Mentmore, but at No 107, Piccadilly, and his widow, a kind-hearted woman who never wearied of doing good to her fellow creatures, followed her husband to the grave in 1877. One of the many charitable causes which she had at heart was the oral instruction of the deaf and dumb, to the furtherance of which she contributed bountifully. Her only daughter and heiress married Lord Rosebery a year after her mother's death.

The house in Piccadilly was occupied for a time by the future Prime Minister before he removed to Lansdowne House, one of three houses in Berkeley Square which Lord Rosebery has lived in at one time or another.

Both he and the late Baron Leopold worthily carried on the Rothschild traditions on the turf, but to dwell at any length on the political or social careers of those who are, or were recently, living forces would cause the present chapter to swell to far too great a length.

No 107 became the Savile Club (a favourite haunt of Robert Louis Stevenson when in London) in 1885, but the names of Blücher, Rothschild and Rosebery will always remain its principal historical assets in the annals of valour, finance and politics.

Not much space remains to notice here the remaining clubs which have sprung up in Piccadilly in recent years.

The club house of the Junior Athenæum, at the east corner of Down Street, was originally built in 1848–49 for Henry Thomas

Hope, of Deepdene, whose only child married the sixth Duke of Newcastle. One of the first houses built in the West End in the French Renaissance style, its handsome iron railing—cast, I believe, in Paris—preserves the crest of the Hope family—the bursting globe—with its punning motto, "At spes infracta." Mr. Hope sold it to the Club about the year 1868. Its owner had been particularly anxious to get rid of a public-house in Down Street, almost opposite his entrance door; but if he were alive now he would find in its place what would probably annoy him quite as much—a Tube Railway Station, open practically day and night, which the public-house never could have been.

The Automobile Club, which from small beginnings has grown to be of such gigantic proportions, was housed for a time in one of the two stonefronted houses built at the west corner of Down Street in the early 'seventies. At No 117 the first Lord O'Neill, Prebendary of Christ Church, Dublin, and a great authority on ecclesiastical music, lived for a time. He was succeeded there in 1882 by Mr. Childers, First Lord of the Admiralty, Secretary of State for War, Chancellor of the Exchequer, and Home Secretary, in rapid succession, under Mr. Gladstone.

His career presents some parallel features to that of Robert Lowe, Lord Sherbrooke. Both had distinguished Colonial reputations before they entered English political life. The "Dictionary of National Biography" labels Childers as a "statesman," and Lowe as a "politician," a definition which seems to award a slight preference to the first-named. In the course of their Parliamentary careers both bent before the storm. Lowe threatened to resign in 1863 because he was not taken into the Cabinet; Childers left his colleagues in 1871, broken in health from a family affliction, and was replaced by Goschen at the Admiralty. Lowe incurred much unpopularity from his abortive attempt to impose a tax on matches, and Childers was widely blamed for his handling of the West End riots and pillaging of shops in March, 1886. These were followed by the resignation of the Chief Commissioner of Police, whose friends stoutly maintained that he had been sacrificed by the Home Office. Many windows in Piccadilly were smashed by the mob at this time. At No. 134, then the residence of Mr Edward Marjoribanks (Lord Tweedmouth), hardly one escaped. The rioters extended their operations as far north as Oxford Street, ransacking some of the shops in South Audley Street on their way.

Between Down Street and old Park Lane is a solid phalanx of clubs, most of them of such recent date as to call for no detailed notice. The most remarkable success has been obtained by the Cavalry Club. Started in 1890 by Captain Wetherall, of the 20th Hussars, as a proprietary club, the venture was at first looked at askance by the Duke of Cambridge, who disliked the idea of confining its advantages to one branch of the service. As time went on, the Commander-in-Chief's views underwent a change, and under the chairmanship of the late General Dickson (12th Lancers) it became a prosperous members' club. In 1909 it was enlarged to about twice its original size; a central hall and staircase were built, and there seems every reason to suppose that when its present lease of 88 years from the Sutton Estate expires, the Cavalry will be found in an equally flourishing condition.

The last Piccadilly club which it will be necessary to mention is the Bachelors', at the east corner of Hamilton Place. Though not an old club, as times go, it has attained a considerable reputation as part and parcel of the social machinery of the West End.

Before it came into existence, a house on this site had been occupied by a variety of aristocratic tenants. The first of them seems to have been Mr Richard Cavendish (formerly Chandler), who was living here so long ago as 1764. Mr Dudley North, another owner, sublet it to, amongst others, the Duke of Dorset and the Duke of Gordon. This latter family, represented by the

Dowager Lady Aberdeen and Mr William Gordon, carried on their connection with the spot until about the year 1816. Sir John Ramsden was here from 1819 to 1839, and his widow until 1857. The last private occupier was Sir Edward Kerrison, and when Hamilton Place was opened up and widened, a portion of the original house was sliced off. In 1881 the Bachelors' was founded by Augustus Lumley and Edward Wolseley. Mr William Gillett, the originator, I believe, of that excellent institution the Bankers' Clearing House, lived in the same house as Lumley, in William Street, Lowndes Square, and ultimately obtained a controlling interest in the new venture. The original list of members lies before me as I write. It contains what was, I believe, an innovation at that date—the private addresses of all the members, a feature which proved a great convenience to ball-givers. A predominating feature of the list is that it contains the names of over 100 members of the Household Brigade, though in later years this proportion has not been so marked. Mr Arthur Balfour was an original member. The fine on a bachelor's marrying produced nothing the first year of the club's existence, but, in its second, it brought in no less than £800. The Bachelors' has every appearance of vitality, filling as it does an admitted want in social London. Some harmless wit—of course, a disappointed candidate for admission—once characterised the younger members as "Gillett's Blades," an apt adaptation to circumstances of a widely advertised article of general utility, which deserves to be recorded in print.

IV

"Old Q," the Star of Piccadilly (and of Newmarket)[107]

The reproduction, in plate 7, of an unpublished drawing by Rowlandson, may serve to introduce a typical Piccadilly celebrity. "Old Q" was, in a very real sense, a connecting link between the seventeenth and the nineteenth centuries. He knew intimately men of his own rank and temperament whose names were household words in the reigns of the later Stuarts, and was himself seen in the flesh by many who were active servants of the State within the last fifty years.[108]

Rowlandson limned him to the life, as he sat, day after day, on the balcony of No 138, toothless and purblind, too feeble any longer to take his walks abroad, "ogling and hobbling down St. James's Street" in his leisured progress to White's. It will be noticed that the artist has refrained from drawing the Duke's house quite accurately and that he has placed the porch at the side, no doubt from a desire to avoid the consequences of a more exact representation.

A confirmed voluptuary, perhaps, but a man not wholly devoid of good, as will appear hereafter, the "Star of Piccadilly," as he was aptly named,[109] has been harshly judged by posterity, principally on account of the longevity of his dissipations and from his having continued the manners and profligacies of the Mohocks and Macaronis well into the nineteenth century, when London society had become, at least outwardly, more decorous than in the days of his misspent youth.

"Black Douglases" there had been in plenty before him who darkened the page of history, though, in the halo of legend which has gathered round this ancient race, the memory of one of "Old Q's" ancestors has been preserved[110] who fell in battle on the plains of Andalusia whilst engaged in carrying the heart of Robert Bruce to the Holy Land.[111] From this chivalrous exploit the Douglases assumed a "human heart crowned" as their hereditary badge, and took the proud motto "*Jamais arrière*," which still adorns their escutcheon. Another branch of the clan, now merged in the Dukedom of Buccleuch, quartering the heart with the arms of Mar within the Royal tressure of Scotland, chose for its motto the single word "*Amo*," thus unconsciously summing up "Old Q's" ruling passion in a word.

In actual human interest few of the clan have surpassed the subject of this brief memoir. He was admittedly a man of taste and artistic perception in an age when art was little appreciated. He was wholly without affectation, kind-hearted, hospitable, and noted for the sincerity of his friendships. He interested the world he lived in (small and circumscribed in its outlook though it was) to a remarkable extent; and, if for no other reason, his memory deserves to be secured from oblivion and his sins of omission, or commission, condoned by the merciful hand of time.

Though Burns and Wordsworth denounced his moral failings in verse, and Leigh Hunt, no less forcibly, in prose, the "degenerate Douglas," who throughout his long life was conspicuous for strong commonsense and resolute will, persevered in the life of pleasure which he had marked out for himself, unabashed by the lampoons which inspired the pens of minor critics, absolutely indifferent to public opinion. He has been likened to the second Duke of Buckingham, so scathingly satirised by Dryden,[112] but, except that he once evaded a duel sought to be forced upon him, his career presents no marked resemblance to that of Zimri. He was more like Charles II in the frankness of his profligacy, but without his callousness. Neither of them, at any rate, made vice appear offensive or virtue ridiculous. "Surely God will not damn a man just for taking a little pleasure out of the way," said Charles II to Bishop Burnet. The "Merry Monarch" was only fifty-four at the time of his death, and had "Old Q," in his turn, died at sixty-five instead of at eighty-five, his dissipations would never have attracted the notice that they have done, for there is always something repellent in the lack of moral sense when found in association with old age. For that reason his closing years appear to us the least attractive of his varied life. When Burns, who always disliked the aristocracy, denounced him for cutting down the woods of Drumlanrig and Neidpath, not forgetting to add that the "reptile wears a Ducal crown," "Old Q" was over seventy and verging on senility. Wraxall, whose picture of him is not on the whole unfavourable, only knew him during the last seven years when bodily decay had set in, and Leigh Hunt did not know him at all except by repute. Therefore the last decade—the senile period so often favoured by moralists in selecting their biographical texts—has been but lightly touched upon in these pages.

"The Dictionary of National Biography" gives the date of his birth as 1724, in which case, to use a sporting metaphor which he would have been the first to appreciate, "Old Q" would have been foaled in the same year as the Godolphin Arabian—one of the corner-stones of the English stud-book. But for once the Dictionary is wrong, as the records preserved in the General Register House, Edinburgh, conclusively prove.[113]

"Old Q" was born on December 5th, 1725, and baptized on the 10th of the same month, at Peebles, a small provincial town not usually associated in the public mind with dissipation or hilarity, although it has been compared, and not unfavourably, to Paris by one of its loyal natives.

His birthplace, formerly the town house of the Hay family, is still in existence as a public institution.

His father died in 1731, and the guardianship of the young Earl of March, as he then became, devolved on his uncle, John Douglas of Broughton. He, too, died a year later and the third Duke of Queensberry, a man of kindly and benevolent disposition, succeeded to the trust.

The boy received his early education, not at Eton, as has been supposed, but at Winchester at a time when that celebrated school was passing through a fashionable phase amongst the aristocracy of the North.

Entering there in 1735 he left five years later, having had amongst his schoolfellows his cousin, Lord Drumlanrig,[114] Lord Elcho, Lord Eglinton and Lord Mar and Kellie, all of them, it will be noted, hailing from North of the Tweed.

It is said that even whilst he was at Winchester young March's escapades in London were notorious, and though he probably passed a portion of his youth under his nominal guardian's roof in Edinburgh and in London, the restraining influence of both his parents[115] was withdrawn at a time when it would have been the most salutary.

When grown to man's estate he was of middle height, smart and dapper in appearance, always faultlessly dressed and remarkable for his piercing dark eyes.[116] Heir to great wealth, and accustomed from his boyhood to unrestrained self-indulgence, young March made his first appearance on the turf at the age of twenty-three under the *régime* of the second Lord Godolphin and Thomas Panton the elder, probably one of the same family which helped to make Piccadilly famous in the days of Shaver's Hall. Panton had been keeper of the King's running horses at Newmarket for a long period, and his name is found in connection with the races there so early as 1719.

In 1748 Lord March's chestnut gelding *Whipper In* beat a bay mare of Lord Downe's over four miles for a hundred guineas, at the Newmarket Spring Meeting. At York a few months later he won a match against Tom Duncombe of Helmsley, owners up, over the same tiring distance.[117]

From that time forward until Trafalgar year, when the Queensberry colours, dark red and black cap, were entered for the last time at Ascot Heath, "Old Q" was the most prominent and successful owner on the English turf, frequently in his younger days riding his own horses and holding his own with the best amateur and professional jockeys of the age.[118]

In 1749 Lord March (and Ruglen) beat his cousin the Duke of Hamilton, husband in after years of one of the beautiful Gunnings, in a match for fifty guineas, and Lord Eglinton in another for the more substantial stake of five hundred.

From these small beginnings he achieved notoriety at a bound when, in 1750, he won a match against time which he made with Count Taaffe, an Irish Catholic who had spent some years in the service of the House of Austria. It was for no less a sum than a thousand guineas, and the conditions were that a four-wheeled chaise carrying a passenger should travel nineteen miles within the hour.

The wager book at White's shows that the event attracted an extraordinary amount of attention for long before its decision. After several experiments Lord March had constructed for him, by a coach-builder in Long Acre named Wright, a chaise in which silk and whalebone were substituted for wood and leather in order, so far as possible, to minimise weight and friction.

The challenger staked out the smoothest mile to be found on Newmarket Heath and regularly trained eight or ten horses over it so as to prevent any possibility of failure on the appointed day.[119] In this historical event in the annals of Newmarket he was associated with his former schoolfellow, Lord Eglinton, who has been met with already in Piccadilly.[120]

The course was *viâ* the Warren and the Rubbing House through the Ditch gap, then bearing to the right round a staked piece of ground four miles in extent and back to the starting point. The off leader was ridden by one Erratt, a groom in Panton's employ, and the three other riders were Lord March's own stable lads. Erratt's mount was called *Roderick Random*, from which it may be inferred that turf nomenclature was tolerably well up to date in 1750, for the first edition of Smollett's immortal novel had been published only two years earlier.

Inside the machine, which resembled a four-wheeled brake, but without the high perch usually fitted to such vehicles by trainers of harness horses, sat a "passenger" dressed in red silk stockings, black cap and white satin waistcoat.

This remarkable match was decided about seven o'clock in the morning in the presence of a large number of spectators, attracted by the novelty of the contest. It is said that the horses ran away with their riders and that they covered the first four miles in the short time of nine minutes! The whole distance was completed in fifty-three minutes and twenty-seven seconds, so that the Scotch peer beat the Irish count with nearly seven minutes to spare. The time was attested by three independent umpires provided with stop-watches, and these were found, on comparison, not to vary so much as one second.[121]

All his life long "Old Q" was passionately addicted to wagers of every description. On one occasion he bet a friend that he would cause a letter to be conveyed fifty miles within the hour. To accomplish this seemingly impossible feat he enclosed the letter in a cricket ball and having arranged twenty expert cricketers in a circle, they threw the ball from one to another with such dexterity and precision that, when the ground was measured on the expiration of the hour, the letter was found to have travelled many more than the stipulated number of miles.

Another of his recorded wagers was with Sir John Lade, one of the ultra-fast set surrounding the Prince of Wales, a noted whip, and a neighbour of "Old Q" in Piccadilly in the evening of his days.[122]

Lade bet a thousand guineas, a much greater sum than he could lay his hands upon after his turf career was at an end, that the Duke could not produce a man who could eat more at a sitting than his own representative, but, at the finish, "Old Q" won by "a pig and an apple pie." Such gluttonous contests were not uncommon in the eighteenth century, and I remember to have heard the late Mr Hugo Meynell-Ingram, of Temple Newsam, who died in 1871, say that they were not extinct in Yorkshire within his recollection.

The betting book at White's discloses particulars of bets made by "Old Q" on a variety of subjects, such as the prospects of marriage within a given date on the part of his friends and acquaintances, the probable extent of their families, and even their expectation of life.

At the date of Lord March's introduction to the fascinations of Newmarket, sport on the Heath had suffered a temporary decline.

The Jockey Club, an institution which has on the whole deserved well of the racing community, had not, it is usually supposed, then been brought into existence, though the actual date of the foundation of the Club is still a matter of some doubt.

The rules of racing, lacking as they did the sanction of constituted authority, varied in different parts of the country. Local stewards and patrons made their own regulations with resulting chaos. There was no supreme court of appeal in cases of disagreement. Even the colours worn by the riders were unregistered, a condition of affairs which lasted until 1762.

There was no official scale of weight for age, although the Master of the Horse for the time being seems to have regulated the conditions of the King's plates run for at Newmarket and elsewhere. There were, as yet, no races for two year old, or even three year old, horses, and the handicap system was unknown.

When handicaps were introduced towards the end of the century they did not obtain any great measure of popularity, but with the institution of five and six furlong scrambles (in which, if a competitor dwells, even momentarily, at the start, his chance is reduced to zero), they became the outstanding and predominant feature in every programme, with a corresponding decline in the number of horses capable of staying over a distance of ground in a fast-run race. Nowadays the number of first-class races run over a course of two, or two and a half, miles may be counted on the fingers, while many of the long-distance races established a few years ago at enclosed meetings like Kempton Park, where there is ample room for such tests of endurance, have been reluctantly abandoned by their promoters owing to the paucity of entries.

It has been stated in print, and with some confidence, that the Jockey Club, of which Lord March was an early, if not an original, member, was formed in or about the year 1750, but it seems to have escaped the notice of the historians of the turf that the *Rules of Newmarket* are expressly mentioned by John Cheny in his *Historical List of Horse Matches* published in 1732. This looks as if the aristocratic subscribers to races at headquarters had already formed some such body for their mutual protection. Moreover, so early as 1727 there was a race confined to horses trained at Newmarket.

Soon after George the Second ascended the throne Lord Godolphin, as we have shown, was racing at Newmarket, and although no actual proof has been discovered of his having been a member of the Club, it seems hardly possible that such a prominent patron of the turf should not have been called to its councils.

The first two Georges, being thoroughly un-English in their tastes and habits, took little or no interest in horse-racing, and the glories of the Rowley Mile had sensibly diminished since the Merry Monarch rode his own horses over the course named after him, and adjudicated, much after the manner of Admiral Rous, the so-called dictator of the turf in a later age, on disputes referred to him for decision. There is proof positive of Charles the Second having ridden "three heats and a course" at Newmarket in 1675 and of his having proved successful through superior horsemanship. There was, however, a race of the value of eight hundred guineas, a very large stake for those days, run for on the Heath in 1730. It was confined to four-year-olds, carrying eight stone seven pounds over the usual distance of four miles.

In 1737, and again in 1738, the "great stake" as it had come to be termed, had increased in value to one thousand guineas, and on both occasions Lord Godolphin was the winner.

In 1730, the successful owner had been Lord Lonsdale, the then head of a celebrated sporting family. The Duke of Devonshire, who had been one of the original subscribers, died before the date of running, and his successor in the title was permitted to take his share in the sweepstakes. No doubt it was decided over the still-existing Beacon Course.

At another meeting at headquarters in the same year Mr. Roger Williams' *Whipper Snapper* ran five times over this trying distance within the hour, carrying a feather weight, for a wager of twenty guineas, and at Lincoln, if Cheny's *Historical List* is to be trusted, there was a race in 1744 for fifty guineas run in one heat over fourteen miles!

There are no such stayers now, the tendency of the age being to cultivate speed rather than stamina, nor are visitors to the Heath again likely to see such a sight as formed part of the day's programme in 1731. Lord Sunderland's running footman[123] then walked the respectable distance of six miles and four hundred yards within the hour for a prize of fifty guineas. The rate of speed would not be thought high at the present day, but the footman presumably covered the distance on the grass and not on a cinder path, which would make a considerable difference in the conditions.

The Rubbing House, referred to above, which stood near the starting post of the Beacon Course, figures in many racing prints and portraits of celebrated horses. It was at least as old as the time of Charles the Second, yet its antiquity did not save it from wanton and wholly unnecessary demolition only a few years ago. It might have been thought that the Jockey Club would have exercised a jealous care in the preservation of its landmarks, but the Red Post on the Old Cambridgeshire hill, which superstitious racegoers used to slap for luck on their way down to the Rowley Mile, has lately shared the same fate.

The Bushes and the Birdcage, the latter so-called from the narrow wire fencing which separates the saddling paddock from the Course, are there still, and the Ancaster and Bunbury Miles remain to preserve the memory of two of the earlier Stewards. Almost everything else at Newmarket is modern, and not always the best at that.

Another curious Newmarket custom, not entirely obsolete, as the present writer can vouch for, is the superstition of raising one's hat on crossing the earthwork known as the Ditch. Failure to observe this precaution is said to be tantamount to certain disaster in the ring.

Could "March Many Weathers" wake from his long sleep and revisit his beloved Newmarket he would find little or nothing to remind him of the place as he knew it, except the exhilarating air, never more enjoyable than when breathed at the July meetings behind the Ditch. The vast crowds which now come down by train to witness the decision of the Cesarewitch and the Cambridgeshire (two great handicaps which provoke more genuine speculation than even the classic events) are conspicuous by their absence in the spring and summer, and I have seen an important race like the Two Thousand Guineas run in the presence of a mere handful of spectators.

The continuator of Defoe's "Tour through Great Britain," paid a visit to Newmarket in 1742, and has preserved for posterity an instructive picture of the scene as it presented itself to his unaccustomed eyes, just before "Old Q" made his first appearance on the turf.

"I had," he wrote, "the opportunity to see the horse races and a great concourse of the nobility and gentry as well from London as from all parts of England. But they were all so intent, so eager, so busy upon what is called the sharping part of the sport, of wagers and bets, that to me they seemed rather like so many horse coursers at Smithfield than persons of dignity and quality. ... These races were instituted with a very good intent, to raise an emulation in our nobility and gentry, to keep up and preserve a race of good horses, ... but as the institution is debased, *it is not the best horse that wins the race, but that which is destined for it by a combination.*"

It will occur to many who read these lines that the criticism is as applicable now as it was 150 years ago to those parasites of the racecourse who infest the rings and enclosures at the various centres of sport, but how to deal effectively with admitted evil is another story too long to be entered upon here.

To "Old Q's" credit be it recorded that, in a turf career of unexampled length, no breath of suspicion ever attached to his name, in connection with the running of his horses, and this although he was a heavy bettor from the first. The moment he discovered that Chifney was not to be trusted he ceased to employ him, although the Prince of Wales affected to believe in his honesty for some time longer.

One of his mentors on the turf was the Lord Tankerville, who, as Master of the Buckhounds, raised Ascot to the dignity of a three days' meeting. From him and Tom Panton, "Old Q" bought *Stadtholder* when he ran at Epsom (in his own name) at the spring meeting of 1749.

He tried over and over again to win the Derby, but, like Lord Palmerston, another Piccadilly celebrity of later date, he was never able to carry off the blue riband of the turf, or the Oaks, and this in spite of his maintaining one of the largest studs in England and devoting his utmost energies to the breeding of bloodstock. In this respect he was less fortunate than his contemporary the third Duke of Grafton (to whom, by the way, judging from their portraits, he bore a certain facial resemblance), for the Grafton scarlet, hailing also from Piccadilly,[124] carried off the Derby three times and the Oaks twice.

"Old Q's" memory is preserved at Newmarket in the Queensberry plate run for at the Houghton Meeting since the Old Cambridgeshire handicap was discontinued and the stand at the top of the town demolished. He deserves to be commemorated by the Jockey Club, for there is no doubt that he and Sir Charles Bunbury (who became a sort of perpetual Steward) did much to place sport at Newmarket on a better and purer footing than they found it, though both of them, after the new fangled short-distance races were introduced, competed in four-furlong scrambles which afford no test of endurance. These, happily, have been discontinued for many years and are not likely to be reintroduced.

The real importance of the Jockey Club dates from the period when its members acquired premises of their own in the town, instead of having to meet at an inn, and even more from their unwearied efforts in acquiring bit by bit the freehold of the Heath and the adjacent training grounds. It stands to reason that until the Club became the owner of the soil it could not arrogate to itself the right, so dreaded by offenders against its rules, of warning off evil-doers.

The modern house in the High Street, now owned by Lord Wolverton, and known as Queensberry House, is built on a portion of the site of "Old Q's" stables, but his actual dwelling-house has long disappeared, as it became ruinous in the middle of the last century.

An assiduous watcher of trials, "Old Q" never let his jockeys know who was to carry his colours until the man was put into the scales to be weighed. A great believer in secrecy in turf affairs, he never admitted any partner to his designs so soon as he felt himself strong enough to stand alone, preferring to take all risks and to concentrate all profits *in propriâ personâ*.

Besides his house and stables in the town of Newmarket he had a large breeding establishment at Saxham, not far from Bury St. Edmunds, which he constantly visited when staying at Euston with the Duke of Grafton.

It was unusual for owners to have permanent houses of their own at Newmarket in the eighteenth century, but Lord Godolphin was one of the exceptions. His house eventually passed into the possession of Dick Vernon, whose name frequently crops up in Selwyn's correspondence. Vernon was regarded by his contemporaries as one of the oracles of the turf. He began life as an ensign in the Guards, took early to racing, and won a Jockey Club Plate in 1753. He built the rooms, which the Club rented, in 1771, and won the Oaks in 1787 with a daughter of *Eclipse*. When proposed for White's, he was blackballed, though out of twelve members present, eight had promised him their votes. After the ballot they assured him, on their honour, that they had all put in white balls, so he was left to the unpleasant conclusion that his proposer and seconder must have been responsible for his rejection. A similar story has been told of elections which went wrong at other Clubs, but it appears to have originated with Dick Vernon's unfortunate experience at White's.

The names of but few of the earlier jockeys have been handed down, but amongst those who rode for "Old Q" was Dick Goodison, who, as not unfrequently happens, developed into a trainer. Erratt, Larkin, Marshall and Arnull were all riding at Newmarket before 1750, and the first-named either leased or sold a portion of the Heath to the Club, from which it is fair to infer that he found his profession a profitable one. It will be recollected that John Watts, after retiring from the saddle, built himself a large house, overlooking the Heath, and many instances could be adduced of similar happenings in recent years.

There were Arnulls in business as trainers at Newmarket within my own recollection, and one of the same family rode the winner of the first Derby. Two, if not three, generations of Chifneys have left their mark on the annals of the turf as indelibly as Fordham or Archer in a later age. Nowadays, I am told that even bookmakers have their permanent residences at Newmarket, occupying them regularly during the principal meetings. It would be interesting to know who was the first professional member of the ring; as a rule gentlemen bet with their friends in the eighteenth century, and amongst those who lost large sums to "Old Q" at one time or another were the "Butcher" Duke of Cumberland (the virtual founder of Ascot) and "Chillaby" Jennings, a virtuoso, who squandered his entire fortune, and died within the Rules of the King's Bench.

From first to last "Old Q" is said to have won upwards of a quarter of a million on the turf, his cool head and shrewd Scotch nature helping him to avoid pitfalls into which less fortunate speculators fell. All the same, he suffered occasional runs of ill luck. In a letter to Selwyn, undated, but probably written in 1766, he said: "The Meeting has ended very ill, and I am now near a *mille* lower in cash than when we parted, most of the White's people are gone to Sir J. Moore's. Bully (Lord Bolingbroke), Lord Wilmington and myself are left here to reflect coolly upon our losses and the nonsense of keeping running horses; and yet, notwithstanding all our resolutions, if we make any, they will end as yours do, after being *doved* at Almack's. Scott has lost near three thousand. I think of going to-night to Bury, to the ball and fair. I wish with all my heart that I was with you, instead of in this d——d place." At the very next meeting he retrieved his losses, with a clear gain of over £4,000.

Before he succeeded to the Queensberry estates Selwyn and "Old Q" frequently helped one another, and the human side of the latter's nature never comes out more strongly than at one of these crises in Selwyn's affairs: "So you have lost a thousand pounds, which you have done twenty times in your lifetime, and won it again as often, and why should not the same thing happen again? I make no doubt but it will. I am sorry, however, that you have lost your money; it is unpleasant. ... As to your banker, I will call there to-morrow; make yourself easy about that, for I have three thousand pounds now at Coutts'. *There will be no bankruptcy, without we are both ruined at the same time.*" Both were members of White's and of Almack's where, in after years, Fox lost so heavily. "Old Q" was also elected to Brooks' in 1764,[125] but when the Ladies' Club at Almack's was founded he was unsuccessful at the ballot. Had he lived a hundred years later than he did, I doubt if he would have viewed with complacency the foundation of a Bachelors' Club at his very doors, for he was always jealous of men younger than himself, especially where the fair sex was concerned.

Before he had been racing for ten years he had a weeding-out sale at his Saxham stud. Eleven brood mares were offered at prices ranging from only forty to 220 guineas, most of them tracing their descent from an Arab stock.

Leaving the purer air of Newmarket Heath and returning for a time to Piccadilly, I find that in early life "Old Q" appears to have sought an honourable alliance with Miss Frances Pelham, daughter of the Prime Minister. Finding that her very moral father disapproved of his suit, he took a house next door to Pelham's in Arlington Street, and added a bow window to his own so that he might the better command a view of his inamorata's coming out and going in. This ardent passion, after lasting for about seven years, flickered out, and the lovers drifted apart. Miss Pelham never married, and predeceased her former admirer after having dissipated the whole of her fortune at the card table.

Somehow or other, "Old Q," though lucky in many ways, never had the supreme good fortune to meet the right woman at the right time. He appears to have paid marked attention to the immaculate Lady Mary Coke, when that lady was in the early days of her widowhood. Being snubbed for his pains, no doubt much to his surprise, he made love as years went on to every pretty woman of his own class, and was accustomed to buy it ready made (in Quin's pungent phrase) from every one of a lower station who offered it for sale. Though Lady Mary boxed his ears and rejected his addresses, the pair remained on terms of considerable intimacy, constantly meeting at the houses of mutual friends to gossip and play cards. Lady Mary, like poor Miss Pelham, was fond of play. She was also a bad loser, which "Old Q" never was. On the authority of the same lady's diary[126] one learns that he paid his addresses at one time to Lady Harriot Stanhope and flirted outrageously with Lady Susan Stewart, a notable beauty, who was currently reported to be desirous of securing a good view of the Green Park should she consent to marry.[127]

Nor was this his final attempt at matrimony. When quite elderly he proposed no less than three times to Miss Gertrude Vanneck, only to be refused again. This lady, a daughter of Sir Joshua Vanneck,[128] was his next-door neighbour in Piccadilly, at No 139, erroneously stated to have formed part of No 138 at one time. It has been supposed to have been used by the Duke as a private seraglio, but he really took it for Lady Yarmouth, the "Mie-Mie" of Selwyn's letters, on her marriage.

Miss Vanneck was also a near neighbour at Richmond, where the Duke took a riverside house about the year 1781. He spent a large sum of money there in alterations and embellished it with a gallery of antique pictures removed from his house at Amesbury.[129] These included the celebrated Vandycks collected by Lord Chancellor Clarendon which had come down to him in lineal descent. They had probably hung in Piccadilly more than a century earlier, when they formed part of the interior decorations of Clarendon House.

The hall at Richmond was hung entirely with the works of the great painter, whilst a collection of legal portraits, also a portion of the Clarendon inheritance, adorned a semicircular corridor, making one think, said Selwyn, that one was in a lawyer's office in Serjeants' Inn rather than a nobleman's private house. Though Horace Walpole criticised the Vandycks unfavourably there is reason to believe that they were absolutely genuine, and some of them may be amongst the masterpieces of that artist owned by Lord Clarendon and now at The Grove, near Watford, Herts.

"Old Q" always affected the *rus in urbe* (though he once told Wilberforce that the Thames bored him), and if he could not be in his beloved Piccadilly he did not like to be far away from it. He cared nothing for his Scotch estates and rarely visited them, preferring Newmarket to Drumlanrig, Richmond to Amesbury, and Piccadilly to all of them.

Despite his neglect of Scotland his political influence in Tweeddale was always considerable. In November 1775 his candidate triumphantly carried an election in his native county although his kinsman the Duke of Buccleuch, who seems to have been jealous of his intervention in political affairs, hoped that long absence from the North would have decreased his local interest. Years after, when he had succeeded to the Dukedom, he managed, in 1790, to get his own doctor[130] returned for the Peebles District of Burghs.

He worked hard to obtain for Selwyn the deputy rangership of the Green Park, but in this he was not so successful, as the coveted appointment was bestowed on Lord William Gordon,[131] and secured to him and his wife for their joint lives. The Ranger's lodge, which stood nearly opposite Down Street in a large enclosure hidden from public view by a high brick wall, was one of the earliest works of Robert Adam. Its proportions were unfavourably criticised, and somehow Adam's classic designs have a way of looking better on paper than in the actual structure.[132]

The Ranger's lodge was pulled down in the 'forties, and the well-modelled figures of stags which stood at the Piccadilly entrance were removed to Albert Gate. The grounds were thrown into the park, and a stone fountain is probably the only remaining relic of the lodge still *in situ*. The mound on which a fine sycamore tree now flourishes was, according to Sir Algernon West, who knew the place in his boyhood, Lady William Gordon's ice-house.

At Richmond "Old Q" found himself within convenient distance of Horace Walpole at Strawberry Hill, of Sudbrook, a charming old house belonging to the Duke of Argyll,[133] and close to that perfect specimen of Jacobean domestic architecture—Ham House by Petersham Common. His own house, which was too large and important to be called a villa, stood nearer to the river than the comparatively modern building known as Queensberry House. Its nearest neighbour was the still existing Trumpeting House, said to have been built for a brother of Queen Anne's favourite, Mrs. Masham. This fine example of a Thames valley mansion of the best class is clearly visible from the railway bridge across the Thames, surrounded by old trees, some of which may have adorned the grounds of the long-vanished Palace of Richmond.

The Prince of Wales and Mrs. Fitz-Herbert were constant visitors at Queensberry House, as was the Duke of Clarence.[134]

"Old Q" did not much appreciate the sailor Prince's society, as he thought his manners decidedly coarse in the presence of ladies, and, notwithstanding his own moral weaknesses, no one knew better than he, with the unmistakable polish of the *vieille cour* which always distinguished him, how a gentleman should behave. According to Selwyn his Grace of Clarence's conversation often verged on indecency, the "Sailor Prince" thinking thereby to gain the reputation of wit. It might have gone down very well on the forecastle deck, but the Richmond ladies did not like it.[135] When the Duke asked if he might put up six of his horses in "Old Q's" stables for three months, the request was respectfully declined. Selwyn seems also to have been afraid that HRH might take a sudden fancy to his house, in order to shelter a lady to whom he was paying his attentions, whilst her own was being painted.

Richmond at the close of the eighteenth century must have been a much pleasanter place than it is now, vulgarised out of all recognition and groaning under the yoke of the jerry-builder, its once fair face disfigured past regeneration by row upon row of cheap and nasty villas and second-rate shops.

The unsettled state of France caused a number of cultivated *émigrés* to take up their summer quarters on the banks of the Thames. Most of them were poor and all were proud. Twice a week "Old Q," who was as much at home in Paris as he was in Piccadilly, kept open house for these exiles, and, in his kindness of heart, he hit upon an expedient by which he was able to afford them a great deal of enjoyment without letting them feel that they were under the slightest pecuniary obligation. "Who cares to go to the Opera to-night?" he would say, "for I am longing to exercise my family privilege!" And, when one of his guests asked him what this privilege consisted of, he added: "That of writing out free admissions to the theatre for any number of my friends." Incidentally he had come to a private arrangement with the Managers of the Opera and the two patent theatres by which his vouchers passed for current coin of the realm. His house-steward had orders to discharge them on their being re-presented, and no one was a whit the wiser.

His dinners at Richmond were served *à la Russe* with a servant at a buffet to carve each joint. He gave his *officier de bouche*, as he called his cook, ninety guineas a year. Selwyn, who was not nearly so well, off, only gave his fifty-two, "and yet," said old Dr. Warner, who was a frequent guest at both tables, "we could live with her!"

Madame de Boufflers, "la Reine des Aristocrates réfugiés en Angleterre," and a rival of Madame du Deffand, was the bright particular star of the Richmond parties. Calonne, a man of incredible facility and a delightful *raconteur*, followed in her wake.[136]

The Comte and Comtesse de Suffren were two other sufferers by the troubles in France, whose society the Duke specially enjoyed. Selwyn has an amusing note of a party which the Comtesse de Balbi gave at the existing Castle Inn, to which "Old Q" and "Mie-Mie" were also invited. "The Duke intends to bring Mr. Grieve[137] with him, and as a member of the *chambre basse* he will pass muster, but he is most wretched at the lingo." In later years the Duke replaced him by a French médecin who had attended Louis XV.

"Old Q" is said to have acquired another house, at or near Richmond, from the Countess of Northampton, and if this was so, it was probably on account of a dispute which he had with the local authorities respecting a portion of his lawn which was claimed by the town. This misunderstanding gave him a distaste for the scene of many varied hospitalities, and he returned to Piccadilly. At his death his Richmond property passed to "Mie-Mie," who promptly disposed of it to Sir William Dundas.

Mention of that lady recalls a still unexplained chapter in the Duke's life. The Marchesa Fagniani, an Italian lady who visited England with her husband early in the reign of George the Third, gave birth to a daughter in 1771, whose parentage was attributed in quarters supposed to be well-informed to George Augustus Selwyn, rather than to her putative father, the Marquis Fagniani.

"Old Q" was also freely named in this connection, but probably with much less reason. Whatever the mystery of her birth, the indisputable fact remains that "Mie-Mie" so endeared herself to Selwyn and "Old Q" that they both left her large fortunes at their death.

Selwyn loved children, and this child in particular. He took the keenest interest in her education and up-bringing, placing her at an early age at an excellent English school, and recovering her, a few years later, from a convent in Paris, to which she had been consigned by her mother. The Marquis Fagniani lost his reason when "Mie-Mie" was only ten years old, and thenceforth, so long as Selwyn lived, her home was with him. When he died in 1791, "Old Q" considered it his duty to assume the parental rights so long exercised by his friend, though whilst Selwyn lived he had been quite content to leave the girl to his care. When a match was arranged for her with Lord Yarmouth,[138] he cut down an oak wood at Drumlanrig, six miles long, in order to provide her with a suitable dowry. He also took a large house adjoining his own in Piccadilly for her and her husband to live in.

This she seems seldom or never to have occupied either in the Duke's lifetime or after his death, but she and Lord Yarmouth, the original of Thackeray's Marquis of Steyne, had, at one time or another, at least three houses in Piccadilly, all of which are mentioned elsewhere in these pages. Lord and Lady Hertford drifted apart, he dying in Park Lane in 1842, and she, so recently as 1856, at a house in the Rue Taitbout in Paris.

"Mie-Mie" was painted by Gainsborough, at Selwyn's instance, in 1775, when that great artist was living at Schomberg House in Pall Mall. A portion of this interesting house exists in its original state, though the eastern wing was ruthlessly destroyed some years ago for an extension of the War Office. Unfortunately the picture cannot now be traced, nor have I been so fortunate as to find any likeness of "Mie-Mie" either in public or private hands.

Returning to "Old Q" and his love affairs, on the other side of the balance to his honourable intentions towards Miss Pelham and Lady Mary Coke must be placed his *liaisons* with the Rena, who so scandalized Lady Mary, with the Zamparini, the Tondino, and numerous *traviatas* of the eighteenth-century stage whose names have not survived.

The Duke was always fond of music and the *coulisses* of the Opera. Contemporary memoirs yield abundant evidence of his activities in this direction. The chief Italian singers of both sexes ("the garlic tribe," as Selwyn called them) on their arrival in London made straight for 138 Piccadilly, where they knew that they were sure of a polite and liberal reception. "Old Q's" box at the Haymarket Opera House was four nearer to the stage than the Prince Regent's, and it was not until after the Duke's death that it was transferred to the Heir-Apparent.

The history of Italian opera in this country has yet to be written, though the great building in the Haymarket will always be associated with the names of Handel and Haydn, many of whose compositions were first performed there. The programme was often of a very miscellaneous character; when opera did not pay, the management varied their attractions with masked balls, and during Lent oratorios were given. Piccini, a rival of Gluck and one of Marie Antoinette's many singing masters, was the most favoured composer: his comic opera *La Buona Figliuola* was performed more frequently than the works of any of his contemporaries, though at the patent houses the insipid melodies of Dr. Arne found much favour. An emasculated version of *Orfeo* was given on the last night of the season in 1770, being described in the bills as a "new serious opera" and labelled as the joint production of Gluck, Bach,[139] and Guglielmi. The price of admission to non-subscribers was half a guinea, the curtain went up at half-past six or seven at the latest, and the management found it necessary to advertise that no visitors could be admitted behind the scenes or on the stage.

This, indeed, was no new managerial difficulty, for nearly a century before Dryden had written:

We beg you last our scene-room to forbear, and leave our goods and chattels to our care.[140]

The Haymarket Opera House was burnt down in 1789, but as it was promptly rebuilt, opera returned to its earliest home, and, with the productions of Cimarosa, it may be said to have entered upon a new lease of life, for his *Matrimonio Segreto* achieved remarkable popularity both in England and in Italy.

The concerts and receptions at "Old Q's" house were attended by the cream of London Society. Lady Mary Coke has placed on record her impressions of a house-warming, or *Soirée de Danse*, which he gave soon after taking up his permanent abode in Piccadilly. "March's great room is gilding, and when finished he is to give a dinner to Lady Sarah (Bunbury), and a concert to a great many more."[141]

For two whole years the house had been in course of erection, and "Old Q" had been paying parochial rates in respect of it pending his removal from Seamore Place. Lady Mary was one of the invited guests, and she wrote in her Journal:

"The house is very fine and fitted up with a great deal of taste. There was three and twenty people; the Duchess of Grafton, the Duchess of Hamilton, the Duchess of Buccleuch, Lady Coventry, Lady Essex, Mrs. Fitzroy, Mrs. Pitt and Lady Susan Stewart. The rest were all men.[142] The supper was fine, but not tedious. When it was over there was music, and five couples danced. Some time ago I should have liked it very much, but now, nothing entertains me. At a quarter after one o'clock, the Duchess of Buccleuch and I called for our chairs and all the party seemed breaking up."[143]

The liveries of the Duke's body-servants were of green and silver, and everything that wealth and a sense of luxury could suggest was requisitioned to entertain his guests at the house-warming.

How much more enjoyable a dancing party of two-dozen must have been than the overcrowding which now prevails at

London balls when fashionable hostesses, with a few praiseworthy exceptions, fill their rooms to suffocation with young people of both sexes, many of them unknown to them, even by sight. It would seem to be an axiom of entertaining in the twentieth century, that success can only be achieved by numbers, with a corresponding disregard for the comfort of the entertained.

A mere catalogue of names is dull reading, little more than a *réchauffé* of the *Court Circular* in its bare facts, but when the list of "Old Q's" invited guests comes to be analysed, how interesting, as a mirror of fashion, it can be made to appear! The drawing-room on the first floor at 138, with a fine ceiling by Angelica Kauffmann still *in situ*, is of moderate size, but, instead of a bare two dozen, it could accommodate a hundred guests without any suspicion of over-crowding.

Lady Mary's record of youth and beauty of high degree in London Society at this period embraced the Duchess of Grafton. This was Anne Liddell, wife of the Prime Minister, only twenty-eight years old, but almost on the eve of divorce.

By 1769, "the smile which blessed one lover's heart, had broken many more," and three days after the dissolution of her first marriage the Duchess became Lady Ossory. It is said that she began a letter to one of her correspondents on the day before the Bill passed the House of Lords, which she signed "Anne Grafton," added a little to it the next day, and signed that "Anne Liddell," did not post it until she had been to church, when she finished it as "Anne Ossory." This episode gave rise to the lines:

> No grace but Grafton's grace so soon,
> So strangely could convert a sinner;
> Duchess a morn, and miss at noon,
> And Upper Ossory after dinner.

Her father[144] is said to have been so mortified at his daughter's conduct as to have expressed a wish never to re-visit London, after the circumstances of her intrigue with Lord Ossory became public property.

The Duchess of Hamilton, so-called by Lady Mary, who probably refused to acknowledge her by her new title, was, at this date, Duchess of Argyll. The youngest of the beautiful Gunnings, she had been married to her first husband, a kinsman of "Old Q," by his private chaplain, the disreputable Kidgell, at Keith's Chapel, in Curzon Street, Mayfair.[145]

According to Walpole, the wedding took place at midnight, the ceremony being performed with the ring of a bed-curtain.

The Lady Coventry referred to by Lady Mary was not the Duchess of Hamilton's equally lovely sister of that name, but Barbara St John, Lord Coventry's second wife, a lady on whom the breath of scandal never blew.

The third Duchess present, her Grace of Buccleuch, was a recent bride, and a Montagu by birth. Lady Essex had been Miss Harriet Bladen, and an old flame of her host. Mrs Pitt was probably the Anne Pitt whose name occurs so often in Walpole's Letters, and, lastly, Lady Susan Stewart, whose flirtations have already been mentioned, was Lord Galloway's daughter, married only two months later (as his third wife) to the Marquis of Stafford.

Lady Sarah Bunbury was apparently not one of the party after all. Had she been present, this great-granddaughter of Charles II would have been the bright particular star of the assembly. George III fell in love with her, and many men of lesser degree did the same. Divorced from Bunbury, a few years later, on account of a scandal in connection with Lord William Gordon, she eventually married Colonel George Napier and became the mother of Sir Charles Napier, the conqueror of Scinde, and of Sir William Napier, the historian of the Peninsular War.[146] It is a pity that Lady Mary Coke omitted to give the names of the mere men summoned to Piccadilly to dance with such a fascinating company of ladies—but, unfortunately for posterity, she always affected to despise the majority of her male acquaintances, unless, indeed, they chanced to be of Royal birth.

On the accession of George III, Lord Bute, one of the most unpopular Prime Ministers of modern times, suddenly increased the number of the Lords of the Bedchamber from twelve to eighteen, for no apparent reason other than to gratify some of his hungry supporters from North of the Tweed.

It was, it should be remembered, the first time within the memory of man that a Scotchman had sat in the seat of power, and, not unnaturally, he offered one of the newly-created posts to his countryman, Lord March.[147]

So far as his political views were known to the Government he had always been reckoned as a staunch Tory, though, as has been said, he cared little for the land of his birth, and seldom visited Scotland except at election times.

In Bute's Administration he became a Knight of the Thistle, and was chosen as representative peer for the Northern Kingdom. He was also Vice-Admiral of Scotland, a sinecure for which he received £1,000 a year. Though he never took a prominent part in the deliberations of the House of Lords, he was a constant attendant at its Debates for forty years, and his interest in politics was almost as keen as his liking for the turf. It was mainly through his agency that Wilkes was put upon his trial for the scandalous "Essay on Woman," which the peers declared, after hearing portions of it read by Lord Sandwich, to be "a most scandalous, obscene and impious libel, a gross profanation of many parts of the Holy Scriptures; and a most wicked and blasphemous attempt to ridicule and vilify the person of our Blessed Saviour." His chaplain, the notorious Kidgell, had surreptitiously obtained some of the proof sheets of the Essay from the printers and shown them to Lord March, who thought it his duty to lay them before the Cabinet. A few days later he was appointed to serve on a Conference between the two Houses to investigate the facts of the publication of the celebrated No 45 of the *North Briton* which more particularly engrossed the attention of the Commons.[148]

And in 1768, when litigation was still pending against this eighteenth-century Bradlaugh, Lord March asked leave of the Lords to join with the Commons in another Conference intended to clear Philip Carteret Webb, the solicitor to the Treasury, from the odious charge of having bribed witnesses to give evidence against Wilkes.[149]

Perhaps the only occasion on which he addressed the House was in the course of a debate[150] on the right of Scotch Peers, created Peers of Great Britain, to vote at the election of their own representatives, it having been contended that he and the Earl of Abercorn had forfeited their right to vote on such occasions.

"Old Q" maintained that by a Resolution passed by the Lords in 1708–9 his ancestor the Duke of Dover's vote as a Scotch Peer had been taken away, whilst by another Resolution of 1711 his right to vote as a British Peer had been abolished. Surely, he contended, his noble progenitor must have been either one or the other! He prayed to be heard by counsel in defence of his rights on the ground that Resolutions passed by the House were neither final nor conclusive. Let the House, he said, but look to its own Journals, and it would see at once how various and self-contradictory they often were. Still, in spite of the Lord Chancellor[151] having expressed his personal opinion that the matter was one which would more properly be regulated by statute, Lord Hopetoun's motion, directing the Resolution of 1708–9 to be transmitted to the Lord Registrar of Scotland for his guidance in cases of future elections, was carried by fifty-one to thirty-five.

Though unsuccessful for the time being, "Old Q" gained his point a few years later. At the 1790 election of Scotch peers the clerks refused to receive the signed lists of the Duke of Queensberry and the Earl of Abercorn, on the ground that they had been created Peers of Great Britain since the Union. The matter in dispute was referred back to the House of Lords, and the whole question threshed out by the Committee of Privileges. The Earl of Kinnoul moved[152] to disallow their votes, whereupon Lord Grenville, Prime Minister of All the Talents, moved and carried the previous question, though only by a bare majority. A further question that the opinion of the judges be taken was carried by twenty-seven to twenty-five and at length, on May 27th, 1793, Lord Cathcart having submitted that the Duke's vote if duly tendered ought to have been counted, the motion was adopted by a small majority, and "Old Q" was adjudged to be within his rights and henceforth unmolested in his claim to a voice in the selection of his fellow countrymen. He managed to retain his post at Court for no less than twenty-eight years, but when the question of the Regency became acute in 1788, he alone of all the Lords of the Bedchamber broke away from party ties and threw in his lot with the Heir-Apparent, with whom and with Fox he had long been on terms of considerable intimacy.

During the prolonged discussions at Westminster on the King's state of mind, the Prince of Wales and his brother, the Duke of York, spent a great deal of their time at No 138, where copious draughts of the new and intoxicating French wine called champagne were quaffed to the success of the approaching Regency.[153]

But for once "Old Q." put his money on the wrong horse.

With the astuteness derived from long experience of the turf he had come to the deliberate conclusion, based on personal enquiries made of Dr. Warren, the Royal physician, that the King had permanently lost his reason.

So far from this being the case, everybody knows that George III recovered his sanity, and that Pitt and the Queen forthwith exerted their influence to remove the more prominent supporters of the Heir-Apparent from their offices and emoluments.

Lord Lothian, another representative Scotch peer who deserted the Court party, was promptly relieved of the command of his regiment, though the King, with characteristic kindness of heart, made up the deficiency of income in his case out of his Privy Purse.

"Old Q's" defection caused a great stir in the fashionable world, and though the loss of a thousand a year was nothing to such a rich man, his *amour propre* was wounded.

He deemed it advisable to withdraw from London for a time, and, during the remarkable and spontaneous exhibitions of loyalty and affection called forth by the King's recovery from his mental disorder, his place in society was vacant. During the summer he plunged into the newly discovered delights of Brighton in the company of the Prince Regent and Mrs. Fitzherbert. Even the loss of our American dominions was forgotten in the popular enthusiasm produced by the necessity for a provisional government, controlled by the Prince and his friends, having being averted.

Under the circumstances Pitt was enabled to resume office amidst general approval, and with augmented power for his country's good.

The illuminations in London in March and April, 1789, were on a scale unprecedented to that time, especially at the West End of the town, although in the poorest quarters nearly every house had its candle. Calonne's mansion at Hyde Park Corner and No 138 blazed with light, and were the observed of all observers, for the Duke, though on the losing side, was a loyal subject. He took his dismissal from the Household with the *sang froid* he displayed when defeated on the turf, and perhaps the death of *Eclipse*, which occurred about the same time, interested him even more than high politics.

The Queen drove up from Kew to see the illuminations and did not reach home till two in the morning, when she found the King still sitting up and in a state of alarm for her safety.[154]

Whether "Old Q." recovered his former intimacy with Pitt is uncertain, but his relations with other Tory ministers continued to be cordial. He was fond of that genial mediocrity Addington, and left him £5,000 in his will.

Pitt's stop-gap Prime Minister, or "the Doctor" as he was familiarly called by his friends,[155] was one of the last of the old port wine school. The official dinners which he gave as Speaker of the House of Commons were famous. They were held in the crypt of St. Stephen's Chapel, after that venerable apartment had ceased to be used as a coal-cellar. Burgundy, champagne, hock and hermitage were served at the banquet, followed by claret, port, madeira, and sherry with the dessert.[156]

1787, 1788, and 1789, if unlucky in politics, were amongst the Duke's best years on the turf. About this time he engaged a Yorkshire jockey called Richard Goodison, known at Newmarket as "Hellfire Dick," whose quickness and resource in race riding were second to none. The Duke had discovered him during one of his many visits to Castle Howard, where he was in the habit of staying with Lord Carlisle for the Northern Meetings.

In 1788 and 1789 the Queensberry red and black cap were carried successfully in 1,000 guineas stakes by *Roscius* and *Dash*, the latter being one of the best horses the Duke ever owned. Only twice before had he carried off a prize of similar value, viz. in 1766 and in 1771 with *Young Hermione* and *Piccadilly* respectively.

Goodison engaged the notorious Chifney to ride for the stable, but the connection proved an unsatisfactory one, his riding of the Duke's horses being, to say the least of it, extremely suspicious. Probably their owner was not much surprised when, a few years later, it was intimated to the Prince of Wales by the stewards that, if he continued to employ Chifney, no gentleman would run against him.

After the Chifney incident the Duke's active interest in racing began to decline, and, though he did not altogether withdraw

1. General view of the eastern end of Piccadilly, *c.* 1840.
From a lithograph by T. S. Boys

2. Clarendon House. From a contemporary engraving by John Dunstall

3. Bath House, Piccadilly, as it stood in 1820, before being rebuilt by Lord Ashburton

4. Old Gloucester House, Piccadilly, now demolished

5. Lady Palmerston. After Sir Thomas Lawrence

6. Lord Barrymore's house, No 105, Piccadilly, in 1792
(before Lord Hertford's alterations)

7. A reminiscence of 'Old Q' and Piccadilly. From a drawing in watercolour by T. Rowlandson

8. 'Old Q' as a young man. By Sir Joshua Reynolds

9. 'Street walkers.' Showing
the junction of Old Bond
Street with Piccadilly.
Published 28 April 1786 by S.
W. Fores, No 3, Piccadilly

10. View towards Piccadilly

11. Royal saloon, Piccadilly. Watercolour by R. Cruikshank

12. Gloucester Coffee House on the corner of Berkeley Street and Piccadilly, *c.* 1828

13. The arrival of the Brighton coach at Regent Circus, Piccadilly

14. Piccadilly from Hyde Park Corner, *c.* 1790

from the turf, he spent less of his time at Newmarket and more in Piccadilly. By degrees he sold off his horses in training and reduced the number of his entries for races to come. One of the last occasions on which he attended a race meeting was in 1801, when he drove down to Egham in a landau and six, only to be mortified by seeing his once invincible colours in the rear.

There was another and more cogent reason for his partial withdrawal from the turf. He resented the irritating defeats which the red and black cap sustained at the hands of the upstart, Lord Barrymore, who shot like a meteor across the sporting horizon in 1787, and managed to lose about £300,000 during the five years in which he figured on the turf.[157] To a man of ten-fold longer experience, it must have been extremely mortifying to see the odds laid on his horses upset as they were on two separate occasions in October, 1788, and 1789, and to find the Barrymore blue and yellow placed in the Derby at the very first attempt.[158]

Neither George Selwyn nor the Duke had any liking for this young Irish lord, whom they regarded as a hare-brained idiot, an undesirable neighbour, and an unsuitable companion for "Mie-Mie," though, from what I have been able to gather of her life, she was a young lady well able to take care of herself. Nor did they desire his company at Richmond, where he invaded the local theatre after giving a series of amateur performances at his home at Wargrave. Selwyn speaks of "that étourdi Barrymore playing the fool in three or four different characters" upon the Richmond stage. The Prince of Wales consented to patronise him when he danced the *pas Russe* with Delpini, and played *Scaramouch* as an after-piece, but "Old Q." sulked and would not go, though he was staying at Richmond at the time.[159]

When Lord Barrymore finally ruined himself in 1792[160] "Old Q" gave £3,050 for the lease of his house in Piccadilly, and 1,300 guineas for the stables, though what use he could have had for either is not apparent.

Before his downfall Lord Barrymore had intended to live at No 105,[161] a much finer house than the one he eventually took, but the disordered state of his finances rendered it impossible for him ever to occupy the mansion erected for him by Michael Novosielski next door to Lord Coventry at No 106.[162]

In the parochial books for 1789 Lord Barrymore's name appears in respect of a house further westward rated at the moderate figure of £60, and he seems to have replaced Novosielski in the occupation of it.[163]

Lord Barrymore's reckless expenditure on the turf and subsequent ruin afford ample scope for condemnation by the enemies of horse-racing, but if young men of sporting tastes were to model themselves on the straightforward lines pursued by "Old Q" for upwards of half-a-century, or better still, on the pattern of Lord Falmouth (who carried off all the classic races with horses of his own breeding, without ever making a bet for any but the most trivial sums), not only would the sport not suffer, but the Anti-gambling League, if it still exists, might find its occupation gone. Lord Rosebery, in a recent speech on the subject of gambling, appeared to condemn the practice of ready-money betting, but for once he rather missed the point, for there can be no doubt that plungers of the type to which Lord Barrymore belonged, to say nothing of smaller speculators, would never lose the large sums they sometimes do if obliged to stake their money at the time. If gambling is ever to be recognised by the legislature (and why, in an age of progress, should it not be, with certain obvious safeguards borrowed from the French model?), to put down ready-money betting would be to begin at the wrong end. The law, as it stands, declares, absurdly enough, that it is an offence to pay before the event is decided, but that to bet on credit and throw good money after bad is permissible. Lord Falmouth did occasionally wager a sovereign or two with his trainer, but, like Baron Mayer Rothschild, another true sportsman, using the word in its best sense, he loved racing for its own sake. His winning record was indeed a remarkable one. He won the Two Thousand Guineas three times, the One Thousand four, the Derby twice, the Oaks four times, and the St. Leger three times. Fred Archer carried his colours in the majority of instances, and his horses rarely, if ever, competed in handicaps. Baron Rothschild's most remarkable run of luck was in 1871, when he won the Derby with *Favonius*, the One Thousand, Oaks and St. Leger with *Hannah*, and finished up the season by taking the Cesarewitch with *Corisande*.

After 1790 "Old Q" returned to Piccadilly for good and all. His social and convivial qualities were lost to Richmond, Newmarket knew him no more, and after "Mie-Mie's" marriage to Lord Yarmouth he seldom left London. He replaced his Scotch doctor, the quondam M.P. for Peebles, by a clever Frenchman named Elvizee, who had been attached to the Court of Versailles. His services were remunerated by the Duke on the Chinese principle. He was to be paid £600 a year so long as his patient lived, but no longer; and he was to live in the house so as to be always within call if wanted. He also engaged a Piccadilly apothecary named Fuller, whose professional attendances between 1803 and 1810 amounted to nearly ten thousand, including 1,700 night calls, out of which he remained with his Grace 1,215 nights. Fuller claimed £10,000 from the Duke's executors, alleging that he had sacrificed his regular business in order to render these exceptional services, and a jury awarded him £7,500.[164] False reports of "Old Q's" death were circulated in 1804, in 1807, and on several subsequent occasions, but a fine constitution, united to a strict attention to diet and sobriety, enabled him to enjoy life (after a fashion) long after he had passed the allotted span of human existence. He continued to attend the House of Lords right up to the close of the century. In 1807 he renewed the Crown lease of his house. In 1809 he made his will, saying that when the contents became public property they would astonish society, which they certainly did. Day after day he was to be seen at the corner of his bow window, and, when the weather was warm and sunny, he would sit for hours together on the balcony, gazing at the stream of humanity passing his doors. Carefully dressed in the latest fashion, he got his muffs (for gentlemen then carried such things) and his stockings from Paris, but to the end he adhered to a three-cornered hat which had been the prevailing *mode* of the eighteenth century. Sometimes, when the rays of the sun were powerful, passers-by would see him shaded by a parasol held over his head by one of his powdered footmen. The last remaining vestiges of a tunnel-like porch which he had constructed to enable him to reach the street level from the first floor, without making use of the principal staircase, have only recently been removed.

One morning, shortly before his death, he sent for his favourite groom[165] whilst sitting at breakfast in his front parlour, and, after questioning him as to his health, asked him how long he had been in his service. "Twenty-eight years, your Grace," said the man. "Then you may retire and live comfortable in ease and independence upon a sum of money which I will give you now, or, if you prefer to stay with me till I die, I will remember you in my will."

Radford absolutely declined to leave his master, and, at his decease, he found himself the owner of several leasehold houses, and all the Duke's horses and carriages. He subsequently became stud groom to George IV at Windsor.

Besides providing for Radford, he left each of his old servants £200 a year, and to those who had only been in his household a short time he bequeathed £50 a year.

In his old age "Old Q" conceived a great admiration for Nelson, with whom he became acquainted through the Hamiltons. The great Admiral was a little suspicious of him, fearing that he might make himself too agreeable to his beloved Emma, but he must have felt gratified, when the Patriotic Fund was established for the benefit of the widows and orphans of the Fleet, to find "Old Q" heading the list with a donation of £2,000. The Duke once gave £1,000, at a Westminster election, of course to the Tory candidate, for he certainly would not have approved of Sir Francis Burdett's democratic views, or the theatrical scenes witnessed in Piccadilly when that idol of the mob was arrested and conveyed to the Tower.

"Old Q" was also an admirer of General Picton, a man of coarse feelings, but remarkable courage. Hearing that he was in want of money to defend himself against a Government prosecution, the Duke sent to ask him if he might be allowed, without offence, to offer him any sum he chose to name under £10,000 towards his expenses. To his credit Picton refused the money, whereupon the Duke left him £5,000 in his will. As everyone knows, Picton fell at Waterloo, but it is not so generally known that he went into action suffering from a wound received a few days before at Quatre Bras, which might, and probably would, have proved fatal in any case. Though suffering intense pain, he refused to disclose the severe nature of the injury, lest he should be prevented from taking his place in the fighting line.

With the great Duke of Wellington I do not think "Old Q" was personally acquainted, though he may have known his brother the Marquis of Wellesley, who came to live at Apsley House about 1808.

Hearing after Trafalgar that Lady Hamilton was in great pecuniary distress, "Old Q" ordered his *chef* to prepare an elaborate repast every day of the week, and had it sent round to her house in Clarges Street. He also placed one of his carriages entirely at her disposal.

In his will he left her an annuity of £500, but this she was never destined to enjoy, owing to the tedious litigation[166] which prevented many of the Duke's charitable bequests from being paid over to the persons he intended them for. His vast estate was dragged into the Court of Chancery and not finally administered until 1816, by which time Lady Hamilton was dead.

The oft-quoted story, related in the first instance by Wraxall, of "Old Q" re-enacting the Judgment of Paris, and the three most beautiful women to be found in London having presented themselves before him, precisely as the divinities of Homer are supposed to have appeared on Mount Ida, must be received with caution,[167] as for many years before his death a number of Grub Street writers made their living by inventing false and malicious stories about him. All of them appear to have been systematically ignored by the person chiefly concerned, though it is not contended for a moment that certain episodes in his life are not deserving of censure, as, for instance, his one-time intimacy with the founders of the "Hell-Fire" Club, a disgraceful *coterie* established at Medmenham by Sir Francis Dashwood in conjunction with, amongst others, Lord Sandwich and Wilkes. It does not, however, appear that "Old Q" was ever a member of that scandalous crew, and, at all events, he drew the line at blasphemy.

His employment, in a confidential position, of the unprincipled Kidgell, cannot be defended except on the ground that "Old Q" had been at school with him and wished to give him a helping hand. His conduct in the affair of the Duke of Hamilton's midnight marriage, and, even more, the methods which he adopted in the prosecution of Wilkes, were sufficient to discredit Kidgell in the eyes of honourable men, and to stamp him as a disgrace to his cloth.

At the period of "Old Q's" life at which we have now arrived he had out-lived nearly all his early friendships. Selwyn was dead, Pitt and Fox had gone over to the majority, and the Macaroni of the mid-eighteenth century was a solitary figure in the more decorous society of a younger generation.

Almost alone in the world, with an ever-accumulating fortune, and no one to leave it to except distant relations, his very isolation becomes almost pathetic. Seeing that he prided himself upon always having £20,000 in cash about him, in addition to a permanent balance of £100,000 at Coutts's Bank, it speaks well for the integrity of his servants that his house was never robbed. He continued to receive visits from political leaders and Ministers of the Crown, such as Addington, and that true English gentleman and model Conservative, William Windham. Every frequenter of Piccadilly in the early days of the nineteenth century must have been familiar with the sight of the old man driving swiftly through the West End in his dark green *vis-à-vis* drawn by two long-tailed black horses, almost always alone, but with two servants behind him and Jack Radford on horse-back bringing up the rear. To the last he retained his love of music, and kept himself fully informed of all that was doing in the operatic world, whilst his purse was ever responsive to the call of misfortune, and his patronage readily accorded to professional worth and talent. At last the resources of nature were exhausted even for "Old Q" and the end came, peacefully enough, on December 23rd, 1810.

All that was mortal of him belongs to Piccadilly still, for, on the last day of the year, his remains were quietly interred in the chancel of St. James's Church under the communion table.[168]

By a strange coincidence the House of Commons was considering on the same day the question of a Regency owing to a recrudescence of the King's malady.

By "Old Q's" directions no inscription marks his resting place, nor would he allow a hatchment to be placed on any of his houses, as was then the all but universal custom, at any rate in the case of persons of high rank. His will disclosed an estate of upwards of a million, and of this sum Lord and Lady Yarmouth ultimately secured over a quarter, as well as the whole of the Duke's valuable furniture and works of art.

He left legacies of £10,000 to at least half-a-dozen people, including various hungry Hamiltons and gay Gordons; in

addition he left £600 a year to the Clerk at Coutts's Bank who
kept his account, a kindly thought which seems seldom to occur
to the modern millionaire; £100 a year to the former leader of
the orchestra at the Italian Opera, and £5,000 to each of the two
hospitals then almost at his doors: St. George's at Hyde Park Corner
and the Lock in Grosvenor Place, both established at a time when
their sites were considered to be outside the metropolitan area. If
only to show how near he was to our own times, here was a man
who had seen the rise of every Administration from Pelham to
Spencer Perceval, who remembered Chatham and Chesterfield in
their prime, had watched the careers of Pitt, Fox and Burke from
the cradle to the grave, and who was still living when Disraeli and
Gladstone drew their first breath.

A link with the past, and a very human link too, was this
"Old Q."

The subsequent history of Nos 138 and 139 is not without
interest, and other ghosts may walk there as well as the Duke of
Queensberry's.

The Duchess of Devonshire, who died in 1824, took both houses,
though I do not think they were ever thrown into one, as has
been sometimes supposed. No 139 (then known as 13, Piccadilly
Terrace) she let to Byron in 1815, and here he wrote "The Bride
of Corinth" and "Parisina," in the intervals of quarrelling with
his wife, and resisting the unwelcome attentions of the sheriff's
officers. Once when one of this objectionable species descended
upon him in Piccadilly, Byron asked if he had nothing of the same
sort for Mr. Sheridan?

"Oh, as for Mr. Sheridan," said the bailiff, "I have this whole
packet for him," producing at the same time a "dismal pocket
book," as Thackeray called it.

"But, my Lord," he added, "I have been in and about Mr.
Sheridan's house for a twelvemonth at a time: a very civil
gentleman he is too—knows how to deal with *us*."

After standing empty for some time, No 139 (originally built for the first Marquis of Cholmondeley) was taken in 1819 by the fourth Earl of Rosebery, grandfather of the present peer, who also belongs to Piccadilly in a sense, for, on his marriage to Miss Hannah de Rothschild, he lived for a time at No 107, before removing to Lansdowne House. His grandfather died in 1868, and the Dowager Lady Rosebery in 1882. Soon after that date the lease of No 139 was acquired by Sir Algernon Borthwick (afterwards Lord Glenesk), the well-known proprietor of the *Morning Post*, a newspaper which increased in value by leaps and bounds when its price was reduced from threepence to a penny. Lord Glenesk died in 1908, and the house is empty at the present time, though no doubt it will soon attract one of the millionaire class, which of late years has made this part of Piccadilly its especial home.[169] No 138, the house always occupied by "Old Q," was taken in the reign of William IV, by the fourth Earl of Cadogan. He it was who added the elaborate *boiserie*, representing the fables of La Fontaine, to the large drawing-room. Though much altered internally, a portion of the wainscoting on the ground floor, and the handsome gilt door-furniture, may date from the period of its first erection. Another occupier in recent years was Mr. Gerard Leigh, the husband of Madame de Falbe. During his tenancy, some time in the early 'seventies, the first strip of wood paving ever seen in London was laid down in Piccadilly, opposite No 138, as an experiment. Mr William Beckett Denison, who died in 1890, came next, and the most recent owner, Mr H J King, succeeded the second Lord Grimthorpe here. Both houses were refronted in stone, in compliance with the requirements of the Crown leases, about twenty-five years ago, but the form of "Old Q's" bow window was retained, although the historic balcony has been altered.[170]

V

From Piccadilly to Berkeley Square and Back Again

When Lady Berkeley of Stratton parted with some of the minor amenities of her mansion in Piccadilly[171] in order to build Stratton Street and Berkeley Street under Evelyn's direction, she also projected a great piazza after the model of St James's Square, to be built upon the surplus land lying to the north of the extensive gardens of Berkeley House.

Nothing, however, was done in connection with the scheme until many years after her death.

In 1739 the irrefutable evidence of the rate-book shows that a beginning had by then been made in this direction.

Some few houses on the east side of the intended Square (known in its unfinished state as Berkeley Row) were completed in that year.

An admiral, Sir Chaloner Ogle, was the pioneer of fashion hereabouts, soon to be followed by persons of greater note.

Thenceforward the new Square—for building operations once begun rapidly spread to the west side—vied in popularity with its slightly older neighbour on the Grosvenor Estate.

The first houses to be completed in Grosvenor Square were rated to the relief of the poor in 1728, though the whole had been planned and talked of some years earlier.

Hanover Square, long a rival to both these abodes of fashion, dates from about 1720, but it has now practically ceased to be a place of private residence, its stately family mansions having gradually been absorbed by clubs, institutions, and business premises, until, at the present day, there is not a single private house to be found in it.

Beloe, in his *Reminiscences of a Sexagenarian*, states that in Sir Robert Walpole's time it was the established etiquette that the Prime Minister returned no visits. On leaving office Sir Robert took the earliest opportunity of visiting his friends in the West End, and when he happened to pass for this purpose through Berkeley Square he found, to his astonishment, that the whole of it had actually been built whilst he was Minister, though he had never before seen it.[172]

Doubt has been thrown upon Beloe's accuracy in making this assertion, but from what has been written above it will be seen that his statement was correct in every particular.[173]

Leaving Piccadilly by way of Berkeley Street, the narrow passage which divides the garden of Devonshire House from that of Lansdowne House deserves a passing glance.

The iron bars at either end were placed there, it is believed, after a mounted highwayman had escaped his pursuers by riding his horse up the steps into Berkeley Street.

George Grenville, who on quitting Downing Street in 1765 went to live in Bolton Street—then often called Bolton Row, from its being for the most part built only upon its eastern side, the western being occupied by the extensive gardens of Bath House—was an eye-witness of the incident.

The precise name of the fugitive highwayman is lost, though the story has been associated with that of Dick Turpin.

Tales of highway robbery invariably gain in the narration if linked with names so familiar as those of Claude Duval, Dick Turpin, or Jack Sheppard; a rascally trio condemned by posterity to bear the burden of even more crimes than they are known to have actually committed.

Jack Sheppard, it may be remembered, lodged in Mayfair at the outset of his criminal career, and only left the neighbourhood after robbing his employer.

Proceeding from Lansdowne Passage to the foot of Hay Hill we are treading on historic ground.

Here, on April 12th, 1554, the day after his execution on Tower Hill, was setup on a gibbet as a terror to rebels the headless trunk of Sir Thomas Wyatt, this being the actual spot where his infatuated followers were repulsed by the Queen's troops.

The site must still have been Crown property at the beginning of the eighteenth century, for Queen Anne granted it to the then Speaker of the House of Commons. But so much clamour was made about this royal gift, as being a bribe of great consequence, that the Speaker hastily sold it for £200, and gave the purchase money to the poor.[174] The Prince Regent and some of his fast friends were once attacked by footpads on Hay Hill, though they can hardly be said to have been robbed, as the party, when called upon to stand and deliver, could only muster half-a-crown between them.

Few perhaps realise to what this spot owes its sylvan-sounding name. To it London vulgarism seems permanently to have affixed the aspirate, notwithstanding the modern tendency to drop rather than to add this appendage.

Hay Hill is really Aye, or Eye Hill, and, as a place name, it has nothing primarily in common with flowery meads and well-stored barns, though there were farms hereabouts well into the eighteenth century. It commemorates, however, one of the most ancient boundaries in western London—the Aye or Eye bourne, a name corrupted by easy transitional changes into T'Aye bourne and Tyburn.

Having its source in the northern heights of Hampstead, the stream ran down through what we now call Marylebone (properly

St Mary by the bourne), and crossed Oxford Street at a spot near the Lord Mayor's Banqueting House, now marked by Stratford Place. Its further course may be traced by South Molton Row, the lower part of Brook Street, Avery (Eyebury) Row, and Bruton Mews, to the foot of Hay Hill.

It then turned south-west, passing at the back of Bolton Row, ran through the low-lying part of Mayfair, and entered the Green Park in the hollow of Piccadilly (where it was spanned by a stone bridge), having fallen more than forty feet in its passage from Oxford Street to this point.[175]

Flowing by, or, as some say, under, Buckingham Palace, near which its waters divided into two or more separate channels, the name of this ancient boundary stream is found scattered along its track through Pimlico to the Thames. Ebury Street and Ebury Square are cases in point, possibly also Tachbrook Street.

No natural feature of the landscape is so hard to obliterate as a watercourse, for which reason mills are almost the oldest description of property in England, it being not uncommon to find a watermill mentioned in *Doomsday Book* still in full working order.

They may be diverted, or buried beneath the surface, but even modern engineering cannot wholly destroy ancient waterways.[176]

So this abiding rivulet—in whose limpid waters our British ancestors may once have laved their painted limbs—though long since lost to view, still pursues its ceaseless course, still ministers to the common good by flushing a sewer. The curious may still descry its polluted stream trickling beneath the manholes and ventilators which mark its prosaic path across the Green Park. Druids may have drunk of its sacred springs, Saxons may have been baptized in its rushing waters, but this much is certain; for centuries it was a notable boundary, and it formed, I think, the westernmost limit of Lord Clarendon's original grant from the Crown in and about Piccadilly.

The neighbouring Westbourne, now degraded into the Ranelagh sewer, had its source in Paddington, quitted Hyde Park at Knightsbridge, and flowed by way of Pont Street (hence the name) and Bloody Bridge to Chelsea. A milestone, which has only lately disappeared, a little to the east of Sloane Square, marked the former site of Bloody Bridge and also the boundary line dividing the Pimlico estate of the Grosvenor family from its great rival in recent years—the Sloane-Cadogan property.

The Aye bourne is shown in most of the older maps of London which include the western suburbs as an open stream, unconfined and uncontaminated as it swept down from the northern heights in a silvery cascade, through the meadow lands of Mayfair, and past the grassy slopes of Hay Hill, to lose itself at last in the wide estuary of the Thames.

To-day, sunk from its high estate, it only survives officially as the King's Scholars Pond Sewer.[177] Three and a half centuries have passed away since the grim sequel to a traitor's death enacted on Hay Hill recorded above.

That gentle eminence then commanded a fair sylvan prospect of pastures and cornfields, gladdened in summertime by the milkmaid's song and the voice of the reaper.

The outlook to-day from the same standpoint, overlooking the gardens of Lansdowne House, regarded in the right spirit, is sufficiently arcadian to recall in some measure the brave days of old, when Tudor kings and queens disported themselves hereabouts with hawk and hound, flew their passage falcons at herons flushed from the Aye bourne's reedy banks, or coursed hares from Hay Hill to the thickets which then covered the site of Bond Street.

But whatever of dignity or the picturesque which remained to it until recent years has now been swept away; the mansions on either side of the hill summit (one of them, known as Ashburnham House, had a long and interesting history of its own) have been pulled down to make way for blocks of residential flats, and whatever old-world charm the spot possessed has vanished for ever.

When Berkeley Square is reached the small house (No 2), recently refronted in stone, deserves notice from its having been occupied for some years before his marriage by Lord Rosebery.

A true son of Mayfair, he was born in a house fronting Chesterfield Street, at the narrower and less fashionable end of Charles Street, readily distinguishable at the present day by its elaborate iron area railing.

No 2, the first of three houses in Berkeley Square which have been inhabited by Lord Rosebery in the course of his career, does not appear to have had any other distinguished occupiers. In 1790 it was a hosier's shop, and the adjoining houses on either side were respectively a linen-draper's and a hatter's.

No 6 on the same side has acquired a fictitious importance, it having been long supposed to have sheltered, at a momentous period of his career, no less an Englishman than the younger Pitt. But the writers who stated so confidently that Pitt lived there overlooked the material fact that what was No 6 when the son of the great Commoner first came to the neighbourhood is now represented by No 47 (to be alluded to more in detail when we arrive at the west side of the Square), a much larger house with an interesting pedigree of its own. The enumeration of the houses in Berkeley Square towards the close of the eighteenth century began with what is now No 52 at the south-west corner and finished at the foot of Hay Hill on the east side. This order of things did not last many years and the houses were numbered afresh as we now know them.

The periodical re-numbering of London streets has led, and will lead in the future, if not discountenanced by the local authorities who settle these petty details, to endless confusion whenever an attempt is made to identify the former homes of men and women prominent in our public life.

An even more irritating instance of this senseless practice is afforded by Hill Street, the Great Gaunt Street of Thackeray, which, since 1868, has been rearranged so that the odd numbers are grouped together on the north and the even ones on the south side. Lord Rosebery has told us that he used at one time to point out No 6 Berkeley Square to his friends, when conversation flagged, in a spirit of almost reverential awe, and of his disappointment when he learnt (from the present writer) that he had lavished an immense amount of unnecessary sympathy and bestowed much spurious sentiment on a house which had no more to do with Mr. Pitt than it had with Lord Macaulay.[178]

Nos 7 and 8 of the present reckoning need no distinguishing label, for are they not known, wherever the English language is spoken, as Gunter's—the oldest confectioner's shop in the West End, if not in all London!

The business was started at No 7 by an Italian pastrycook called Dominicus Negri in 1757. Twenty years later the title of the firm was Negri and Gunter, but from 1779 onwards the name of Gunter, with its great reputation for turtle soup, ices and ball suppers, has stood alone in the parochial books.

Unless it be Fribourg and Treyer, the tobacconists in the Haymarket, who were certainly in business there in the reign of George I, and who have had the good sense to retain their original bow-windowed shop-front, I do not know of any commercial undertaking in the West End with a longer pedigree than Gunter's. The original shop was enlarged in 1835, in the heavy style prevailing at that period, by the inclusion of the adjoining premises at No 8. Even in Piccadilly, with traditions a century older than any which Berkeley Square can show, there is not to be found a single instance of a shop still flourishing at the same address definitely known to have been established in the reign of the second George. Such claims have been made, though without any real foundation, in cases within my own knowledge. Yet after careful investigation, involving the closest scrutiny of the successive ownership of business premises not only in Piccadilly, but in its immediate neighbourhood, from the earliest date of which any record has been preserved, I have not been able to find that—apart from hotels and restaurants of luxurious type rebuilt on former sites of inns and taverns—these pretensions rest on any substantial basis. There is at the present day a bun and tea shop in Piccadilly, at the corner of New Bond Street, boldly advertising on its outer walls, but without a scintilla of real evidence to support the contention, that it was established in 1688.

As a matter of fact, it only became a baker's shop, specialising in "Uxbridge Rolls," about the year 1780 [see illustration on the opposite page], though it is conceivable that a similar business may have been carried on at another address by a shopkeeper who parted with his interest for a consideration. There are a large number of shops in London which are trading to-day on reputations built up by others, after years of honest toil and endeavour, simply because the newcomers have bought not only the goodwill but the name of the original firm.

On investigation it will often be found that a business which the usurper claims as his very own originated in a quarter far removed from the locality selected by his successor in the title.

I have seen in a street dating only from the latter half of the nineteenth century a shop-front inscribed with the misleading label "This business was established in the reign of Queen Anne." And perhaps it may have been by some one else, but the all-important element of continuity, considered from the topographical point of view, is lacking.

Passing by the next house in a necessarily rapid perambulation of the Square, it is to be noted that Lord Clyde was living at No 10 shortly before his death. No 11, Horace Walpole's house in the closing years of his life, deserves closer attention. Its exterior has escaped extensive modernisation and presents much the same appearance as it did when first built for Sir Cecil Bishop in 1741.

Sir Cecil died in 1778, and Walpole, who had long been on the look-out to acquire a house in the Square, bought it in the course of the winter of that year. It remained in his family for exactly half a century, and might still have been owned by a Walpole had not the third Earl of Orford (of the new creation) lost it in the course of a night's high play at cards to Mr Henry Baring, the father of the late Lords Revelstoke and Cromer.

This same Lord Orford's daughter, the late Lady Dorothy Nevill,—one of Watts's loveliest sitters in the days of her youth,—believed but was never quite sure if she was born there or not. It was from her own lips that I learned of the family misfortune which occasioned her father's and mother's removal from No 11, and of the keen regret which they felt on leaving the Square. Whether she was really born there, and I think she was all too young to have entered the world in the reign of George the Fourth, Lady Dorothy passed the later years of her long life within a stone's throw of her father's old house, at No 45, Charles Street. There she entertained an ever-increasing circle of friends, political, literary and merely social, especially at Sunday luncheons, over which she presided with much charm and distinction.

No 45 was brick-dust or terra-cotta coloured when Lady Dorothy lived there, but I notice that it is now, 1919, being converted into a whited sepulchre.

Mr Baring, whom, as we have seen, superseded the Walpoles at No 11 by the hazard of the die, was supposed to have one of the best cooks in London. If not actually *the* best, he was at all events one of three acknowledged holders of the *cordon bleu*, the others being respectively in the service of Lord Granville and Mr Speaker Brand. Becquinot was the name of Lord Granville's *chef*, and Cost that of the Speaker's, but I have forgotten the name of the genius who ruled over the kitchen in Berkeley Square.

Mr Baring died in 1848, and the house is now in the occupation of Mr. Vernon Watney, who succeeded the late Earl of Clarendon here. Some iron bands and chains to strengthen the hall-door were placed there by Horace Walpole at the time of the Gordon riots and still remain *in situ*, but there is little of the interior left which can with confidence be ascribed to the period of his tenancy.

No 12, the largest house on this side, has had an even more interesting history than the home of the Walpoles. It was built for Admiral Sir John Norris, known in the Service as "Foul Weather Jack," and he lived here from 1740 till his death nine years later. Then came the Keppels, who occupied it, with occasional intermissions, for nearly a hundred years.

George, third Earl of Albemarle, Commander-in-Chief at the Havanna, was the first of the family to settle here. This was in 1767. His brother, Admiral the Hon. Augustus Keppel, second in command to Sir George Pocock at Havanna, and court-martialled in 1779 for his share in that expedition, also lived here when in town. On the news of his acquittal being made known he became *instanter* a popular hero.

Rioting of a more or less harmless description followed swiftly, not so much from an innate love of disorder, but as if to emphasise the condemnation of Government indifference to popular sentiment. It seems that sentiment, which counts for so much, is little understood by the ordinary official mind in this or any other age.

The windows found not to be illuminated in Keppel's honour were broken indiscriminately, whilst the houses of unpopular Ministers were attacked and, in some instances, wrecked. The Admiral was presented with the freedom of the City, received the thanks of the House of Commons, and when he attended a banquet at the London Tavern his coach was drawn through the streets by bluejackets and enthusiastically cheered.

Another, and in his case more enduring, test of popular appreciation was the blossoming of a crop of public-house signboards named after him. This crop is not even yet entirely withered, for there are still Keppel's Heads to be found in many places both in and out of London. Every naval officer knows the one on the Hard at Portsmouth (where licensed premises abound to an extent unknown elsewhere), affectionately known in the Service as "The Nut."

In October, 1782, Horace Walpole records another outburst of democratic frenzy which swept through Berkeley Square, this time because the mob chose to think that Lord Rodney's victories over the French some months earlier were not being sufficiently appreciated in high quarters. "He paraded through the whole town to his own house at this end[179] with a rabble at his heels breaking windows for not being illuminated, for which no soul was prepared, as no soul thought on him, but thus our conquerors triumph. My servants went out and begged these Romans to give them time to light up candles, but to no purpose and were near having their brains dashed out."[180] All his windows were smashed by a volley of stones as he sat in one of the first-floor rooms fronting the Square.

"I have told you before of the savage state we are fallen into; it is now come to such perfection that one can neither stir out of one's house safely, nor stay in it with safety," he wrote to the same correspondent.

The long connection of the Keppels with this house came to an end in 1849, and it was next occupied by Mr Charles Prideaux Brune, Mr Henry Petre, and, in more recent days, by the late Sir Edward Levy Lawson, raised to the peerage as Lord Burnham in 1903.

Transferring our attention for a moment from Berkeley Square to the Street of Ink, otherwise Fleet Street, we find that in the year 1855 two brothers of the name of Levy, with no previous

experience of the newspaper world, bought from Mr Serjeant
Sleigh a paper called the *Daily Telegraph*, then in a moribund
condition, there being something less than £5 in the cash-box
when they took it over. The elder of these brothers, Lionel Levy
Lawson, was a manufacturer of printer's ink carrying on business
in Bouverie Street, nearly opposite the present offices of the paper.
The first issue of the *Daily Telegraph and Courier*[81] had been on
Friday, June 29, 1855. It was printed in Exeter Street and published
at 253 Strand. The advertisements, at first very few in number,
were confined to the front page.

The new proprietors promptly reduced the price to one penny
(it had originally been two pence), and it was the first London
morning newspaper to be published at so low a figure. On Friday,
September 14, there had appeared in its columns the following
notice to subscribers: "On and from Monday next, the 17th, the
Daily Telegraph, same size and quality of matter as at present, will
be published at the price of one penny." Two days later the paper
congratulated itself on the fact that it had been enabled to narrate
"the state of affairs at Sebastopol," and "to place in the possession
of our readers, nearly a fortnight ago, the same intelligence as
the *Times* has but just communicated to its readers." If they
did occasionally contravene the amenities existing between the
older organs of public opinion, the new proprietors, by perfectly
legitimate methods, gradually built up what is the most valuable
asset to any newspaper—a gigantic advertisement business. This
the *Daily Telegraph* apparently still retains, in spite of insidious
attempts on the part of its imitators to wrest this initial advantage
from it. In its earliest issues under the new proprietary the paper
proclaimed its readiness to accept advertisements at half the rates
charged by the *Times*.

The bait took, not without exciting something approaching
consternation in Printing House Square and Wellington Street,
and from the 'sixties onwards the circulation of the paper increased

by leaps and bounds, owing to an immediate response on the part of the advertising public to these counsels of perfection.

In the days of its youth it was read from Whitechapel to Wimbledon, and its purchasers took kindly from the first to the roaring of the "young lions of Peterborough Court" (Peterborough Court as a London place name has now entirely disappeared owing to the extension of the *Daily Telegraph* offices), as they were facetiously termed in the Street of Ink. Whilst the abolition of the paper duty greatly stimulated journalistic enterprise, it must not be supposed that the collection and transmission of news, as apart from advertisements, was neglected by its astute owners. On the contrary, they attracted to their service a retinue of picturesque, if somewhat sensational, writers, working in harmony with one another, who studied the idiosyncrasies of an ever-increasing circle of readers educated, by imperceptible stages, to believe in what the *Daily Telegraph* had to tell them day by day. Constantly introducing new features of interest, by devoting more and more space to the drama, the Turf, and the artistic world than was then customary in contemporary journalism, the favourite organ of Suburbia (if such a word is to be found outside Peterborough Court in its earlier days), the first of the penny papers gradually attained a wider influence and importance. The foundations of the great commercial enterprise so truly laid by the brothers Levy were strengthened in more recent times by the broader outlook on public affairs and the generally sound political instincts developed by the late Lord Burnham. A true friend and a generous employer, he strengthened the position of his paper by securing special correspondents of tried capacity, in some cases recruited from the service of Printing House Square, and it was his reward in the fulness of time to see his newspaper achieve actually the largest circulation in the world.[182]

The small house next door (No 13), recently vacated by Lord Carnarvon, has been superstitiously rechristened No 12A. Presumably its new owner regards thirteen as an unlucky number.

It has had a great number of occupiers since it was first built for the Hon. Mrs. Jane Lowther in 1742. Some of them were men and women of note in their day, others have left no distinguishing mark on the sands of time, but if ever a memorial tablet is placed on its modest front, it should be to the honour and renown of Mr Edward Bouverie, who lived in it for twenty years from 1765. He it was who planted the plane trees which are the Square's greatest ornament.

The finest of their kind in London, not even excepting those in the great piazza of Lincoln's Inn Fields, the Berkeley Square planes are massed, not in pairs, but by the dozen. They show no appreciable sign of decay after flourishing for nearly one hundred and fifty years, but one of the largest was unfortunately blown down a few years ago during a violent gale. The plane is the ideal tree to resist the deadly fumes of London smoke, from its annual habit of shedding its bark, but it does not readily bear transplantation, as I can testify from personal observation. In my early childhood a riotous mob clamouring for Reform broke down the railings of Hyde Park on the Park Lane side, and I remember being taken by my father to the scene of destruction and seeing them lying on the ground near Grosvenor Gate. This was the occasion when a Home Secretary wept at the audacity of a London mob in resisting the authority of Whitehall. When the question of replacing the railings came to be considered, a great public improvement was effected by widening the roadway and setting the rails some few yards further back from Park Lane. This necessitated the removal of a large number of plane trees which fringed the old Park boundary, but, in the process of transplanting them to new sites, many died, and those that survived show to this day signs of stunted growth. In more recent years the late Mr. Ferdinand Rothschild moved large forest trees with great success at Waddesdon, but he had at his disposal greater mechanical resources than were available at the time of the Park Lane improvement. Admiral Rous, handicapper to the Jockey Club, often spoken of by ill-informed writers as the Dictator of the Turf—though he laid no claim to the title and deprecated its use—lived at No 13 from 1859 till his death in 1877. He wrote several excellent articles on racing topics in The Times at the request of my uncle John Delane, with whom he was on intimate terms.

For years the Admiral was a familiar figure and welcome guest at the luncheon parties in Ascot week which Delane gave at his house adjoining the Royal Enclosure, from which it is separated only by the high road. Few of the friends who met there in each recurring month of June are still in the land of the living, and perhaps the only survivors to-day are the evergreen Lord Coventry (Master of the Buckhounds under many Administrations and a great upholder of Ascot traditions) and Lord Rosebery. Many letters from the Admiral's pen on the state of the English Turf in the 'sixties and 'seventies are in my possession, but, having devoted so much space to racing at Newmarket and elsewhere in the chapter on "Old Q," I am unable to deal further with this aspect of the national life within the limits of the present volume.

The Lowthers, on the opposite side in politics to the Walpoles and Keppels, seem to have taken root in the Square at an even earlier date.

No 14 was first built for Lord Lonsdale in 1740, and Lord Brougham, who was fond of changing his London residence, was here for a couple of years at the very beginning of Queen Victoria's reign.

The tenure of No 16 is intimately bound up with the name of the original ground landlord. The fifth and last Lord Berkeley of Stratton, who died in 1773, left Berkeley Square to Mrs Anne Egerton, sister of one Bishop and daughter of another, for her life, with £60,000 in ready money. To his distant relative, Earl Berkeley of Berkeley Castle, he left £20,000, all his plate and pictures, four large estates in Somerset, two in Dorset, and, after Mrs. Egerton's death, the freehold of Berkeley Square, estimated to produce about £15,000 at the expiration of the then existing leases. Mrs Egerton lived to enjoy this sudden accession to wealth for about fifty years.

It is curious to note the persistent fondness of the naval profession for this quarter of the town. No 17[183] was first occupied in 1739 by Admiral Sir Chaloner Ogle, who distinguished himself in 1722 by ridding the coast of Guinea of pirates. He hoisted his flag as Rear-Admiral of the Blue in the "Augusta" in the course of the summer of 1739, joined Admiral Vernon in the disastrous attack upon Cartagena in 1742, and succeeded him in the command after Vernon's recall.

This house, practically unaltered since Ogle's day, was the last London home of Montagu Corry, Lord Rowton, Disraeli's confidential friend and secretary.

Originator of the philanthropic scheme for the benefit of the working classes, his name will always be associated with the Rowton Houses.

Sir Squire Bancroft, the *doyen* of the English stage, and his equally talented wife—one of the theatre's brightest ornaments before and after her marriage—lived at No 18 from 1883[184] till 1916. Their tenure of these two houses coincided with the period of their many managerial triumphs at the old Prince of Wales's and the Haymarket Theatres.

No. 18 was probably garden ground attached to No 17 until about 1785, whilst the existing No 19, now empty and offered for sale, really belongs to Bruton Street, in which is still the entrance door.

To cross the road is to recall another interesting and much older link with the stage, for at No 20 (rebuilt about 1795 and with No 21, but now again two separate houses) lived Colley Cibber, actor, manager of Drury Lane, Poet Laureate and

adapter of Shakespeare, from 1741, when he paid £50 a year for
the house, until his death in 1757. He was therefore one of the
earliest settlers in the Square. As he was not always to be found
at home on quarter day, the rate-collector was directed, I learn
from the parochial books for 1746, to call upon the Laureate "at
White's Chocolate House."

Cibber's poetic effusions have long since faded from the
public memory, but a single line from his pen, introduced in his
adaptation of " Richard III" for Drury Lane:

"A horse, a horse, my kingdom for a horse!"

has become such a stage tradition that nowadays no actor of the
title *rôle* would think of omitting it. Theatrical audiences have
become so accustomed to it that they accept it as the actual
language of Shakespeare and would resent its exclusion from the
text, and I remember to have heard Sir Henry Irving say that
he found it one of the most telling lines in the play when he
produced it at the Lyceum.

I believe that "Off with his head, so much for Buckingham" was
another of Cibber's embroideries. *Apropos* of this the irrepressible
H J Byron suggested as a punning motto for a box-office clerk:
"So much for Booking-em."

And so, though Shakespeare never wrote either of the lines,
poor Colley survives on the boards he loved so well and trod
nearly two centuries ago. After this who can assert that the actor's,
or rather, in this case, the adapter's, art is an evanescent one?

The mother of a gentleman who died not many years since,
well recollected Cibber standing at the parlour window of his
house at the Bruton Street corner, drumming aimlessly with his
fingers on the frame.[185]

Lyrics and the drama are here found in appropriate association,
for, at the large house in the Adam style, rebuilt about 1794–95 on

the site of Colley Cibber's former abode and the adjoining No 21, lived for many years Lady Anne Barnard.

A Lindsay by birth, she became the wife of Mr Andrew Barnard, who died in 1807. After his death the house was once more subdivided, a rearrangement which still exists.

Lady Anne, who died in Berkeley Square after a long illness in 1825, wrote the words of "Auld Robin Gray" (named after the old Balcarres herd) to a taking air even now familiar to that extremely conservative section of the musical public, the frequenters of ballad concerts. She first acknowledged its authorship in 1823 to Sir Walter Scott, who subsequently edited it for the Bannatyne Club.

The former shrines of oratorio and the old English ballad— Exeter Hall in the Strand and St James's Hall in Piccadilly—have been demolished in recent years and their sites absorbed by modern hotels. But the ballad habit persists to a remarkable degree and its votaries are still made happy on occasional Saturday afternoons when the Queen's Hall and the Albert Hall are not required for higher things.

No 22 has little or no historical associations which need detain us, but it has a distinctly Scottish pedigree, having been the abode of various Lindsays and Hoziers in succession since the reign of George the Fourth. No 23, a small house, was first occupied in 1748 by Viscount Dunkerron, son of the Earl of Shelbourne of that day. Dying in 1750, he was succeeded here by the Hon. Richard Leveson-Gower, of whom Horace Walpole has a story to relate.

"Lady Cath Pelham was telling Mr Nugent of a mad dog, whereon young Leveson, looking at Nugent, said, 'I have seen a mad dog to-day, and a silly dog too.' 'I suppose, Mr. Leveson, you have been looking in the glass.' 'No, I see him *now*,' upon which they walked off together but were reconciled." This was in 1750. Three years later young Leveson was dead, but I do not remember what fate befell Mr Nugent. The house was a solicitor's office for fifty years (Richard Sarel 1789–1839) and afterwards a dentist's. Lord Alfred Paget, an especial favourite with Queen Victoria, was another occupier between 1857 and 1860.

Lord Alfred, though not a sailor, was passionately fond of the sea.

A yacht called the *Alma* which he owned was wrecked somewhere off the British coast. He escaped with his life, though only after a somewhat lengthy immersion. Soon after this misadventure Lord Alfred had occasion to go to Cowes, and took the earliest opportunity of paying his respects to the Queen. Owing to the loss of his wardrobe he went up to Osborne in the clothes in which he had so narrowly escaped drowning.

When ushered into the Royal presence he stammered out: "Ah, ma'am, look at your poor Alfred now!"

The loss of his yacht had been a severe finaticial blow to him, and somehow this reached the Queen's ear.

A few days afterwards Lord Alfred received a cheque for an amount equivalent to the yacht's value, with a charming letter from Her Majesty, in which she said:

"The enclosed is a gift which none but your Sovereign can offer, and one which you, her subject, cannot refuse."

Though he escaped a watery grave on this occasion, Lord Alfred ultimately died on board another yacht of his called the *Violet*, in 1888.

No 24, the house in the extreme north-east corner, has had at least two dozen owners or occupiers, none of them, however, staying very long. Of these the only famous one was Sydney Smirke, the architect of the great circular reading-room at the British Museum. This was on the whole his most successful work. The dome, which exceeds in diameter that of St Paul's Cathedral, is practically identical in dimensions with that of the Pantheon.

Smirke also designed the new Inner Temple Hall, and either built or remodelled, in conjunction with his brother Robert and

George Basevi (the creator of Belgrave Square), several of the club houses in Pall Mall and St James's Street. He lived at No 24 from 1841 till 1856.

No 25, long known as Thomas's Hotel, was in the possession of one Tycho Thomas (probably the founder) so long ago as 1798. Charles James Fox was one of its early patrons. When he lived in Piccadilly, Fox lodged with his bosom friend Fitzpatrick over a grocer's and oilman's shop on the south side of the street. This was Mackie's, in the block between Duke Street and St James's Street and nearly opposite the Burlington Arcade. The name has long disappeared from the list of Piccadilly tradesmen and all the houses thereabouts have been rebuilt within recent years, but singularly enough there is at the present day a grocer's shop on the same site (Nos 171 and 172) to carry on the tradition of "Mackie's pickles." Thomas's Hotel enjoyed a considerable reputation a generation or so back, as a family hotel of the old-fashioned type, quiet, respectable, and rather expensive. Having outlived its usefulness it was rebuilt a few years ago, together with a small adjoining house, as a block of residential flats.

The remainder of the north side was occupied until the reign of George IV by business premises, mostly at low rentals. One of them, the only one which need be mentioned here, was a clock and watchmaker's, named Dwerrihouse, a member of a family of high repute in the annals of his trade.

Four large houses of no architectural merit or pretensions have obliterated the memory of the humble shopkeepers who toiled here in the closing years of the eighteenth and the beginning of the nineteenth century. All of them, viewed from the outside, are ugly and commonplace, yet who can tell what vital human interests, what absorbing emotions and domestic crises, their brick walls have screened from prying eyes since first they took shape and were inhabited by men and women of wealth and substance, if not of outstanding public interest!

Their owners' names may not have achieved a niche in that temple of fame, the "Dictionary of National Biography"— nevertheless, these dull Georgian mansions sheltered in their day many lesser lights in the firmament of social London.

No 27 was first occupied by Colonel and Lady Laura Meyrick, and, after them, by the Duke of Beaufort. No 28 was for years the town house of the first and second Lords Ormathwaite, and, subsequently of the thirteenth and fourteenth Dukes of Somerset. No 29, the largest of the four, was built for the first Lord Wenlock (Paul Beilby Lawley Thompson, who lived here from 1824 to 1852).

Sydney Smith, who has placed it on record that the parallelogram between Oxford Street, Piccadilly, Regent Street and Hyde Park enclosed more intelligence and human ability, to say nothing of wealth and beauty, than the world ever collected in so small a space before, wrote: "Lord Wenlock told me that his ground-rent cost him five pounds a foot; that is about the price of a London footman six foot high—thirty guineas per annum."[186] After the Lawleys had vacated No 29, it passed into the possession of the seventh Duke of Marlborough, who died in it. Within the last two decades the late Mr Albert Brassey lived here, and the house is now inhabited by his widow.

No 30 was continuously inhabited by the members of a single family named Pinney until a quite recent date.

The quiet side of the Square, a region where, if anywhere in the West End, "greatness breathes her native air," remains to be noticed.

Still one of the choicest spots in habitable London, where, nowadays, only men of abundant means can command a place of abode, the catalogue of former residents bristles with names well known in every walk of public life. First Ministers of the Crown, Proconsuls, distinguished soldiers and sailors, social celebrities of both sexes, have made their homes here during the last seven reigns. Every grade of the Peerage, from the Duke of feudal ancestry to the mushroom Baron of the day before yesterday, is represented. Here it may not be inappropriate to remark that it speaks volumes for the persistence of the hereditary element in the British Constitution that in the last thirty years no fewer than two hundred and ten brand-new Barons have been created (over one hundred of them within the last ten years), forty-three Viscounts, twenty-three Earls and ten Marquises! Even before these lines appear in print it is probable that these figures will require revision and amplification, for, as yet, the fountain of honour shows no sign of becoming dried up. For all practical purposes some twenty Peeresses in their own right will shortly have to be included and, if the Scotch and Irish Lords not being Peers of Parliament, are counted in, the actual number of the Peerage, without reckoning the Episcopal bench, now amounts to the stupendous total of seven hundred and fifty or thereabouts—actually more than the aggregate of the reformed House of Commons which has just been called into existence.

Of late years the *nouveau riche* and the successful man of business have left their indelible trade-mark on this once wholly aristocratic quarter; but, even now, there are houses here which have been inhabited by only one, or at most two, families since Berkeley Square first came into existence.

The Vestry of St George's took the new mansions under its especial protection as soon as they were completed. I find from a minute in the parochial books, made on April 11th, 1745, that a Committee, appointed "to take a view of the west side of Berkeley Square and the streets adjacent," recommended, as necessary for the safety of the inhabitants, that a watchman should be placed there forthwith. One John Norman was appointed, and his box was ordered to be fixed "near the Square and facing Hill Street, and to take care of the houses from the Coffee House[187] to the bottom of the Square, Hill Street and the mews."

No 34 now merged in Mount Street, stood on the Grosvenor Estate, and was the last of Lady Mary Coke's many residences in London. Author of an absorbingly interesting journal, vivifying at every page the dry bones of social and political life in the eighteenth century, it seems incredible that her name did not find a place in that monumental work, the "Dictionary of National Biography."

In her earlier days Lady Mary rented No 43 in the Square, and towards the close of her life she had a small house in Hill Street, for which she paid £250 a year, in order to be near her sisters—Lady Greenwich and Lady Betty Mackenzie. No 34 remained in her possession until her death in 1811.

The next house (No 35) is the first belonging to the Fitzhardinge-Berkeley Estate on this side of the Square.

It was built in 1742 for Sir Charles Frederick, Surveyor-General of the Ordnance. No 36, recently rebuilt and stone-fronted, has had a great variety of owners, most of them ladies, of whom the first was a Lady Frances Williams, who I find was living here from 1744 to 1761.

It became a doctor's house in the middle of the last century, and was occupied for a few years by Lord Northcliffe, founder of the *Daily Mail*, then known as Mr Alfred Harmsworth.

No 37, incorporated with No 38 by Lord Jersey about 1822, was for a short time, in 1754 and 1755, the residence of the second Duke of Chandos, not the "princely" Chandos of Canons fame, but his youngest and only surviving son.

There was nothing in the least princely about him; on the contrary, he and his wife, according to Mrs Delany, were the ugliest couple in England, and it is on record that George II called him "a hot-headed passionate half-witted coxcomb."

He married, as his second wife, at Keith's Chapel in Mayfair on Christmas Day, 1744, one Anne Jefferies, who had been his mistress for some years previously.

It is said that she was sold, with a halter round her neck, by her original husband Jefferies, an ostler at the Pelican Inn, at Newbury, and that she was bought in the open market by the Duke.[188]

No 38, now Lord Rosebery's, has a very interesting pedigree. It appears for the first time in the parochial books for 1744, when its estimated annual value was only £180.

Its first owner was the third Duke of Manchester,[189] and his successor in the title, George, fourth Duke, Lord Chamberlain in the Rockingham Administration, also lived here.

He did not, however, stay long in the Square, for Lady Mary Coke, who kept a watchful eye upon everybody's movements in the same *monde* as her own, wrote in December, 1768:

"Did I tell you that the Duke of Manchester has bought Lord Pomfret's house.[190] As he intended having a house in town I'm surprised he sold his own, which was in a much better situation."

Wraxall, in his usual spiteful manner, spoke of the Duke as not wanting in talent, but as being a man of very dissipated habits.[191]

Robert Child, head of the great banking establishment at Temple Bar, began what was to prove a much longer family connection with No 38, after the Duke of Manchester's departure.

The Childs were goldsmiths, before they became bankers, at the sign of the Marygold, and so, I believe, were the Hoares, their near neighbours in Fleet Street.

Sir Francis Child, who has been called, with some reason, the father of his profession, was born so long ago as 1642. He lived at Fulham, no doubt in order to be within easy driving distance of his business in Fleet Street. After the Marygold became a bank, the ledgers of the firm, full of entries of goldsmiths' accounts and pawnbrokers' pledges, were stored, as they became obsolete, in old Temple Bar. Robert Child came to Berkeley Square, as a young man in 1768. Shortly before his death he had a shock from which he never recovered.

The story runs that the young Lord Westmorland, known to his intimate friends as "rapid" Westmorland,[192] greatly admired the banker's only daughter, but without openly declaring his intentions.

Dining one night with Mr Child at No 38, he said to his host "If you were in love with a girl, and her father would not let you marry her, what would you do?"

"Do? Why, run away with her, of course!" was the prompt reply.

Young Westmorland, who was only twenty-two, forthwith planned an elopement with Miss Child, and, on a May morning in 1782, she walked deliberately out of her father's house carrying in her hand a small parcel.

A little school-room maid, whom she had taken into her confidence, had a hackney coach waiting round the corner to convey her young mistress to the protecting arms of her expectant lover.

He, also, was in readiness with the orthodox postchaise which figures in so many of the elopement stories of the period. This she entered without demur or delay and away they drove in hot haste towards Gretna Green.

As soon as her flight was discovered in Berkeley Square a hue and cry was set on foot. Mr Child, quite accurately guessing his daughter's probable destination, went off in pursuit in a second postchaise, preceded by a mounted messenger who, by dint of hard riding, managed to overtake the runaways somewhere near Rokeby, in Yorkshire.

"Shoot, my Lord, shoot!" cried Miss Child, who seems to have been a strong-minded girl for her age—she was only seventeen at the time—whereon Lord Westmorland frustrated any attempt at discussion by firing a couple of pistol shots at the approaching messenger.

Mr Child, rapidly nearing the scene of action, saw his trusty servant's horse fall dead by the roadside, whereupon he turned back, realising that further pursuit was hopeless. He declared, subsequently to the marriage, which was solemnized over the border, that no one bearing the name of Westmorland should ever be his heir. Yet, unwilling to disinherit his own descendants, he left the whole of his vast fortune to the first daughter of the runaway pair who should be christened Sarah and take upon herself the name of Child.

Mr Child died at the early age of 43, less than three months after his daughter's elopement, nor did the young Lady Westmorland enjoy a long married life. She died, aged only twenty-eight, at the Lodge in the Phœnix Park, Dublin, during her husband's Vice-Royalty of Ireland. Lord Westmorland married again, and not so happily, and lived till 1841, having become totally blind in his old age.

Under the terms of Mr Child's will Lady Sarah Sophia Child became his sole heiress, and by her marriage with Lord Villiers, afterwards fifth Earl of Jersey, the estate of Osterley, which had been acquired by Sir Francis Child in the reign of Queen Anne, was brought into her husband's family.

If G.E.C.'s "Complete Peerage" is to be trusted, Sarah, Countess of Jersey followed closely in her mother's footsteps. That usually accurate synopsis of the British Orders of Nobility states that she was married, also in the month of May, at Gretna Green.

Wherever the ceremony took place, and it has been asserted by some authorities that she was married privately at her father's house in the Square, the bride can only have been eighteen on 23rd May, 1804—the accepted date of the wedding. One of the most beautiful women of her day and a recognised leader of society, immortalised by Disraeli as "Zenobia," Lady Jersey was one of the last of the lady patronesses of Almack's. She died at No 38 in 1867, aged 81, leaving a fortune of £300,000, derived, as we have shown, from the great private banking-house at Temple Bar.

When the long connection of her family with the Square came to an end, which it did in 1871 on the death of Mr Frederick William Villiers, Lady Jersey's last surviving son, the house was taken by the first Earl of Londesborough. After him came, in 1888, Lord Rosebery, who acquired the freehold and rebuilt the façade from the designs of a Scottish architect with the usual Caledonian predilection for dull red sandstone. He altered the interior in many ways, enlarging Countess Sarah's ball-room at the back of the house, but the exterior would have looked better than it does had it not been disfigured by Commonplace plate-glass windows out of keeping with the historic associations of a mansion with a pedigree rapidly approaching its second century.

This is not the time or the place to dwell upon Lord Rosebery's political career, or that of any living statesman, but his long and honourable connection with the Turf supplies a parallel with the racing achievements of Lord Jersey.

Both won the Derby three times, Lord Jersey in 1825 with *Middleton*, in 1827 with *Mameluke*, and in 1836 with *Bay Middleton*.

Lord Rosebery's three winners were *Ladas* in 1894, *Sir Visto* in 1895 and *Cicero* in 1905. *Sir Visto* also carried off the St. Leger, after being knocked out in the ring, as I well remember, on the morning of the race, though he subsequently returned to favouritism.

I do not find that Lord Jersey's colours were ever borne successfully in the great event at Doncaster, but his record in what may be called the minor classic contests is better than Lord Rosebery's, so far as a comparison is possible at the present time.

Still it is to be hoped that the famous Mentmore stud will send out, for years to come, horses of as high a class as *Cicero* and others who have carried the primrose and rose hoops. So far, in a turf career of nearly half a century, Lord Rosebery has only triumphed twice in the Two Thousand Guineas, as against *five* successes standing to Lord Jersey's credit. He first won it in 1831, and again in four consecutive years—1834, 1835, 1836 and 1837—until it was commonly said that it was hopeless to try and lower his colours over the Rowley Mile, however they might fare elsewhere.

Up to the present Lord Rosebery has only tied with him in the One Thousand and the Oaks, each winning the Newmarket race twice and scoring a single victory in the "ladies' race" at Epsom. It may be that Lord Jersey's phenomenal success was due to the fact that he never ran his horses as two-year-olds, preferring to bring them out fresh and better developed a year later. In adopting this policy he contended that a horse gained in stamina by not being run off its legs before reaching something like maturity; and, though his opinion was not widely shared by his contemporaries, experience proved that he was fully justified in the views which he held so tenaciously. His first big winner was, I think, *Cobweb*. She won both the One Thousand and the Oaks of 1824, and was a great success at the stud. One of her foals was *Bay Middleton*, and, at the mature age of twenty-three, she produced *Clementina*, who, in due course, won the One Thousand for the late Mr George Payne.

The next house, No 39, was built for yet another Duke, Peregrine Bertie, 3rd Duke of Ancaster, a pillar of the Turf in the middle of the eighteenth century. His second wife, who had a fortune of £60,000, was Mary, daughter of Thomas Panton of Newmarket, whose name occurs elsewhere in these pages. Horace Walpole, who had no liking for the sport of Kings, called her, quite inaccurately as it happens, "the natural daughter of Panton, a disreputable jockey." All the same the lady became Mistress of the Robes to the immaculate Queen Charlotte in 1761 and retained that position until her death.[193]

Her husband's name was mentioned for the Lord Lieutenancy of Ireland, but Lord North put his foot down and declared that it would be impossible to send such an egregious blockhead into such a responsible situation. Ultimately the Duke's sporting tastes were rewarded with the Mastership of the Horse. One of the founders of the Jockey Club, his name is commemorated at Newmarket to this day by the Ancaster Mile.[194]

No 40, in Waterloo year the residence of the 4th Duke of Newcastle, was rebuilt, rather successfully from an architectural point of view, by Messrs George and Peto for the late Mr William Severin Salting, younger brother of George Salting—the well-known art collector and benefactor of the National Gallery, the British Museum, and the South Kensington Museum. The brothers were of Danish origin, their father having been a native of Copenhagen. George Salting was a collector in the true sense of the word, for his whole life was spent in accumulating the choicest treasures of art which came into the market, and although he spent enormous sums on his various hobbies he contrived somehow to leave a fortune of over a million at his death.

The gloomy-looking stuccoed house at the corner of Hill Street (in which it was formerly reckoned), was Admiral Byng's from 1744 until a one gun salute summoned him to his doom at Spithead. Shortly after this tragedy had been enacted the house was let to Lady Raymond.

"We had a tempest of wind and snow for two hours beyond anything I remember. Lady Raymond's house in Berkeley Square is totally unroofed; and Lord Robert Bertie, who is going to marry her, may descend into it like a Jupiter Pluvius."[195] Lord Robert did marry Lady Raymond and became the next tenant. He was in the "Ramillies" with Byng and gave evidence on his behalf at the trial of the Admiral. No 42, the house at the opposite corner (and like No 41 originally rated in Hill Street), was built for Margaret, Countess of Coningsby. Its owners since then have been too numerous to mention in detail. For many years Sir John Cam Hobhouse, Lord Broughton, the author of a voluminous political diary, lived in it. His daughter and co-heiress Charlotte married the 4th and last Lord Dorchester and brought the house into the Carleton family. Lord Dorchester, who was one of the founders of Hurlingham, fought a duel in Spain in 1847 and died in the house fifty years later. Some of Lord Broughton's books are, or were quite lately, in the library here.[196]

No 44, built by Kent for Lady Isabella[197] Finch, is one of the most perfect eighteenth-century London houses remaining in practically an unaltered state.

In the rate-book for 1745 it was assessed at £130, and apparently Lady Bell had something of Colley Cibber's aversion to the payment of rates, for a note in the parochial archives runs: "Says she has not been in ye house long enough and will not pay."

The "Great Chamber" on the first floor, the ceiling of which was painted by an Italian artist, probably Amiconi or one of his pupils, is one of the loftiest and best-proportioned saloons in the West End.

It was the scene, according to Walpole, of a "funeral loo" party in 1764, attended by the Duke,[198] Princess Emily and the Duchess of Bedford[199] in addition to himself.

Lady Bell, one of the "black funereal Finches," at the end of a long night's play at cards, was owed by William Pulteney, Earl of Bath, one of the more substantial ghosts of Piccadilly, exactly half-a-crown.

He sent it to her next day with the wish that he could give her a crown. Whereon Lady Bell, "browner than strawberry in late summer," replied that, though he could not give her a *crown*, he could give her a *coronet*, and that she was very ready to accept it. But there was at least one other rival for his hand since Lord Bath had become a widower—in 1758.

Mrs Anne Pitt, a half-crazy sister of the great Lord Chatham, coveted the prize for herself, and wrote to Lady Suffolk: "My Lord Bath is here, very lively, but I have not seen him, which I am very sorry for, because I want to offer myself to him. I am quite in earnest and have set my heart upon it, so I beg seriously you will carry it in your mind, and think if you could find any way to help me. Do not you think Lady Betty[200] and Lord and Lady Vere would be ready to help me if they knew how willing I am? But I leave all this to your discretion, and repeat seriously that I am quite in earnest."[201]

Lord Bath did not marry either of these ladies and died a few years after their attempts to capture him and his fortune. The next mention of this interesting house of which we have any knowledge is from the pen of the indefatigable Lady Mary Coke, who wrote in 1773: "Lord Clermont has bought the house in Berkeley Square that belonged to Lady Bell Finch."

Two Viscounts Clermont lived here in succession, of whom the first was a keen sportsman who won the Derby in 1785 with *Aimwell.* After them came Mr Charles Baring Wall, the 4th Marquis of Bath of the Thynne family, Sir Percy Burrell, Mr George Thomas Clark of Tal-y-Garn, Co. Glamorgan, his son Mr Godfrey Lewis Clark, and his grandson.

Nos 45 and 46, uniform houses with massive fronts of Portland stone, retaining their original link extinguishers, are unique in the annals of the Square from the continuity of their ownership. Both of them have been inhabited, since first they were erected, by only two families.

So remarkable a coincidence in London topography justifies me in setting out their pedigrees in detail:

No.45

William Ker, Earl of Ancram	
(afterwards 4th Marquis of Lothian)	1750–1760
Robert Clive, 1st Baron Clive of Plassey	1761–1774
Margaret, Lady Clive	1775–1780
Edward Clive, 2nd Lord Clive and	
1st Earl of Powis of the new creation	1781–1839
Edward Herbert, 2nd Earl of Powis	1840–1848
Edward James Herbert, 3rd Earl of Powis	1849–1891
George Herbert, 4th Earl of Powis	1892–

No. 46.

Edward Bligh, 2nd Earl of Darnley	1745–1747
John Bligh, 3rd Earl of Darnley	1748–1781
Mary Countess of Darnley	1782–1794
John Bligh, 4th Earl of Darnley	1795–1831
Edward Bligh, 5th Earl of Darnley	1832–1835
Humphrey St John Mildmay	1836–1853
Mrs St John Mildmay	1854–1862
Humphrey Francis Mildmay	1863–1866
Henry Bingham Mildmay	1867–1905
Rt. Hon. Francis Bingham Mildmay	1906-

Over 150 years of continuous residence by a single family speaks volumes for the fascination which this corner of habitable London has exerted on successive generations of the governing class of this country. Dukes have flitted from one Square to another, Prime Ministers have vacillated, as is their wont, between Downing Street, St James's, Mayfair, and Belgravia, but No 45 Berkeley Square has proved an irresistible attraction to the descendants of the heaven-born General Clive for over 150 years. Well may the name of the Earl of Powis inscribed on the brass plate of its entrance door proclaim the fact to all and sundry who pass it by.[202]

The tour of the Square is nearly complete, but some outstanding names call for special remembrance.

At No 47, and not (as we have shown) at No 6, there was to be found, at a momentous period of his career, one of the greatest of Englishmen. The house had been taken (after being relinquished by the Freeman family, for whom it was built in 1745) by John, second Earl of Chatham, and I find William Pitt writing to the Duke of Rutland on November 22nd, 1783: "For fear of mistakes I must tell you that I am at a house which my brother has taken here, and not at Shelburne[203] House."[204]

On December 17th Fox's India Bill was thrown out in the House of Lords. The King forthwith commanded his Ministers to return their seals of office. At the same time he requested Pitt to undertake the task of forming an alternative Administration. On the morning of Tuesday, December 23rd, the decisive moment arrived, and Chatham's son, still only twenty-four years of age, became First Minister of the Crown and spent the Christmas season in settling the composition of his Cabinet in the library of his brother's house. A red-letter day, if ever there was one, in the annals of Berkeley Square!

In the following March, Pitt removed to Downing Street, nor did Lord Chatham remain many years at No 47 after his brother's departure.

Passing over some intermediate occupiers, an immense gulf is fixed between the supremely great man who made this particular house his temporary home in 1783 and its tenure (some time in the early nineties) by a German company-promoter named Steinkopff.

Managing director, though not the actual discoverer, of the Apollinaris mineral water, this enterprising alien drifted on the flood tide of financial achievement into this seat of the mighty, and rebuilt the house in its present form. Dr Ernest Hart, editor of the *British Medical Journal*, had supplied the idea, the late Mr George Smith, the publisher, advanced the capital, and Edward Steinkopff contributed the business capacity which made the company the great financial success it was, and, I believe, still is.

He was not, as has been supposed, a Jew, for his father was a Lutheran pastor in Mecklenburgh.

In 1897 Steinkopff, who was at one time also the proprietor of the *St James's Gazette*, with the late Mr Frederick Greenwood as its editor, sold his interest in the Apollinaris Company for a sum of over a million sterling. In 1906 he died, and the house, which he made a perfect store-house of the arts, is now the property of his daughter, Mrs Stewart Mackenzie of Seaforth.

No 48 was built for William Henry Zulestein de Nassau, fourth Earl of Rochford, a nobleman of Dutch ancestry with little or no German taint in his blood, whose family had come over with the Prince of Orange and become naturalised in England.

The Lord Rochford of 1745 was quite English. Educated at Westminster School, he married an English wife, as his father had done before him. He became Secretary of State for both the Northern and the Southern Departments and represented the Court of St James's at Turin, Madrid and Versailles.

Charles, second Earl Grey took the house in 1825, and let it in 1831 to Lord Brougham. Returning to the Square after Reform had been carried, Lord Grey found that the ex-Chancellor had been a very undesirable tenant, for "Never was a house left in a more filthy condition."[205] Lord Grey died in 1845 and his widow parted with the house to a Mrs Leslie. In 1867 it became the town house of the Thynnes of Longleat, Marquises of Bath, a family not to be confused with that of Pulteney, Earls of Bath, whose name occurs so frequently in these pages.

Elizabeth, Duchess of Hamilton and Brandon married, as her second husband, Richard Savage Nassau, brother of the Lord Rochford mentioned above, and joined the family party in the Square at No 49. This house, a perfect Georgian structure of the better class, is practically unspoilt externally and internally. It was for many years the London house of the old Suffolk family of Thornhill, and, more recently, of the late Dean of York and his widow, Lady Harriet Duncombe.

In 1902 Mr William Salting removed to it from No 40, and it is now in the occupation of Mrs Salting, who has preserved, with rare discrimination and unerring taste, every feature of interest which it contains.

Dean Duncombe is almost the only, if not the only dignitary of the Church to be found in the Square's history, nor has it ever been a favourite perching place with the legal profession. Lord Brougham is one of the few exceptions, and he never stayed very long anywhere until he came to an anchor in Grafton Street in the evening of his days.

No 50, the so-called haunted house, has had many occupiers, none of them, I believe, ghostly ones. The first inhabitant was a General Frampton, whom I find living here from 1745 to 1749. George Canning was here in 1807, and the Hon. Miss Elizabeth Curzon paid the rates from 1841 to 1859, after which date the house stood empty for about twenty years.

Ridiculous rumours as to its being haunted grew up as years went by. At one time it was said to be tenanted by a gang of coiners who were in the habit of entering by an underground passage leading into it from the Mews at the back. A later version of the supposed mystery attaching to it was that shrieks were to be heard echoing and re-echoing from its dingy walls by nocturnal passers-by. Some of these credulous people, mostly young men returning home from Mayfair ball-rooms in the early hours of the morning, would pull the bell-handle and go away convinced that there was something uncanny about the house simply because the call was never answered! The explanation is that it belonged to an eccentric lady who paid the rates with unfailing regularity but never cared to take up her abode in the Square.[206]

In 1880 the Earl of Selkirk, who, to my certain knowledge, ridiculed the idea of its being haunted, took the house, and it was till quite recently in the occupation of his widow.[207]

Except to mention that the third Earl of Albemarle was at No 51 for a few years before he removed to the east side (see the account of No 12), the one next to it (No 52, first built for Hans Stanley in 1745) is only memorable from its having been the residence (from 1874 till his death in 1885) of Field-Marshal Lord Strathnairn, one of the bravest of the brave men who helped to save India in the dark days of the Mutiny.

The little house round the corner, now numbered 52A, really belongs to Charles Street, and No 53, on the south side, an ideal residence for a bachelor, was for over forty years the home of Sir Henry Edwards, known to his friends as "the Bart," who died in 1897.

Lansdowne House, one of the finest eighteenth-century mansions in London, alone remains to be noticed before this chapter, already swollen to too great a length, can be brought to its fitting conclusion.

Henry Fox, writing to Lord Shelburne (afterwards Marquis of Lansdowne), 29th June, 1761, gives the topographer valuable information concerning the site whilst it still lay open and unappropriated:—"I see you have ordered Mr Adam to look out for space to build a Hotel upon. The late Lord Leicester and the late Lord Digby were about a fine piece of ground for that purpose, *still to be had*, the garden of which, or the Court before which, may extend all along the bottom of Devonshire[208] Garden, though no house must be built there; the house must be where some paltry old stables stand at the lower end of Bolton Row."

This clear statement goes far to explain what I could never understand until Fox's letter supplied me with the clue, why Lansdowne House was not built north and south instead of in the cramped position which it occupies, facing due east and with little or no ground at the back of it. Some stipulation on the part of the ground landlord led, no doubt, to this—the finest example of the many private palaces designed by the brothers Adam in town or country—being deprived of that southerly aspect which would have rendered it an even more desirable place of residence than it is.

Although the site had been, as we have seen, recommended to Lord Shelburne in 1761, Lord Bute was before him in negotiating for its acquisition. In the end, though the house was built to his order between 1765 and 1767, Lord Bute remained constant to South Audley Street.

Lansdowne House is said to have been sold to Lord Shelburne for £22,000, or £3,000 less than it cost to build. This must surely have been an under-estimate, though it should be stated that the chief glory of the house as it stands to-day, the noble sculpture gallery, was not added until some ten years later, whilst the library dates only from 1790. Some wit remarked that the house had been "built by one peace and paid for by another," in allusion to the unpopularity which attached to the names of the original owner and his successor for their conduct, at an interval of twenty years, in translating a state of exhausting war into a condition of unsatisfactory peace.

Lord Bute resigned almost immediately after the signing of the Peace of Paris in 1763, and Lord Shelburne did the same after the Peace of Versailles in 1783.

It is said that the latter would even have been willing to cede Gibraltar to Spain, if compensation had been offered, but he was fortunately overruled in the Cabinet. Almost every article of the treaty was fiercely assailed in Parliament, and the Minister soon bowed before the storm.

We, who have just seen the conclusion of the most terrible war in history, know that no Peace which it is in the power of Ministers to devise can ever be wholly satisfactory to a nation, and more especially to a combination of nations, taking part in a life-and-death struggle for the domination of the world. No cessions of territory or rectification of frontiers, no exaction of indemnities or imposition of penalising conditions upon the vanquished, can ever be a full and adequate compensation for the appalling loss of blood and substance, the wanton waste and long-drawn agony of the past five years. Leagues of nations, however admirable in theory, will assuredly break down in practice. The one and only security for England and her Allies is to make it certain, so far as human foresight can provide, that they are never again found unprepared.

I must now return (after this brief divergence from mere topography into the troubled sphere of European politics) to the peaceful atmosphere of Berkeley Square and that green oasis in the surrounding desert of bricks and mortar—the garden of Lansdowne House at the foot of Hay Hill.

This was the spot at which our survey of the Square was entered upon, and from which the return to Piccadilly must be made.

The greater part of the site upon which Lord Bute began to build (at first, I think, from the designs of the elder Brettingham) belonged originally to Lord Berkeley of Stratton, but a portion of the garden ground was leased from the Curzon family and others, whilst the passage-way between Bolton Row and Berkeley Street[209] formed the subject of a separate lease granted by Will Pulteney, Earl of Bath, shortly before his death. The whole of Lord Bute's purchases and leases were assigned to Lord Shelburne in 1768, and the property is now entirely freehold.

The present owner courteously placed at my entire disposal an exhaustive collection of deeds, documents and letters relating to Lansdowne House from the time of its acquisition from Lord Bute.[210]

Amongst them is a bill of the brothers Adam, dated October, 1765, for the "plans and elevation of Shelburne House in Berkeley Square, *with all the alterations made from Lord Bute's design.*" Included in the items is a sum of £546 3s. od., received from Lord Bute "for articles which were left unexecuted by his Lordship."

The sum total of the payments to the Adams for work done under their superintendence was only about £8,000, but the interior decorations by Cipriani, Zucchi and Rigaud, the finest of their kind in London, were paid for separately.

Further works were carried out between 1770 and 1800 by

Henry Holland and George Dance, who was responsible for the library; and in the 19th century by Smirke and others.

The greater part of the antique statuary was brought from Rome by Gavin Hamilton, who had a practically unlimited commission to buy anything really good which came into the market. Hamilton entered upon his congenial task with such diligence and success that at last Lord Shelburne had to cry a halt, for even in those now remote days of low prices for works of art of the highest class the annual bill ran into many thousands of pounds. The library was placed under the care of Joseph Priestley, and it was in his rooms at Lansdowne House that he made his great discovery of oxygen.

In 1805 Lord Shelburne, 1st Marquis of Lansdowne, died in Berkeley Square, as did his successor in the title only four years later. The 3rd Marquis was born in the family house, and to him is mainly due the formation of the priceless collection of pictures which adorn its walls and also those of Bowood.

Ranging as it does from Raphael, Murillo and Velasquez to Hogarth, Reynolds and the mid-Victorian painters, it includes a round dozen examples of Sir Joshua's best work. Perhaps the most widely known is the "Strawberry Girl," so familiar to all of us in an engraved form.

There is also a wonderful portrait of Laurence Sterne by the same master hand.

I am loath to part company with Berkeley Square, conscious as I am that I have omitted to mention many who have helped to make it famous; but the return to Piccadilly must be made.

VI

Piccadilly Terrace (Hyde Park Corner) the Acme of Fashion for a Hundred Years

Until nearly the end of the eighteenth century the houses in Piccadilly west of Hamilton Place, or Hamilton Street as it was then called, were of small account. They were mostly second-rate inns or taverns designed, primarily, for the convenience of drovers attending the cattle markets formerly held in Brook Fields. But some there were at which country gentlemen arriving in London from the West Country put up their horses and, at the same time, refreshed the inner man.

The oldest and the best known of these inns was the "Hercules Pillars," probably so called from an earlier tavern of the same name in Fleet Street. It had a history dating from the seventeenth century, for it is referred to by Wycherley,[211] and here it was that Fielding made Squire Western put up when in hot pursuit of Tom Jones. Apsley House stands on a portion of the site.[212]

The "Triumphal Chariot" was another much frequented by pleasure-seekers coming to and from Hyde Park. It stood at or near the west corner of Hamilton Place, which, at the time of which we speak, was entirely composed of small houses at very low rentals, widely differing in character from the imposing mansions which now comprise its western side.

A *cul-de-sac* until 1871, Hamilton Place occupies the site of a piece of ground filched from Hyde Park and granted by the Crown in 1693 to Elizabeth Hamilton, widow of James Hamilton, Ranger of the Park *temp*. Charles II, whose name occurs frequently in the Grammont Memoirs. After the grant had been renewed in 1757 to George Hamilton, the whole of the property (with the exception of Apsley House, which is shown in a MS. plan of the year 1773 preserved in H.M.'s Office of Woods) was re-granted to William, Earl of Shelburne, who at one time intended to build a mansion here but changed his mind. In 1693 it comprised only seven small houses and a stable to which, in after years, was added a brewhouse overlooking the Park.

Dudley North, or Dudley Long North, to give him his full name, a prominent Whig M.P. whom we have already met with at No 140, lived for a time at the first good house built on the west side of Hamilton Place,[213] but he soon deserted Hyde Park Corner for Brompton, where he died in 1829.

A house on the site of No. 141 Piccadilly, the west corner of Hamilton Place and often reckoned therein, was projected for Lord Montgomerie *circa* 1796, but apparently it was not proceeded with, and the corner site remained unoccupied for some years. The existing mansion, lately re-cased in stone, was built for John Scott, 1st Earl of Eldon, the well-known Lord Chancellor, and first occupied by him about 1818.

Piccadilly has never been a favourite place of abode with the pillars of the law. Lord Chancellors Eldon and Bathurst, and Sir Fitzroy Kelly are among the few exceptions, all three being numbered amongst the more eminent inhabitants of the Terrace.

The son of a Newcastle "coal fitter," John Scott, Lord Eldon, began his London life in Cursitor Street, Chancery Lane. Many years later the self-made Chancellor, pointing out his former home to a friend, said:—"That was my first perch. Many a time have

I run down from there to Fleet Market to buy sixpennyworth of sprats for my supper."

His gains at the Bar during his first year amounted to just nine shillings and no more. Yet by sheer merit and prodigious application to his profession, with no one to push him, he won his way to the Woolsack, leaving at his death a fortune of £700,000.

Before coming to the West-End he lived in Carey Street and in Bedford Square. He was not remarkable for hospitality and when all his windows were broken in a Corn Law riot in 1815 someone was unkind enough to say that the Chancellor had at last begun to keep open house!

Soon after he came to an anchorage in Piccadilly he was much annoyed at hearing that a section of Queen Caroline's friends intended to buy a house for her use in Hamilton Place, where it was intended she should keep a pseudo-Court with the mob to stand guard over her. Lord Eldon, who did not at all relish the idea of having her as a neighbour, threatened Lord Liverpool with his immediate resignation if the Government made itself a party to the proposal, and on learning that a voluntary subscription was on foot to carry out the scheme, he defeated the purchase by becoming the owner of the house, at a considerably enhanced price.

He died in Piccadilly on January 13th, 1838, in his 87th year, and his remains lay in state here. The funeral proceeded by road to Encombe, resting at Bagshot, Winchester and Wimborne on the way, and not until the 26th of the month was his body laid in the family vault at Kingston.

The second and third Earls of Eldon continued to live at No 141, and after them there came another self-made man in the person of the late George Herring, follower of the turf, financier, and, in his later years, philanthropist.

Herring's mother kept an Alton ale shop in Newgate Street. He and his brother William were precocious youths and they started a betting list (the late Mr George Hodgman began in the same way in a court off Fleet Street), offering the odds to all comers at a time when books were opened long before the date of decision of the principal races, and when it was possible to back a horse for the Chester Cup[214] at any time during the winter. They did so well at this form of speculation that when George appeared as a witness in the Palmer poisoning trial in 1856 and was asked, "What is your occupation?" he was able to say: "I am independent."

When still quite a young man he became an assistant to Fred Swindell, the bookmaker, and eventually commissioner to Sir Joseph Hawley. He had a narrow escape when *Blue Gown* won the Derby in 1868. The horse had previously been scratched for the Two Thousand, so as to give him and his friends a chance of getting out.

On the morning of the race Herring persuaded Sir Joseph, who preferred the chances of *Rosicrucian* and *Green Sleeves*, to save on *Blue Gown*, as he had done from information received at the last moment.

Thenceforward Herring worked a number of important commissions, and had the reputation of helping himself to a portion, at any rate, of the long odds he was able to secure.

He managed to ingratiate himself with a number of aristocratic patrons of the turf, and did a good deal of business for the "Romeo" Lords, of whom the late Earl of Devon, then known as Lord Courtenay, was one of the principals.[215] Always obsequious and business-like, Herring scraped acquaintance with several big German financiers at Baden Baden, amongst others Mr Bischoffsheim, and through him procured an introduction to the late Baron Hirsch which proved very advantageous.

He now severed his connection with the Victoria Club, gave up bookmaking and commission working, went into the City, did well there, and ended by making a large fortune and buying Lord Eldon's old house. Both these self-made men began their careers east of Temple Bar, to end them in the chosen abode of fashion in the west. Fred Swindell, who taught Herring most of what he knew, and finished up in Berkeley Square, used to say that he went to live there so that he might see for himself who called on Admiral Rous. It was racing which put John Gully into Ackworth, and which enabled Harry Hill to buy it afterwards, but Herring is one of those rare instances of a man succeeding late in life in the City, after having been for the greater part of his career a racing man with no especial knowledge of stocks and shares. Mr. John Corlett, who was kind enough to give me most of the above information, informed me that the last horse Herring ever backed was his *Let Go the Painter*, a very disappointing animal, not only to his owner but to his friends. In his later years Herring, who was not by any means insensible to Royal influence, became a munificent contributor to King Edward's Hospital Fund, and, dying in 1906, left over a million, the greater part of which he bequeathed to charitable objects.

The story of the next house[216] is the story of the rapid social elevation of a single middle-class family, and, as a romance of the Peerage, it is almost without a parallel.

The Burrells may be called without exaggeration an exceptionally fortunate race. Towards the close of the eighteenth century, when almost unknown in fashionable society, their daughters, without any of the beauty or personal charm of those celebrated Irish beauties, rivalled the matrimonial achievements of the Gunnings by a series of equally brilliant alliances, all of them contracted within an even shorter period.

Peter Burrell, a sub-governor of the South Sea Company and a Director of the Royal Exchange Assurance Society (one of the first, if not actually the first of its kind), was the son of a plain Commissioner of Excise, who died in 1756. His sole patrimonial inheritance consisted of a small property at Langley, in the parish of Beckenham. When he entered the House of Commons as

Member for Haslemere he lived first in Mark Lane and then in
Leadenhall Street. In his later years he ventured as far West as
King Street, Covent Garden, but even that locality had ceased
to be fashionable when he went there. For the last two years of
his life he represented Dover. His only brother, Merrick, entered
into partnership with one of the Raymonds of Saling Hall, Essex,
and having become fairly well known as a merchant in Copthall
Court, Throgmorton Street, he prospered sufficiently to become
a Governor of the Bank of England, and was created a Baronet in
1766. Like his elder brother he entered the House of Commons,[217]
of course in the Tory interest.

Peter Burrell the second had the good fortune to marry an heiress
from Hackney, one Miss Elizabeth Lewis. In 1769 he was appointed
Surveyor of the Crown Lands, an extremely lucrative office held
in after years by George Selwyn. This Peter who had, with a son
to be mentioned hereafter, four daughters, seems to have been the
real founder of the family fortunes. Like his father before him he
had Parliamentary aspirations and he represented first Launceston
and then Totnes in the House of Commons. He fixed his town
abode in Upper Grosvenor Street, but almost immediately after
he became a Government official, he acquired the site of the still-
existing Gwydyr House in Whitehall. In 1770–1771 he succeeded
in obtaining at a very low rent a lease of two plots of land with
frontages to the street and to the Privy Garden, the chief portion
of which had, up to that time, been in the occupation of the Lord
Steward's lamplighter, and used for the safe custody of the wheels
belonging to the State lottery. Burrell advised their removal to
Ely House, and on this preferential site, after agreeing to pay the
lamplighter ten pounds a year as compensation for disturbance,
he built a capital mansion, at a cost of £6,000, from the designs
of John Marquand, a Government official, who is sponsible for
most of the later eighteenth-century maps and plans preserved
in the Office of Woods. The site of Gwydyr House was liable to

inundation from the Thames at spring tides, and this entailed a
heavy preliminary expense in planking and piling.

The Crown Surveyor's three youngest daughters became
successively Countess of Beverley, Duchess of Northumberland
and Duchess of Hamilton. The latter, having been divorced by
her husband, married Lord Exeter,[218] a peer who had a somewhat
varied experience of matrimony. Having divorced his first wife in
1791,[219] he married three months later Sarah Hoggins, the well-
known "peasant Countess," of Tennyson's "Lord of Burleigh,"
from whom the present holder of the title descends. Countess
Sarah died in 1797, and in 1800, in the course of the same
month in which her former husband died, Elizabeth Burrell
became Lord Exeter's third wife. Lady Beverley and the Duchess
of Northumberland, both of them married to Peers claiming
descent from one of the proudest families in England (though
it is true that their connection with it was subsequent to the
metamorphosis from Percy to Smithson), had no such untoward
happenings in their married lives, and at their deaths they found
honourable burial in Westminster Abbey.

The only remaining Miss Burrell became the wife of Mr Richard
Bennet, of Babraham.

The Surveyor of Crown Lands did not long enjoy the profits
of his office, or his new house, for he died in 1775. His only son,
whom we may call Peter Burrell the third, was born in Upper
Grosvenor Street, July 16, 1754. He married, at the early age of
twenty-four, Lady Priscilla Bertie, she being then only seventeen,
eldest daughter and co-heir of the third Duke of Ancaster and
Kesteven, by Mary, daughter of Thomas Panton of Newmarket,
whose name occurs elsewhere in these pages. Horace Walpole,
who was inclined to sneer at the rapid elevation of the Burrells,
speaking of them as "broken merchants" before they blossomed
into Government officials, declared that it was Lady Priscilla
who fell in love with young Burrell during a chance meeting

in the South of France, and that she insisted on marrying him *malgré lui.*[220] However this may have been, within six months she not only inherited[221] Grimsthorpe Castle—one of the most delightful houses in all East Anglia, and unquestionably the finest country seat in Lincolnshire, carrying with it the greater part of the valuable Ancaster estates—but there also reverted to her the feudal office of Great Chamberlain of England and the hereditary Barony of Willoughby de Eresby, a dignity dating from the reign of King Edward the Second.

Plain Mr. Burrell was knighted in 1781, when only twenty-seven years of age, in order to render him eligible to execute the office of Chamberlain by deputy, the judiciary having decided that it could not be satisfactorily performed by anyone of lesser degree. In this capacity he presided at the trial of Warren Hastings in Westminster Hall. But his good luck was not yet exhausted. Sir Peter Burrell, as he had now become, succeeded (in 1787) to a Baronetcy on the death of an unmarried great-uncle, and in 1796, on the forty-second anniversary of his birth, he was raised to the peerage as Lord Gwydyr. Even his title was taken from a portion of his wife's property, coming to her as it did from her great-grandmother Mary, daughter and heiress of Sir Richard Wynn, of Gwydyr, Co. Carnarvon. This signal mark of Royal favour was not directly traceable to any of those obvious sources which occasionally conduct mediocrity to social eminence.

Favouritism, feminine charm and beauty as exemplified in his home circle, conspicuous Parliamentary ability, length of official service, or such interest as depends on the responsibilities attaching to a great inherited estate—all these were wanting in Peter Burrell's case. Yet not only did he take his place amongst the hereditary Peers of England, but he was entitled to claim precedence of nearly all of them by right of office.

Wraxall says that he had a good address, accompanied by great elegance of deportment, but there must, I think, have been something more in the man than the mere words convey. His portrait by Gainsborough, sold in London a few years ago for a large sum, represents him as a young man of pleasing, if somewhat effeminate, appearance.

From having no permanent place of abode in London at the outset of his career,[222] he burst upon an astonished aristocracy in one of the best positions in Whitehall. Later on, as the family fortunes increased, his son, who for the purposes of this narrative may be called Peter the fourth, built for himself a mansion in the best part of Piccadilly, which remained in the possession of his descendants until 1865. He first inhabited the house on the Terrace in 1809, and eleven years later, his father, having entirely deserted the paternal estate at Langley for his wife's stately home at Grimsthorpe, died at Brighton of gout in the stomach.

He was buried with great ceremony at Edenham, the resting-place of countless Willoughbys, where his memorial bust, strangely out of harmony with the magnificent series of mediæval monuments surrounding it, may still be seen. After being occupied for many years by the Charity Commission, Gwydyr House, the last of the older Whitehall mansions, has been swallowed up by the Board of Trade. After the death of the first Lord Gwydyr it was occupied for a time by the Duke of Leeds. On the Duke's removal to St James's Square it became the temporary home of the Reform Club whilst the clubhouse in Pall Mall was in course of erection. This was from 1838 to 1840. It was next occupied by the Commissioners of Woods and Forests, who rented it from Lady Clare, Lady Willoughby's daughter. From 1869 to 1871 it was the office of the Poor Law Board. The Commissioners of Works then rented it at £1,300, and the Local Government Board immediately preceded the Charity Commission here.

The 4th Lord Gwydyr, who died so recently as 1909, aged nearly 100, remembered being rowed from Whitehall in his grandfather's barge to see George IV crowned in the Abbey. Present at the

coronation banquet in Westminster Hall, he saw William IV,
Victoria, and Edward VII crowned, and just failed to live into the
present reign. The title is now extinct, after little more than one
hundred years of crowded existence.

There seems to be no fixity of tenure for London statues, for in
1898 Grinling Gibbons' finely-modelled bronze figure of James II
was, most unnecessarily, removed from its original position behind
the Banqueting House to the garden of Gwydyr House. But the
deposed king was not destined to stay there long. The authorities
considered the new Admiralty building at the end of the Mall—
one of the most hideous of modern Government offices—a
more appropriate site, and James was torn from Whitehall to be
replaced by Lord Clive, who never lived there at any time of his
life. The statue has now been removed to a more appropriate site
near the India Office overlooking St James's Park.

The 2nd Lord Gwydyr and 21st Lord Willoughby (Peter Burrell
the fourth) married yet another heiress, Clementina, daughter of
James Drummond, Earl of Perth. She annoyed old Lord Eldon,
her next-door neighbour on the Terrace, by reproducing the
instrumental amenities of the Highlands in Piccadilly. "I am
sometimes tormented," he wrote, "by the noise of Lady Gwydyr's
Scotchmen playing under my windows upon the Scottish
instrument called the bagpipes, but there is music in that droning
instrument compared to the babel of lawyers' tongues."

Lord Willoughby and his wife died within a month of each
other, and the Crown lease of No 142 was sold for £24,700.

After being occupied for a time by the late Mr John Snowdon
Henry,[223] it passed into the possession of Miss Alice de Rothschild,
having been owned by only two families since its erection more
than a hundred years ago.

Artists have never been numerous in Piccadilly but at a house,
now No 143, designed by the brother Adam, who were responsible
for the greater number of the Terrace houses, there came to live

in 1795 Sir Nathaniel Dance Holland, an original member of the Royal Academy. To its first exhibition he contributed portraits of George III and his Queen, but I have no knowledge of their present whereabouts. He became acquainted and, as some say, infatuated, with Angelica Kauffman whom he met whilst travelling in Italy. Towards the end of his life he eschewed painting and went into politics, and he was a member of the House of Commons at the time of his death in 1811. His widow parted with the house to James Haughton Langston[224] and after his death his widow Lady Julia sold it to Baron Ferdinand de Rothschild, son of Baron Amschel of Vienna. He came here on his marriage, and lived in Piccadilly for more than thirty years.

Baron Ferdinand cared more for art than business, but when the late Lord Rothschild was raised to the Peerage he entered the House of Commons and represented the Aylesbury divison of Buckinghamshire until his death in 1898. He bequeathed many of his unrivalled *objets d'art* to the British Museum, of which he was a Trustee. At Waddesdon he erected a fairy palace on what had been up to the time that he acquired the property nothing but ploughed fields. He was, I think, one of the first, if not actually the first, to remove large forest trees from their original positions by means of hydraulic jacks. Having been transported one by one for long distances, they were replanted round about the new house, and, strange to say, with such care and thoroughness was the work accomplished that most of them lived.

The next two houses on the Terrace, going westward, were also built in 1795 from the designs of the brothers Adam.

No 144 was first occupied by Sir Drummond Smith of Tring Park.[225] Strange as it may appear the name of Smith has hardly occurred elsewhere in these pages, if at all. Sir Drummond died in 1816 and his widow, who was a Monckton by birth, in 1835. The Crown lease was then bought by Thomas Wentworth Beaumont[226] and his descendant Lord Allendale, late Captain of the Yeomen of the Guard, is the third of his race and name to live here. Wentworth and Beaumont are great names in the territorial history of England, and I notice that in Burke's Peerage Lord Allendale is credited with a descent from the Bellmonts, Lords of Whitley Beaumont,[227] though this exalted pedigree did not appear in the pages of Burke when his family was numbered only among the landed gentry. I fancy that the Beaumonts of to-day are in no way related to the great feudal lord who, having obtained large grants of land in the County of Lincoln, was ennobled by Edward II and became Constable of England.

The rapid social advancement of a junior branch of this ancient family was partly, if not pnincipally, due to a fortunate alliance in the 18th century of Thomas Richard Beaumont[228] with Diana, the eldest of three natural daughters of Sir Thomas Wentworth Blackett, Bart, who died unmarried in 1792.

The fusion of the Beaumonts of Whitley with the commercial strain of the Blacketts amalgamated certain valuable mining properties and broad acres in the neighbourhood of Hexham. It also ensured the County of Northumberland being worthily represented during a long series of years by one or other of its members. A Blackett, who became Mayor of Newcastle, sat for that town in 1673, but the historic names of Beaumont and Wentworth are to be found in the records of Parliament from the very earliest times. In recent years the Beaumonts of Whitley have not been remarkable for the consistency of their political opinions. The first of them to take up his abode in Piccadilly was a Tory in his youth, but about 1820 he became a strenuous partisan on the other side.

He lost his seat at the general election of 1826 and in consequence of some angry words uttered on the hustings at Alnwick between him and Mr Lambton they fought a duel on Bamburgh sands.

Both fired simultaneously at twelve paces without injuring one another, whereupon their seconds declared that honour was satisfied and the incident terminated. Nowadays a similar misunderstanding would probably have resulted in a sordid action for damages, much washing of dirty linen in public, and no material advantage to anyone but the lawyers engaged in the case.

This Mr Beaumont was one of the founders of the "Westminster Review," a still-existing monthly publication, which, when competition was not so acute, had some slight political influence.

A more interesting association with No 144 is the fact that it was here that Lord Palmerston lived for one brief year before settling down at Cambridge House.

A shooting box belonging to the Beaumont family at Allenheads is said to be the highest inhabited country house in England. Standing in a most delightful situation no less than 1400 feet above sea level, it commands a view over the Northumbrian hills and dales which is all but unique in this country.

No 145, which like its neighbours has completely lost, at all events as regards its exterior, any vestige of the Adam style (owing to the Office of Woods requiring the tenants to reface their holdings with stone as the leases fall in) was built for Sir John Smith-Burges, yet another of George the Third's baronets.

In such slight estimation was the neighbourhood of Hyde Park Corner held at the close of the 18th century that its annual value was computed at only £210 in 1795, a lower assessment than that of any house in the immediate vicinity.

Lady Smith-Burges married the fourth Earl Poulett in 1816, and at her death the lease was acquired by the Marquis of Northampton, a man of varied abilities, accustomed to think for himself in an age when political independence was little understood. He was President of the Royal Society and many other learned bodies, and a writer of long-forgotten verse. In his official capacity he gave a series of entertainments in Piccadilly which were attended not oniy by men of science but by the élite of London society.

In his youth he sat in the Commons as member for Northampton. It would seem as if there was something inherently Radical in the atmosphere of that Midland borough, for Lord Compton, as he then was, shocked his family by coming out as an independent reformer, only to be stigmatised by his contemporaries as unpractical and cantankerous. Such, however, is the invariable fate of a reformer born out of time. Having retired to Italy, he warmly espoused the cause of the victims of despotic government in Lombardy and Naples. Returning to England, after succeeding to the Peerage, he astonished the House of Lords, much as he had shocked his relations when member for Northampton, by trying to tack a clause on to the Reform Bill designed to amend the law which, until only the other day, obliged members of the House of Commons to vacate their seats on appointment to office under the Crown.

Lord Northampton was advised by Lord Ellenborough and by Lord Grey (who expressed himself as favourable to the proposal) to endeavour to effect his object by means of a separate Bill. This he proceeded to do,[229] but withdrew the measure when some of his brother peers declared that it was beyond their province to interfere with the domestic affairs of the Lower House.

Nearly a century has elapsed since Lord Northampton's well-meant attempt at remedial legislation, yet this harmless reform is still not wholly accomplished though often pressed upon the attention of the Government of the day irrespective of party.

The Comptons, unlike the Beaumonts, have been, on the whole, fairly consistent Whigs, though since the great cleavage of parties in 1886, on Mr. Gladstone's conversion to Home Rule, some of the family have transferred their political allegiance to the Liberal-Unionist camp, whose stronghold was until lately to be found in Birmingham and the surrounding Midland fringe.

The aristocratic Whiggism of the Comptons was replaced in Piccadilly by a representative of the great brewing interest controlled by the late Lord Burton—one of the Gladstonian peers who ultimately found political salvation in the ranks of the Opposition. Mr Hamar Bass, dying in 1898, was succeeded by Sir William, the 2nd Bt, who still owns the house, though it is at present occupied by Baron Albert Goldschmidt de Rothschild.

Nos 146 and 147 were originally one large house, first occupied, in its undivided state, by the French Ambassador, the Count d'Adhémar. According to Wraxall the Embassy in Piccadilly was a rallying point of pleasure and social activity, whilst the business affairs of the post were managed principally by the Count's secretary Barthlemy. Every Sunday evening in the winter season d'Adhémar opened his house to his friends and even when he was attacked by a paralytic stroke he would not allow his usual weekly reception to be abandoned. Whilst his guests punted at faro the Ambassador lay in an adjoining room attended by his physicians. His recovery proving merely temporary, the Chevalier de la Luzerne replaced him at the Court of St James's and the house, after being extensively altered and improved, was next tenanted by Monsieur Charles Alexandre de Calonne whom we have met with already at "Old Q's" hospitable board. The site of the French Embassy had been leased by the Crown to Sir R. Barnard and, though nearly £10,000 had been expended on it, Calonne intended to spend £4,000 more. But by 1793 he was practically ruined and the contents of the mansion, with the exception of the pictures, were sold by auction on the premises. The sale took place on May 13, 1793, and the auctioneers, Messrs Skinner and Dyke, described the house in preliminary notices in the newspapers as being at "the extremity of Piccadilly."

Calonne came to England owing to his having been banished from France where, as Controller General of Finance, he managed so badly that the annual deficit of the Treasury only four years after his appointment amounted to 115 million francs. In 1802 he died in poor circumstances after having been permitted by Napoleon to return to his native land.

The house was now subdivided and Calonne's lease was acquired by Sir Drummond Smith and Sir John Smith-Burges, who seem, like Pulteney and Clarges in an earlier age, to have had a finger in every speculation in house property hereabouts.

The eastern portion[230] passed into the possession of John Craufurd of Auchenames, whilst the Western half[231] was taken by Sir Charles Cockerell. Both their names appear in the rate-book for 1795 when the estimated annual value of both houses was only £150. 'Fish' Craufurd, as he was nicknamed at Eton, was a Whig M.P. and a friend of Charles James Fox. He belonged to that group of fashionable young men who frequented White's and Brooks', and made it the business of their lives to play for high stakes. The 'petit Craufurd' of Madame de Deffand's letters was witty and vivacious but affected and insincere. He died unmarried in 1814 and was succeeded in Piccadilly by Sir Edmund Antrobus, a partner in Coutts's, and the second of the great banking firm to settle in the neighbourhood.

The name of Antrobus is not to be found in the pages of the 'Dictionary of National Biography' but in association with those of Coutts, Trotter, and Marjoribanks it was long a power in the Strand. Sir Edmund bought "Old Q.'s" estate at Amesbury where recently the family name has been somewhat prominently before the public in connection with the future of Stonehenge—that immemorial monument of antiquity which "Old Q" owned so long but assuredly never valued.

The Antrobus connection with Piccadilly extended over more than seventy years, and the next owner of the house was Sir Charles Day Rose, who died with tragic suddenness. He was a son of the Canadian statesman well-known in London society a generation ago. The lease was then acquired by the late Sir Sigismund Neumann.

Sir Charles Cockerell, the first owner of No 147, was an eminent East Indian civil servant. For 25 years he lived in Bengal, and having been rewarded for his services with a Baronetcy he went into Parliament. On the death of his widow in 1851 the house was taken by Sir Fitzroy Kelly, or "apple-pip Kelly" as he was called from his ingenious defence of the arsenical poisoner Tawell, who was hanged in 1845.

He is said to have been the first criminal arrested by means of the electric telegraph, a subject which Frith seized upon for one of the sensational pictures which passed for art in early Victorian days. Kelly was, I think, the "Bar" of Mr Merdle's dinner parties in "Little Dorrit."

He began his London life at No 3 Serjeants' Inn, Fleet Street, where he had a relative of my own, his junior in the Ipswich Election petition of 1835, as his next-door neighbour.[232] As his practice grew Kelly came west of Temple Bar. He migrated to New Street, Spring Gardens, a favourite haunt of lawyers in the forties, owing to its proximity to the Courts at Westminster. Lords Abinger, Cranworth and Campbell were all living there at one time. After he became Solicitor-General, in succession to Thesiger, one of his rivals in Westminster Hall until a year before, Kelly removed to Piccadilly.

Baron Lionel de Rothschild, the last surviving member of the second generation of English Rothschilds, bought the remainder of Sir Fitzroy's lease and threw Nos 147 and 148 into one house, circa 1860–1863.

The old No 148 has a longer history behind it than any of the Terrace mansions with the exception of Apsley House—its immediate neighbour on the west. It was built for Wilbraham Tollemache, afterwards sixth Earl of Dysart, about the year 1782. Lord Dysart died in 1821, and his sister in 1840,[233] at the patriarchal age of ninety-five. She was therefore old enough to remember the time when there was not a single private house in Piccadilly west of Mr Pulteney's.[234] Lady Dysart's nephew, Admiral Tollemache, who died in the year in which William the Fourth ascended the throne, was the last of his family to occupy the house on the new Terrace. Soon after his decease it was taken by Baron Lionel Nathan de Rothschild, the "Sidonia" of "Coningsby," who, as already stated, rebuilt it[235] between 1860 and 1863.

The process of reconstruction, from the designs of an architect named Marsh Nelson, must have been a leisurely one for Delane alludes to it in his diary as "Rothschild's new house" when noting a dinner engagement for the month of May, 1864. It contains a handsome white marble staircase and spacious reception rooms, but the exterior with its ugly plate-glass windows is more commonplace than pleasing. Moreover it dwarfs Apsley House, which, with all its faults, has a better façade.

Baron Lionel, the last of the second generation of English Rothschilds, died at a good old age only a few months before the Editor of *The Times*, who so strenuously befriended him in his long and plucky attempt to enter Parliament. The coming of his family to the West End has been fully treated of in Chapter III, so that it will be unnecessary to recapitulate the facts attending the early struggles of the great financial house to obtain representation in the House of Commons. Observant visitors to Westminster between 1847 and 1858 must have been aware of the unsworn representative of the City of London sitting below the Bar—in the House but not of it—compelled by its rules to withdraw when notice was taken of the presence of strangers. Yet this incomplete member, who controlled the exchanges of Europe from his armchair in New Court, excited a greater influence on behalf of his constituents than many a more active voter. Baron Lionel was defeated at the Liberal *débâcle* of 1874, because he had the courage to tell the electors of the City of London that if Mr Gladstone abolished the Income Tax, as in his election address he declared he would do if returned to power, the country would be defrauded of some nine millions. As the estimated surplus could not, in Rothschild's opinion, amount to half that sum, the moiety would have to be made up by new taxes in the form of licence duties, a self-denying ordinance which failed to commend itself to the City. The net result of Mr Gladstone's desperate bid for a renewal of confidence on the part of the electorate was that England, for the first time since 1841, saw a Conservative Government in power as well as in office.

At the close of his life Baron Lionel carried off the Derby—on its one hundredth anniversary—with *Sir Bevys*.

The horse, which ran in the assumed name of "Mr Acton," started at a long price. The going was heavy, and Fordham, whose only success in the great Epsom race it was (though he had ridden in some twenty other Derbies), made the best of his way home on the upper ground, known to the *cognoscenti* as the Thormanby track, winning easily at the finish. Lord Rosebery's *Visconti*, another outsider, was third, much to the delight of his owner, who had backed him for a place. By a singular coincidence the Rothschild colours were also carried in the race by a horse called *Squirrel* which finished absolutely last. The winner was led in by Baron Lionel's youngest son, the late Baron Leopold—well known and deservedly popular on the Turf—in the compulsory absence of his father, who was seldom or never seen on a racecourse, owing to his having completely lost the use of his walking powers some twenty years before. *Sir Bevys'* Derby was run on the 28th May, 1879, and within a week the winner's future engagements were rendered void by the death of his owner (at No 148) after a short illness. The horse was actually on the way from Newmarket to Paris to run for the Grand Prix at the time.

Baron Lionel's connection with Piccadilly extended over forty years. Latterly he suffered from rheumatic gout, yet almost until the day of his death he visited New Court and took his accustomed drive to Gunnersbury. Liberal but not extravagant, except in the cause of charity, he possessed a well-stored mind united to a singularly tenacious and receptive memory and the soundest and promptest decision in all business matters. As a social power he may not have been so conspicuous as his brother, the Lord of Mentmore, but in New Court he was, unquestionably, the guiding spirit of the firm. Shortly before his own retirement Delane, who kept a watchful eye upon "necrologies awaiting their victims," as he was wont to call them, entrusted the compilation of Baron Lionel's biography to the veteran Dean of Canterbury, still, happily, in the land of the living and displaying his accustomed energy in obtaining funds for the necessary repair of his Cathedral Church. It is considerably more than half a century, as I write, since Dr Wace joined the staff of *The Times*, and I believe that he is now the only surviving member of the great Delane dynasty in Printing House Square. "I find Wace very useful. I put him, indeed, before Brodrick and how we should have got on without him is beyond my conception."[236] The editor told Mr Wace, as he then was, to be careful to avoid anything like adulation of wealth in his memoir, adding, in one of his admirable letters of guidance, that in his opinion, "though it cannot be said that the Jews have added much to Parliament, the removal of their exclusion, was, no doubt, very necessary to its character, for it could not be considered the representation of the whole nation so long as one influential body was excluded."

It is given to but few men to see their sons attain to the dignity of Lord Chancellor. Sir Thomas More's father is said to have been one of these, and in 1771, old Lord Bathurst, when he was not far short of ninety, was another. Apsley House, or "No 1, London," as a Frenchman is said to have directed a letter to the great Duke, was built by the brothers Adam between 1771 and 1778 for the "weak but worthy" Chancellor, Henry, second Earl Bathurst. During these seven years he held the Great Seal, and, singularly enough, the Adams were building at the same time No

20 St James's Square, for Sir Watkin Williams Wynn, to replace the old home of the Chancellor's father.[237] Till within a month of his death Lord Bathurst rode out for two hours every morning and drank his bottle of port after dinner. He used to allude to his son, Lord Apsley, as the "old gentleman," and would sit up till the small hours of the morning enjoying himself after the Chancellor had retired to bed. The son, who was one of the least distinguished holders of the Great Seal, at all events within recent times, was, however, honest and diligent.

In 1770 Lord Apsley, as he then was, began to nibble at the site of the house which, after one hundred and fifty years, is still known by his name. A gate-keeper's lodge, granted in that year to Mrs Anne Gilbert, widow, at a yearly rental of £34, was the first of several plots of ground which he eventually secured from the Crown. But before he could begin to build he was obliged to buy out another widow who kept an apple stall at the Park corner. The site had been given by George II to an old soldier named Allen who fought for him at Dettingen. This stall, which is marked in a print of the year 1766, was long a bone of contention between Mrs Allen and the Chancellor. In the end she filed a bill against him and he gave her a considerable sum of money to abandon her claim, whereon someone, probably a brother lawyer, spitefully remarked that: "here was a suit brought by one old woman against another and that the Lord Chancellor has been beaten in his own Court."[238]

In the course of 1771 Lord Apsley secured a lease of two adjoining plots. One of these, filched from the Park, was demised to him for thirty-six years at a yearly rent of only £4! and on the whole extent of his holding he proceeded to build, at a cost of £10,000, a plain red brick house paying £110 in all to the Crown.[239] He was more or less his own architect, though he condescended to consult the brothers Adam in the matter of the interior decorations. The result was not altogether a success, for when the first floor was built it was

found not only that the Chancellor had overlooked the necessity
of a staircase to reach the second storey, but that no provision had
been made for offices and stables. In 1775 he petitioned the Crown
for leave to improve his property by building on the former site of
the "Hercules Pillars" immediately to the east of his new house.
He had already purchased the remainder of the Crown lease and
pulled down the inn which stood on a portion of the land granted
to the Hamilton family in the seventeenth century.

The Chancellor's son and heir[240] succeeded his father in
Piccadilly in 1794. He was Secretary of State for Foreign Affairs
for two months in 1809, and is said to have been the last man in
fashionable society to wear a pigtail. He adhered to the practice
until 1828, when, on becoming President of the Council, he cut
it off and sent it round to his ministerial colleagues in a despatch
box.

The Bathursts deserted Apsley House in 1807, and did not
return to Piccadilly for a century.[241] "No 1, London" was next
occupied by the Marquis of Wellesley soon after his ungenerous
recall from India by the Company whose revenues he had more
than doubled during his tenure of office.

His early education began at Harrow, but his stay at the grammar
school on the hill was a short one. Having been implicated in
barring out an unpopular headmaster, he was taken away by his
father and sent to Eton in 1771 or 1772. There were several other
migrations to Eton in consequence of the same affair.

Instances are rare of boys having been at two public schools,
but Sir Joseph Banks is a case in point, and I have heard of a
boy who, after spending six unprofitable years at Harrow, passed
another and, it may be hoped, more useful six at Eton.

Lord Wellesley boarded at Miss Mary Young's house, and here,
too, was his even greater brother Arthur, when it was kept by her
sister, Mrs Naylor. In Maxwell Lyte's "History of Eton College"
it is stated that the great Duke was at Ragenau's, but this appears

to be inaccurate, though his sons Lord Douro (afterwards second Duke), and Lord Charles Wellesley both boarded there.[242]

Eton was always very near to Lord Wellesley's heart, and, by his express desire, he was buried in the College Chapel. That the Duke ever said that the battle of Waterloo was won on the playing-fields of Eton I believe to be one of many picturesque fictions which have crystallised around his name. He did, however, take part there in a memorable fight with a boy called "Bobus" Smith, whom he signally defeated. Otherwise his career at Eton was uneventful.

His elder brother, when one of the senior Oppidans, spoke so well at the Election of 1778, in reciting Strafford's last speech, that he drew tears from an audience which included George III.

"Your Lordship," said David Garrick, "has done what I could never accomplish—made the King weep."

Lord Wellesley did not stay long at his first coming to Piccadilly, for he was sent Ambassador to the Central Junta of Spain to concert measures for the Peninsular War, his brother, Arthur being appointed to the command of the troops.

In the course of the next year he was back at Apsley House, and became Secretary of State for Foreign Affairs in Spencer Perceval's brief adminstration. Thus within the brief space of twelve months Apsley House earned the distinction of sheltering two Foreign Ministers. Lord Wellesley assumed office at an important crisis. England was completely isolated. Every other European Government groaned under the Napoleonic yoke, which it was his brother's destiny to overthrow. In 1815 and 1816 the great Duke rented No 4 Hamilton Place, and in January of the next year he acquired the leasehold interest of Apsley House. His brother, after completing his second Vice-Royalty of Ireland, withdrew to Marble Hill, Twickenham, and then to Brompton, being little seen in London in his later years. But in Piccadilly the Duke spent as many years as Nelson spent days, for I cannot discover that the hero of Trafalgar was ever resident in the street except for short and infrequent visits to the Hamiltons[243] between 1801 and 1803.

In 1830, after protracted negotiation with the Crown, the Duke bought the freehold of Apsley House for the moderate sum of £9,532, though even this he thought too high a figure.[244] It is a fallacy to suppose that it was a gift from the nation, though the estate of Stratfieldsaye, formerly the property of Lord Rivers, was bought for him at immense cost by a grateful country.

As the great Duke of Marlborough had been rewarded with a "Palace" nothing less would satisfy the popular sentiment in the case of Wellington. But there was now no Vanbrugh to design a Blenheim, and the whole history of the erection of Stratfieldsaye is a ghastly record of failure and opportunity misused. An adaptation of Lord Rivers' old house was finally preferred, as against an entirely new building, but the site selected was unsuitable, low and damp, and the design was conspicuously lacking in architectural merit or grandeur. Part of the house may date from the sixteenth century, when it belonged to the family of Dabridgecourt; but it has been so much altered and enlarged that it is difficult to say how much of the original building remains. In 1795 Lord Rivers added the long gallery, the dining-room, the library, the present billiard room, the Duke's sitting-room, and two ground-floor bedrooms. He also raised the ceiling of the hall, in which the great Duke's banner from St George's Chapel now hangs. The Duke built the first-floor rooms and the attics to the two wings; also rooms for the Duchess over the dining-room, and a tennis-court.

In the course of the alterations there was discovered under the steward's rooms in the north wing a paved chamber containing a large copper. This is supposed to have been used by Lord Rivers as a place in which to prepare food for his dogs, and a number of sheep bones and other *débris* found below the drawing-room points to there having been a pond on the site before the space was enclosed in the house. Here is a description of the "Palace" written not long after the great Duke's death.

"The house is plain and very comfortable—not at all splendid. Capital bed rooms and a great number of small low sitting rooms; a few Spanish pictures of, I should say, questionable merit; but a vast number of engravings absolutely covering walls—few good but all interesting; the park flat and dull with a large piece of water and a cascade; the cookery good and the wine admirable and abundant—in short very good quarters, though, to my taste, more pleasant in summer than now. Our party consists of the Duke and Duchess, Lady Charles Wellesley, Lord W. Osborne, Lord Arthur Lennox, Colonel Bruce, Strzelecki, Murchison, Sir A. Cockburn and Alfred Montgomery, but there are some more coming to-day. They had a *battue* yesterday at which six guns killed 198 head, about as many as they had killed on Tuesday."[245] This would not be thought much of a *battue* nowadays, but country gentlemen had more moderate ideas of a good day's sport fifty years ago than in this age of mammoth bags. In 1865, when Delane made one of a shooting party at the same place, he wrote: "We had one of the two best day's shooting I ever saw. Yesterday 219 head of pheasants were killed by six guns, and to-day 370. I don't remember the number of hares and rabbits. I believe I am only answerable for about 40 pheasants, but the Master of Lovat to-day shot 31 pheasants and 25 hares without missing a shot or moving from one place. The Duke shot to-day 80 pheasants to his own gun."

But it is time to leave Stratfieldsaye and return to Piccadilly.

The Duke cased the old red brick building with Bath stone and considerably extended the accommodation of the interior, adding the whole of the west wing towards Hyde Park, in which to hold the annual Waterloo banquet. The classic portico and heavy entrance gates date from the same period. Though he had not much knowledge of art or architecture, the Duke had a happy knack of admiring and being contented with his own belongings. He employed Benjamin Wyatt, the designer of Drury Lane Theatre, who had probably been recommended to him by George the Fourth, both in Piccadilly and at Stratfieldsaye.

His main alterations at Apsley House were completed about 1829, in which year there is a print of the house much as it stands to-day.

In 1831, in the midst of the popular excitement following on the abandonment of the first Reform Bill, the Duke's windows were broken by an angry mob which did considerable damage in the West End, not only to private houses, but to clubs and shops which were found to be unilluminated.

On the night of April 27th, Parliament having been dissolved four days earlier, Sir Robert Peel's house in Whitehall Gardens was attacked. A Bishop who lived in St James's Square saw the mob coming and saved his windows by hastily placing candles in them, but when the rioters reached Apsley House a volley of stones crashed through the windows. The Duke's servants fired over the heads of the crowd in order to frighten them, but without much effect until the ringleaders learnt that the Duchess was lying dead in the house.[246]

London mobs, if unreasoning, are seldom inhuman, and when the leaders heard that the Duke's was a house of mourning they went away to Park Lane and amused themselves by wrecking Lord Londonderry's house instead. In their indiscriminate haste they submitted the houses of many staunch supporters of Reform to a similar fate.

The windows of Apsley House were broken more than once, and in May, 1832, shortly before the triumph of Reform, the Duke had bullet-proof iron blinds or shutters put up and tested them himself by firing at them with a rifle.

A few years after they had been placed in position he was rapturously cheered by a crowd which insisted on following him up Constitution Hill. Having little sympathy with democratic aims, and being wholly uninfluenced by popular demonstrations, the Duke rode leisurely into the courtyard, pointed to the shutters, bowed to the mob and went indoors. His successor, the "son of Waterloo," as he loved to be called, a somewhat eccentric man who took little part in public life, altered the house considerably in 1853 from the designs of Philip Hardwick. He and his Duchess, twice Mistress of the Robes to Queen Victoria and a celebrated beauty, continued the magnificent hospitalities begun by the great Duke, and the Apsley House balls in the 'sixties were among the most brilliant given in London up to that date.

Since the second Duke's death the house has undergone but little alteration externally or internally, save for a better arrangement of the pictures and trophies. The great Duke's bed-room remains much as he left it, and is a comfortless apartment on the ground floor with no fewer than seven doors in it. In its extreme simplicity it resembles the death chamber at Walmer Castle. The nucleus of the collection of foreign pictures[247] which adorn the walls was the spoliation of some of the Spanish palaces by Napoleon's brother, Joseph Buonaparte. He was in process of removing them, with other works of art, to Paris when they fell into Wellington's hands at the battle of Vittoria. An enormous amount of loot was obtained by camp followers and non-combatants at the same time, whilst the British Army is said to have literally trodden on gold and silver coins intended for the pay of French soldiers who abandoned them in their flight. When King Ferdinand's throne was restored he showed his gratitude to the Duke by begging him to keep the pictures, and at Apsley House they remain to this day.

Sir William Allan's painting of the battle of Waterloo was bought by the Duke out of the Scotch Academy exhibition of 1843 and hung in a prominent position. "Good, very good, not too much smoke," was his comment, much in the laconic style in which he answered a little boy who ventured to ask him what Waterloo was like: "Damned hot whilst it lasted," was all he would say.

To Creevey, in response to a similar enquiry, he said: "It was the nearest run thing you ever saw in your life. By God, I don't think it would have done if I had not been there."

When necessary he could administer a snub better than most men and when an importunate visitor (I have been told that he was an American) had the audacity to ask him: "Were you surprised at Waterloo, Duke?" he replied with a withering glance: "No, but I am now."

The enormous enhancement in value of freehold property at Hyde Park Corner in recent years shows what a wise purchase the Duke made when he acquired Apsley House less than a hundred years ago. St George's Hospital is said to have changed hands recently for a sum not far short of a quarter of a million. It would be an ideal site for a Metropolitan opera-house, though theatrical enterprise does not as a rule flourish in the West End, but it is said to be the intention of the purchaser to erect a gigantic hotel in this unique position overlooking two parks and the gardens of Buckingham Palace. In the event of the scheme maturing, it is difficult to see how a profitable return can be secured on the capital outlay, for there are limits even to the paying capacity of visitors to modern *hotels de luxe*; but whatever building ultimately replaces the hospital it is to be hoped that due regard will be paid to its design and that an architect will be found who is capable of doing justice to the site and its enormous possibilities.

I would rather have St George's Hospital replaced by an opera-house worthy of the musical fame of London than see Devonshire House, the home of generations of Berkeleys and Cavendishes, transformed, through the lure and greed of gain, into a vast hotel or a towering block of residential flats.

All cast-iron, concrete, plate glass and imitation marble, heaped storey upon storey (fireproof, perhaps, but art-proof for certain), these monstrous sky scrapers of the Western World, however appropriate to New York, would be utterly out of place in Piccadilly.

This street of precious memories has already one huge caravanserai on the former site of the old Angel Inn.[248]

Another, as yet a steel skeleton unclothed in stone, is in course of erection in the dip where the Tyburn stream, now disguised as a sewer, debouches into the Green Park.

At present the Park Lane Hotel, as it is without much reason to be called, resembles nothing so much as the ribs of a battleship on the stocks, it having been impossible to make progress with the masonry during the war.

Devonshire House, though not a beautiful building by any means, is not without a certain dignity of its own which we can ill afford to lose. Its ample forecourt tells the story of a vanished age when men of means built leisurely and spaciously and regarded elbow room as essential to their wants.

Clarendon, Burlington, and Sunderland built after this fashion, deliberately entrenching themselves behind high sheltering walls for the double purpose of privacy and security.

All these have disappeared, but the massive brickwork which screened Lord Berkeley of Stratton's mansion from the vulgar gaze in the reign of Charles the Second has endured to this day.

Pepys in a sense assisted at its birth, noting in his immortal diary the laying of the first brick.

The scarcely less observant Evelyn, who was called in to advise on the planting and laying out of the gardens, would have grieved to see it share the untimely fate of Clarendon House.

The old wall narrowly escaped destruction in one of the air raids during the Great War, when considerable damage was done to house property in the immediate vicinity. This wall, at all events the lower portion of it, is by far the oldest thing remaining in Piccadilly, and it would be nothing short of vandalism to raze it to the ground.

Londoners capable of appreciating the historic value of our few remaining private palaces, and I believe they are an ever-increasing number, should raise their voices in indignant protest, ere it be too late, against the threatened demolition of Devonshire House.

Let them consider the loss of prestige and interest to the neighbourhood which will inevitably follow should some architectural monstrosity of American origin replace this landmark in the social history of London.

Assuredly the disfigurement caused by a modern Tower of Babel, soaring skywards in the very heart and centre of the West End, would outweigh the advantages which its myriads of bedrooms might have to offer to weary pilgrims in search of a London lodging. Probably, however, before these lines can appear in print, Apsley House will be the sole survivor of the ducal mansions which once abounded hereabouts.

In bidding farewell for the present to Piccadilly and to Berkeley Square (an offshoot of the parent tree), I am proud to have identified, for the first time, Nelson's temporary abode in the street which sheltered Wellington for many long years. It is all but certain, however, that they never met in it, for the Duke's connection with Apsley House did not begin till after Trafalgar was fought and won.

Nor until now has it been definitely established where Sir Walter Scott stayed in Piccadilly, when visiting his friend Mr Dumergue.

Pitt and Fox have been found living, for brief periods in their respective careers, in Berkeley Square, wherein also the heaven-born General Clive made his London home.

The names of first Ministers and advisers of the Crown from the days of Clarendon to those of Palmerston have been inscribed on the street's long roll of honour and renown.

Personalities so sharply contrasted as "Old Q"and Lady Burdett-Coutts have helped, in widely different fashion, to make social history in Piccadilly, their lives all but overlapping and extending, between them, over portions of three centuries. Successive generations of Rothschilds and Barings, representing the acknowledged aristocracy of the financial world, have lived here side by side in amicable rivalry; whilst lesser-known plutocrats, mostly, I regret to say, hailing from Germany, have humbly followed in their wake. Mediocrity and genius, the dissolute and the virtuous (of both sexes), Art, Literature, Commerce, the Drama and Sport have all contributed their quota to the sum total of Piccadilly's abiding interest. For in this unique street, little more than a mile in length from the Haymarket to Hyde Park, is to be found an epitome of English social life, from the days of the second Charles to those of King George V, whom God preserve!

Notes

CHAPTER I

1   At the southern end of Whitcomb Street, on its eastern side, and in Monmouth Court adjacent, there were standing until quite recently, some of the oldest houses in the West End. This street retained, in part, its earlier name of Hedge Lane, when Rocque drew his great map of London in the reign of George II.

2   Coutts's Bank, prior to its removal to the former site of the Lowther Arcade, stood on the south side of the Strand on a spot formerly occupied by Britain's Burse, or the New Exchange, demolished in 1737.

3   The Chamberlain's accounts of the Royal Parish of St Martin-in-the-Fields.

4   Common.

5   "Accounts of the Churchwardens of St Martin-in-the-Fields, 1525–1603," edited by Mr. Kitto, 1901. It is a matter for regret that this valuable transcript, abounding as it does in topographical historical information, stops short at the death of Queen Elizabeth, and it is to be hoped that at some future date the record will be continued, at all events, to the close of the seventeenth century.

6   Compare Blount's *Glossographia*, 1656, and Edward Phillips' (Milton's nephew) *New World of Words*, 1656, in which it is distinctly stated that the ordinary took its name from the Dutch.

7   This document, which was proved in May, 1623, is still to be seen at Somerset House.

8   Higgins may conceivably have been in partnership with Robert Baker.

9   The *Athenæum*, July 27th, 1901.

10 *Calendar of State Papers, Domestic Series*, 1629–31, page 428.

11 Lady Shrewsbury, widow of the seventh Earl, was a munificent benefactress to St John's College, Cambridge, where a statue to her memory was erected so recently as 1864. She died in April, 1632, and was buried beside her husband at Sheffield.

12 *Calendar of State Papers, Domestic Series*, 1636, page 150.

13 Admirably reproduced in facsimile by the London Topographical Society.

14 This was established by one Kelsey in 1611–12. "Churchwardens' Accounts of St. Martin-in-the-Fields."

15 *The Earl of Strafford's Letters and Despatches*, by William Knowler, 1740. Vol. I, p. 262.

16   The ex-Kaiser Wilhelm, who unveiled the Victoria Memorial, is said to
      have admired it greatly; but, with the exception of the fountains at its base,
      the design is unworthy of its site and the great Queen it is intended to
      commemorate. An overpowering mass of white marble, clumsy statuary, and
      tawdry gilt excrescences, it has been not inaptly likened to a bookmaker's
      wedding cake!

17   I. Edward VI, C. 12, s. 14.

18   Cobbett's *State Trials*, Vol. VI, pp. 1310–1350. In the long and interesting
      account of this remarkable trial, the Tudor statute, under which any peer,
      upon claim made, was held to be a clerk convict who might make purgation
      for his offence, is not specifically mentioned. It was successfully pleaded at
      the trial of the Duchess of Kingston for bigamy in 1776, and not finally
      repealed until 1863.

19   Standing Orders of the House of Lords, No. LXV., passed in January, 1689.

20   *Hatton Correspondence*, Vol. I, p. 158.

21   *Lords' Journals*, Vol. XIII, p. 131.

22   The town house of the Earls of Pembroke was at Durham House in the
      Strand, where the Adelphi now stands.

23   *Lords' Journals*, Vol. XIII, p. 139.

24   *Lords' Journals*, Vol. XIII, pp. 384–387.

25   There is a representation of the crime upon Tom Thynne's monument in
      Westminster Abbey.

26   The greater part of St James's Market, famous, according to Gay, for the
      quality of its veal, was destroyed on the formation of Waterloo Place.

27   Delaune's *State of London*.

28   Farquhar, the dramatist, discovered her at the age of sixteen behind the bar
      of the Mitre Tavern in St James's Market.

29   *The Earl of Strafford's Letters and Despatches*, 1740. Vol. I, 4, 435.

30   The Earl of Pembroke.

31   *Calendar of State Papers.* Domestic Series, Charles I, May 30th, 1636, p.
      462.

32   *Calendar of State Papers. Domestic Series*, Charles I, 1657–58 January 32, p.
      213. From a survey, made under the Commonwealth and now preserved in
      the Public Record Office, I gather that Mrs Baker's title was also called in
      question.

33   No. 73 of the Augmentation Records in the Public Record Office.

34   *History of the Rebellion*, Bandinel's edition 1826, Vol. I, p. 422.

35   Now Panton Street.

36   In 1686.

CHAPTER II

37   Published shortly before the Restoration.

38   Sackville Street appears to have derived its name from a Captain Sackville,
      whom I find living there so early as 1676.

39   An inn the site of which it is now impossible to identify.

40   *The History of St James's Square*, 1895.

41   Edward Somerset, second Marquis of Worcester.

42   One of the sacred buildings, which Somerset is said to have threatened with destruction was St Margaret's, Westminster, but while the Protector undoubtedly confiscated ecclesiastical property, Clarendon at least bought and paid for what he required.

43   An allusion to a gilt globe which surmounted the central cupola.

44   Lady Berkeley was the daughter of Sir Andrew Riccard of St Olave's, Hart Street, Governor of the East India Company. Lord Berkeley was her third husband.

45   In 1698.

46   Afterwards Duke of Buckingham.

47   Tradition asserts that it was painted by Verrio to deceive Gibbons.

48   Afterwards the first Earl Spencer. Born 1734. Died 1783.

49   At £4 per annum.

50   Prime Minister in 1783, and again from 1807–1809.

51   The 1st Lord Shelburne, ancestor of the Marquis of Lansdowne.

52   Now represented by the Windham Club.

53   Before it was acquired by Lord Spencer, Clarges's house was inhabited for a time by the 3rd Lord Berkeley of Stratton. He died soon after coming to live in it, and subsequent occupiers were Count Tallard, and the 2nd Duke of Queensberry. It then became the Venetian Embassy before its removal to St James's Square.

54   Lady Wentworth, writing to her son, November 23rd, 1708, said: "My dearest and best of children, I have been to see a very good house in St James's Square. … It was my Lord Sunderland's. It was too little for them"; and, on November 26th, she added: "My old Lady Bristol gave it to her daughter Sunderland, then she let this young Lord and his Lady live some years in it, and after she had sold it they hired it for a year." Lady Wentworth's son, Lord Stafford, did not, however, take it, and the first Duke of Portland went to live in it in 1710.

55   The London County Council has recently placed a medallion on No10 recording the names of the three Prime Ministers who have lived there; Lord Chatham from 1759 to 1762, Lord Derby from 1837 to 1854, and Mr Gladstone in 1890.

56   Piccadilly Terrace, beyond Hamilton Place, was a development of much later date.

57   Applebee's original *Weekly Journal*, April 29, 1721.

58   See Boyle's *Court Guide* for 1792.

59   Susan Starky, a servant maid of his brother James.

60   The *Dictionary of National Biography* states that Lord Pulteney died, at the early age of seventeen, in 1743, but this is an obvious error, for he sat in the House of Commons from 1754 to 1763.

61   Daughter of the first Sir Richard Sutton.

62   In 1793 I find the name of John Bearing (*sic*) entered in the parochial rate-books as the occupier of No 48, Charles Street, Berkeley Square, now the residence of Lord Burghclere.

CHAPTER III

63   Now part of the Royal Thames Yacht Club and included in the freehold
     property of Mr Burdett Coutts.

64   Directed by the first Marquis of Headfort, and Mr John Maddocks, who
     married Lord Craven's sister.

65   See the account of Shaver's Hall in Chapter I.

66   Now let on lease by the trustees of the Sutton Estate to the Naval and
     Military Club.

67   Charles Greville, writing in 1834, describes a tenants' festival which he
     attended at Petworth as being one of the most genuine exhibitions of
     cordiality between employer and employed at which he ever assisted. 4,000
     invitations were issued, but as many more came. The old Peer could not
     endure the thought that there should be anybody hungering outside his
     gates, and he went out himself and ordered the barriers to be taken down
     and admittance given to all.

68   Adolphus Frederick, born 1774, died 1850, father of the late Commander-in-
     Chief. His widow survived until 1889, dying at the great age of ninety-one
     at York House, St James's Palace. That rather mean-looking building, carved
     out of the old groom porter's lodgings, in which the Duchess lived and
     died, though thought good enough to house the present King and Queen
     on their marriage, was long discontinued as a Royal residence, but was in
     1919 fitted up for HRH the Prince of Wales. It had occasionally been placed
     at the disposal of distinguished foreign visitors to our shores. Within recent
     years the President of the French Republic and the son of the Mikado were
     accommodated there, and on the outbreak of the great European war Lord
     Kitchener occupied it for a time.

69   See page 109.

70   Hanged at Stafford in 1856.

71   Sir Frederick Evelyn, Bart., of Wotton, lived here from 1777 till his death in
     1812.

72   It was until 1918 the residence of Sir Bertram Godfray Falle, the colleague of
     Admiral Lord Charles Beresford in the representation of Portsmouth.

73   The old "White Horse" inn, dating from the seventeenth century, stood at
     the south-west corner of the street which commemorates it.

74   The Marquis of Salisbury's house, No 20 Arlington Street, is built of the
     same material.

75   Another occupant was Sir Frederick Adair Roe, Chief Magistrate at Bow
     Street. He lived here from 1835 to 1866, and his widow until 1883.

76   See *Gentleman's Magazine*, March, 1816.

77   Now the St James's Club

78   There is a leaden cistern in the area with the date 1761 and the initials H H
     upon it.

79   The 7th and 8th Earls.

80   Augustus Charles Joseph Flahault de la Billarderie, Grand Chancellor of the
     Legion of Honour 1864–1870. Born 1785, died 1870.

81 See Henry Greville's *Diary*, June 7, 1861, for an account of her share in the famous flight of the Princess Charlotte from Warwick House.

82 September 8, 1870.

83 Charles Cecil John Manners, afterwards sixth Duke of Rutland, died unmarried, 1886.

84 The letter on the opposite page, though unimportant in itself, is interesting as being perhaps the only one now in existence written by Nelson from Piccadilly.

85 Still flourishing in the same street and in the same family after more than 120 years (though not on its original site), and now better known for its pictorial association with British sport than for the satirical prints which formed its principal stock-in-trade in the eighteenth century.

86 No 110 remained in the possession of the same family until 1892, when Mrs Augustus Villiers (Georgina Harriette Elphinstone, daughter of the last Viscount Keith), who had lived here ever since Queenie's death, also died in it. Mrs. Villiers was the third wife of Lord William Godolphin Osborne, of Tulliallan Castle.

87 His next brother, who had a club-foot, was called "Cripplegate," his youngest "Newgate," and his sister, from her command of vigorous language, "Billingsgate".

88 Madid, now almost obsolete as an adjective, signifies moist or humid.

89 The principal town house of the Seymour-Conway family in Manchester Square was acquired before the end of the eighteenth century, but as it was sometimes let to foreign embassies, its owners often sought other quarters.

90 Richard fourth Marquis of Hertford, who died unmarried in 1870.

91 In 1822.

92 In 1813.

93 *Fleet Street in Seven Centuries*, by Walter G. Bell, 1912, p. 368, one of the most valuable of recent contributions to the history of Old London.

94 Over Sir John Bennett's shop.

95 There is an excellent illustration of it as it stood in Fleet Street at p. 315 of Britten's *Old Clocks and Watches and their Makers*, 3rd edition, 1912.

96 Richard fourth Marquis of Hertford. Born 1800, died in Paris unmarried in 1870. He added extensively to the collection of works of art begun by his father and continued, after his death, by Sir Richard Wallace.

97 Lord Redesdale adds that the ancient Milanese family from which Mie-Mie presumably sprang was accustomed to spell the name as Fagnani and not Fagniani. The latter is, however, the version adhered to in all the English accounts I have had access to and I have therefore not thought it necessary to depart from it here.

98 Now the Savile Club.

99 Lady Brownlow's *Reminiscences of a Septuagenarian*.

100 Mayer Anschelm Rothschild of Frankfort, born 1743, died 1812.

101 His name first appears in this position in the *London Post Office Directory* for 1810.

102 See Delane's diary, June and July, 1847. "Called by appointment on the Rothschilds who are very anxious about the City election and are pressing for support" (June 18). "Got up late and went to Rothschild's house in Piccadilly to assist him in preparing his address. Saw there Sir Anthony and the Baroness. Having finished the address advised him to take Lord John Russell's opinion upon it" (June 26). "Saw the Rothschilds again to approve some omissions Lord John had suggested in his address" (June 28). "To my great relief Rothschild, after several variations of the numbers, was this day returned for the City. I saw the Baroness afterwards in a state of almost frenzied delight and gratitude" (July 29). "Saw Rothschild with his brothers Anthony and Nathaniel in the City and was overwhelmed with thanks" (July 30).

103 Separately noticed in Chapter VI.

104 On the death of Nathan Mayer Rothschild's widow in 1851.

105 About the year 1851.

106 Cristoforo Moro, sometimes confused with the original Shakespeare's Othello, was Doge of Venice from 1462 to 1471.

These fine mediæval lanterns, surmounted by the lion of St. Mark, formed part of the equipment of the Bucintoro at the annual festa of *La Sensa* or Wedding of the Adriatic, a ceremony which ended only with the Republic itself.

CHAPTER IV

107 William Douglas, 4th Duke of Queensberry. Born 1725, died 1810.

108 Tregonwell Frampton, "the father of the English turf," who trained the King's horses at Newmarket in 1695 was born in 1641, and was living when "Old Q" was born, whilst Lord Godolphin, who was still racing when the Duke made his first appearance on the turf, was born in the reign of Charles II. Lord Palmerston was a Minister of the Crown for some years before the Duke's death, and the third Earl of Clanwilliam, a distinguished diplomatist, who died so recently as 1879, remembered having seen him in Piccadilly.

109 We believe by Crabbe though the ascription has never been satisfactorily established.

110 Sir James "The Good," knighted on the field of Bannockburn for conspicuous valour. With only sixty horsemen he pursued the fugitive King of England to Dunbar, guarded though he was by an escort five hundred strong.

111 The Royal heart is now said to repose, not in the Holy Sepulchre at Jerusalem, but at Melrose.

112 And also to that indefatigable sensualist John Wilmot, Earl of Rochester.

113 The *Complete Peerage*, now appearing in an improved and enlarged form under the able editorship of Mr. Vicary Gibbs, gives the correct date of birth. This monumental work on the historic Peerage is a striking tribute, if any were needed, to the abiding interest in the hereditary principle, rudely

shaken though it has been by recent legislative action, after desertion, in its own Chamber, by those who should have been its stoutest defenders.

114 Lord Drumlanrig was accidentally killed a few years later, and his younger brother also dying at an early age, Lord March ultimately succeeded to the Dukedom on the death of the husband of Prior's "Kitty ever young," in 1778.

115 His mother (Lady Anne Hamilton) died in 1748, whereby her son succeeded to the additional Earldom of Ruglen with a large landed estate in the counties of Edinburgh and Linlithgow.

116 The Duke of Buccleuch has a portrait of him at the age of about eighteen painted by Allan Ramsay. His portrait by Sir Joshua Reynolds at Hertford House, is reproduced on the ajoining page.

117 The author of that interesting and generally accurate work *The Jockey Club and its Founders*, published in 1891, has apparently antedated this event by three years. See page 114 of Mr. Robert Black's book.

118 Lord March's colours were at first all white, but were soon changed to a variant of the Douglas tartan. Unrepresented on the racecourse at the present day, they may have been used for a short time by the Marquis of Queensberry who died in 1900, author of the well-known rules of boxing called after him. "Young Q's" biography should be undertaken when the events in which he figured can be seen more in perspective, but the successful treatment of his life would require rather special qualifications.

119 August 29th, 1750.

120 See p. 55.

121 An oil painting of the match, probably by Seymour, with portraits from life of the principal persons engaged, changed hands at auction some few years ago, but its present whereabouts is unknown to the writer. The match also achieved wide notoriety through the medium of a print, published by Pond, a diligent compiler of turf statistics, copies of which are sufficiently common to render a reproduction in these pages unnecessary.

122 Sir John Lade lived at a house now merged in the site of the Lyceum Club, and the Margrave of Anspach succeeded him there.

123 One Thomas Butler.

124 The Turf Club at the corner of Clarges Street and Piccadilly was the former town house of the Dukes of Grafton. It is well shown in a drawing by Sandby in the Crace Collection at the British Museum.

125 His proposer was Sir George Macartney, our first Ambassador to China.

126 Privately and sumptuously printed for Lord Home by his brother the late Mr. James Home.

127 In 1768 Lady Susan married the first Marquis of Stafford and died in 1805.

128 Ancestor of Lord Huntingfield, one of the few members of the English peerage of Dutch ancestry.

129 The Amesbury estate, including the world-famous Druidical circle of Stonehenge, passed into the possession of the Antrobus family, but has, quite recently, been acquired for the nation owing to the liberality of a private individual.

130 William Grieve.

131 Brother of Lord George Gordon, the originator of the Gordon riots.

132 Selwyn had been deprived of his sinecure office as Paymaster of the Works
     under Burke's scheme of economical reform, though, a little later, he was
     rewarded with the equally unarduous and lucrative post of Surveyor-General
     of the Crown lands.

133 Now converted into a golf club.

134 Afterwards King William the Fourth.

135 G A Selwyn to Lady Carlisle, November, 1790.

136 Her daughter-in-law, the Comtesse Emilie de Boufflers, was guillotined
     in 1794. She was herself imprisoned but released after the death of
     Robespierre.

137 His doctor, mentioned above.

138 Francis Charles Seymour-Conway, afterwards third Marquis of Hertford.
     Born 1777. Died 1842.

139 Not the great John Sebastian.

140 *Vide* also Etherege in the *Man of Mode*, where one of the characters says of
     Dorimant (John Wilmot, Earl of Rochester): "I'll lay my life there is not an
     article but he has broken; talked to the vizards in the pit, waited upon the
     ladies from the boxes to their coaches; gone behind the scenes and fawned
     upon those little insignificant creatures, the Players."

141 George Selwyn to Lord Carlisle, February 2nd, 1768.

142 Unmentioned by name.

143 Journal, March 12, 1768.

144 Lord Ravensworth.

145 Keith was at the time a prisoner in the Fleet, and Kidgell, who had been
     at Winchester with "Old Q," acted on this occasion as his deputy. What
     were his precise duties as the Duke's chaplain it would be difficult to say,
     but it is on record that the Duke was a great admirer of Voltaire, whom he
     considered to have done more real good by his writings upon tolerance than
     all the priests in Europe. See his letter printed at p. 17 of *George Selwyn and
     His Contemporaries*, by John Heneage Jesse, 1843, Vol. II.

146 She died in Cadogan Place, quite blind, having outlived all the companions
     of her youth, in 1826.

147 He did not become Duke of Queensberry until 1778, nor a British peer (as
     Lord Douglas of Amesbury) until 1786.

148 "Old Q" writing from Newmarket to George Selwyn at this time, said: "He
     (Wilkes) deserves to be put in the pillory for his abuse of the Government,
     and I should be very glad to see him severely punished."

149 *Vide Journals of the House of Lords*, December 12th, 1768.

150 May 18, 1787

151 Lord Thurlow.

152 May 13, 1793.

153 A very early mention of champagne occurs in one of "Old Q's" letters to
     George Selwyn, in November 1766. "I have not yet received some champagne
     that Monsieur de Prissieux has sent me, but I expect it every day." It is

possible, however, that champagne was not at that date an effervescing wine, but that it partook of the still variety known as yin d'ay.

154 See the "Diary of Thomas, Earl of Ailesbury," printed in the *15th Report of the Royal Commission on Historical Manuscripts*, Part VII, p. 303.

155 Ministre soi-disant, et médecin malgré lui.

156 Lord Colchester's Diary, February 1796.

157 As he was also an inhabitant of Piccadilly no apology is required for introducing him here.

158 The Duke ran horses in the Derby on no less than seven occasions, viz., in 1781, 1783, 1786, 1788, 1790, 1792, and 1796, but was never once so fortunate as to be in the first three.

159 August 1790.

160 He died only a year later, in his twenty-fourth year.

161 See the account of Hertford House, now the Isthmian Club, at p.117, Chapter III.

162 Novosielski was more of a scene painter than an architect, but his name appears as such on the view of No 105 given on p. 117 of this volume.

163 It stood on the site of what was until a few years ago No 114, when it was pulled down to make way for a new hotel facing the Green Park. This building, now in course of erection, has swallowed up all the numbers between the Savile and the Junior Athenæum Club, obliterating several houses of some historic interest.

164 The name of John Fuller, Chemist and Druggist, 34, Piccadilly, appears in the *London Directory* for 1800.

165 Jack Radford, who habitually stood booted and spurred on the pavement in Piccadilly in readiness to execute his master's orders and to carry notes to any of his acquaintance whom he recognised from the balcony.

166 Set on foot by Lord Yarmouth, who, with other beneficiaries, disputed the legality of some of the numerous codicils to the will.

167 The same remark applies to other orgies in which he is alleged to have figured in extreme old age.

168 Gerard Andrewes, the Dean of Canterbury, was Rector of St James's at this time.

169 Since these words were written No 139 has been acquired by Baron d'Erlanger.

And also to that indefatigable sensualist John Wilmot, Earl of Rochester.

170 No 138 is now (1920) the new premises of the Lyceum Club.

CHAPTER V

171 Berkeley, now Devonshire, House.

172 Vol. I, p. 291.

173 Mr. Wheatley, by the way, blundered badly when he wrote in *London, Past and Present*, that the ground of the Square was laid out and the buildings began in 1698 *in the reign of Queen Anne*!

174   *Annual Register*, 1769, page 86.

175   Brick Street, between the Isthmian and St James's Clubs, was formerly called Engine Street, from a water-wheel designed to regulate the waters of the Tybourne at times of exceptional rainfall.

176   Walbrook and the Fleet River in the City of London are cases in point.

177   So called from a turbid pool adjoining the Westminster Playing Fields at Vincent Square, and drained on the reclamation of Pimlico for building purposes.

178   The existing No 6 was one of the first houses to be completed in the new Square, a Mr Thomas Brudenel coming to live in it in 1739, the first recorded year of its separate existence.

179   Rodney lived in Hill Street when he was a Captain and in Queen Anne Street and Hanover Square in his later years.

180   Walpole to Sir Horace Mann, November 26, 1782.

181   There was an earlier London *Telegraph* in 1796.

182   So early as September 20, 1855, the *Daily Telegraph* had declared that its circulation exceeded that of any London morning newspaper with the exception of the *Times*, and that it was then greater than that of any four morning newspapers put together. Its advertisement rates were then unprecedently low—two lines for a shilling, soon after increased to eighteen pence. On November 2 of the same year, it was able to declare that its circulation was greater than that of all the other papers put together, leaving out the paragraph about the *Times*.

183   For many years the last house northward in the block below Bruton Street.

184   When they removed from Cavendish Square.

185   Fitzgerald's Garrick, Vol. I, page 104, note.

186   Theodore Hook's idea of the real London was somewhat more circumscribed.

187   Probably in Mount Street or Davies Street.

188   Notes and Queries, 4th Series, vol. vi. p. 179.

189   Died 1762.

190   It was in what is now, from a residential point of view, an unfashionable quarter, Wigmore Street.

191   He died in 1788, and his widow, Elizabeth, eldest daughter of Sir Francis Dashwood, removed to No. 14 on the opposite side of the Square and remained there till her death in 1832.

192   John Fane, tenth Earl of Westmorland, K.G., Lord Lieutenant of Ireland.

193   Mary, Duchess of Ancaster died in 1793.

194   The next owner of the house was William Henry Lambton, M.P. for Durham and father of the 1st Earl of Durham, and others who have lived in it were various members of the great and good family of Smith; Sir Henry des Vœux; Charlotte, Lady Carrington; the 8th Viscount Downe, and Mrs Hartmann, to whom King Edward VII lent the White Lodge in Richmond Park; and Lord Queenborough.

195   Horace Walpole to George Montague, February 22nd, 1762.

196   No 43 has already been mentioned in connection with Lady Mary Coke.

197 Bell.

198 ? of Cumberland.

199 Horace Walpole to the Hon. H.S. Conway, June 5, 1764.

200 Germain.

201 Letters of Henrietta, Countess of Suffolk, 1824, Vol. II, page 251.

202 So far as I know Lord Powis is the only peer whose name is thus recorded in
     London. A house in the Stable Yard of St James's Palace, formerly belonging
     to Lord Warwick, had a similar inscription until quite recently, but it
     has now disappeared, leaving this sole distinction, as applied to a private
     residence, to Berkeley Square.

203 Lansdowne.

204 Other letters dated from the same address were written by him on December
     23rd and 30th, 1783, February 17th and March 10th, 1784.

205 *Life of Haydon*, Vol. II, p. 360.

206 There were in the days of my childhood two small houses, with melancholy,
     uncared-for gardens in front of them, presenting an even more dilapidated
     appearance than No 50 Berkeley Square, in St George's Place, Knightsbridge,
     on the site of the late Lady Baden-Powell's house.

207 Lady Selkirk died whilst these pages were passing through the press.

208 House.

209 Now Lansdowne Passage.

210 I could wish that other families had preserved their archives as carefully and
     tabulated them as skilfully as has been done by Lord Kerry, but I have found
     that, with some notable exceptions, owners of historic houses in the West
     End care little about their pedigrees, and, once they are assured that their
     title to the property is a good one, they take but a faint interest in who may
     have preceded them.

CHAPTER VI

211 In the "Plain Dealer," 1676.

212 There is to this day, in Greek Street, Soho, a public house of this singular
     name.

213 It is plainly shown, as the largest house in the street, in Horwood's admirable
     Map of London, 1795. North's house was then No 15, and the total number
     of houses seems to have been twenty-two. In later years these were reduced
     to half a dozen, and latterly, when the east side had practically disappeared,
     to three large houses, or four, if the one at the Piccadilly corner is included,
     all of them on the western side.

214 Usually run for in the month of May.

215 Youngest son and eventual heir of the 11th Earl of Devon. Born 1836. Died
     unmarried, 1891.

216 No 142.

217 As Member for Grampound.

218 Tenth Earl and 1st Marquis.

219 Emma, only daughter and heir of Thomas Vernon, of Hanbury, Co. Worcester.

220 The marriage took place at her mother's house in Berkeley Square, February 23, 1779.

221 Her brother, the 4th Duke of Ancaster, having died unmarried, July 8, 1779, in his twenty-third year.

222 In 1776 he became one of the Tory members for the little borough of Haslemere (a constituency which his grandfather had represented from 1722–1754), though, when his main interests were transferred to Lincolnshire, he sat for Boston.

223 M.P. Lancashire, S.E. Division.

224 M.P. Oxford City, 1826–1863.

225 Now the country home of Lord Rothschild.

226 Born 1792, died 1848.

227 A titular dignity unknown to the College of Arms.

228 M.P. Northumberland, 1795–1818.

229 On June 14, 1832.

230 Now represented by No 146.

231   No 147.

232 John Bury Dasent, Judge of County Courts. Born 1808, died 1888.

233 At Ham House, Richmond.

234 Bath House.

235 With No147.

236 Delane to Dasent, September 2nd, 1863.

237 Allen, 1st Earl Bathurst.

238 Lord Campbell's *Lives of the Chancellors*, Vol. V, p. 449.

239 There is a view of it in the Crace Collection at the British Museum.

240 Henry, 3rd Earl Bathurst, born 1762, died 1834.

241 See the account of No. 139 in Chapter IV.

242 Information kindly supplied to the author by Mr R.A. Austen Leigh, Editor of the earlier Eton school lists.

243 At No 103

244 See Appendix to *8th Report of the Commissioners of Woods and Forests*, pp. 32–42.

245 Delane to Dasent, January 3, 1861.

246 The Duke was unable to go to the House of Lords on the day of the Prorogation in consequence of the critical state of the Duchess, and on the next day, April 24th, she died.

247 Admirably catalogued a few rears ago by Evelyn, Duchess of Wellington, and privately printed in two quarto volumes.

248 In more recent times the St James's Hall and Restaurant.

Also available from Nonsuch Publishing

For forthcoming titles and sales information see
www.nonsuch-publishing.com